D0477963

John Walkenbach's
Favorite Excel® 2010
Tips & Tricks

by John Walkenbach

1,048,576 Rows
16,384 Columns

17,179,869,184 cells

WILEY

Wiley Publishing, Inc.

John Walkenbach's Favorite Excel® 2010 Tips & Tricks

Published by
Wiley Publishing, Inc.
111 River Street
Hoboken, NJ 07030-5774

www.wiley.com

Copyright © 2010 by Wiley Publishing, Inc., Indianapolis, Indiana

Published by Wiley Publishing, Inc., Indianapolis, Indiana

Published simultaneously in Canada

No part of this publication may be reproduced, stored in a retrieval system or transmitted in any form or by any means, electronic, mechanical, photocopying, recording, scanning or otherwise, except as permitted under Sections 107 or 108 of the 1976 United States Copyright Act, without either the prior written permission of the Publisher, or authorization through payment of the appropriate per-copy fee to the Copyright Clearance Center, 222 Rosewood Drive, Danvers, MA 01923, (978) 750-8400, fax (978) 646-8600. Requests to the Publisher for permission should be addressed to the Permissions Department, John Wiley & Sons, Inc., 111 River Street, Hoboken, NJ 07030, (201) 748-6011, fax (201) 748-6008, or online at http://www.wiley.com/go/permissions.

Trademarks: Wiley and the Wiley Publishing logo are trademarks or registered trademarks of John Wiley & Sons, Inc. and/or its affiliates in the United States and other countries, and may not be used without written permission. Excel is a registered trademark of Microsoft Corporation in the United States and/or other countries. All other trademarks are the property of their respective owners. Wiley Publishing, Inc., is not associated with any product or vendor mentioned in this book.

LIMIT OF LIABILITY/DISCLAIMER OF WARRANTY: THE PUBLISHER AND THE AUTHOR MAKE NO REPRESENTATIONS OR WARRANTIES WITH RESPECT TO THE ACCURACY OR COMPLETENESS OF THE CONTENTS OF THIS WORK AND SPECIFICALLY DISCLAIM ALL WARRANTIES, INCLUDING WITHOUT LIMITATION WARRANTIES OF FITNESS FOR A PARTICULAR PURPOSE. NO WARRANTY MAY BE CREATED OR EXTENDED BY SALES OR PROMOTIONAL MATERIALS. THE ADVICE AND STRATEGIES CONTAINED HEREIN MAY NOT BE SUITABLE FOR EVERY SITUATION. THIS WORK IS SOLD WITH THE UNDERSTANDING THAT THE PUBLISHER IS NOT ENGAGED IN RENDERING LEGAL, ACCOUNTING, OR OTHER PROFESSIONAL SERVICES. IF PROFESSIONAL ASSISTANCE IS REQUIRED, THE SERVICES OF A COMPETENT PROFESSIONAL PERSON SHOULD BE SOUGHT. NEITHER THE PUBLISHER NOR THE AUTHOR SHALL BE LIABLE FOR DAMAGES ARISING HEREFROM. THE FACT THAT AN ORGANIZATION OR WEBSITE IS REFERRED TO IN THIS WORK AS A CITATION AND/OR A POTENTIAL SOURCE OF FURTHER INFORMATION DOES NOT MEAN THAT THE AUTHOR OR THE PUBLISHER ENDORSES THE INFORMATION THE ORGANIZATION OR WEBSITE MAY PROVIDE OR RECOMMENDATIONS IT MAY MAKE. FURTHER, READERS SHOULD BE AWARE THAT INTERNET WEBSITES LISTED IN THIS WORK MAY HAVE CHANGED OR DISAPPEARED BETWEEN WHEN THIS WORK WAS WRITTEN AND WHEN IT IS READ. FULFILLMENT OF EACH COUPON OFFER IS THE SOLE RESPONSIBILITY OF THE OFFEROR.

For general information on our other products and services, please contact our Customer Care Department within the U.S. at 877-762-2974, outside the U.S. at 317-572-3993, or fax 317-572-4002.

For technical support, please visit www.wiley.com/techsupport.

Wiley also publishes its books in a variety of electronic formats. Some content that appears in print may not be available in electronic books.

Library of Congress Control Number: 2010929318

ISBN: 978-0-470-47537-9

Manufactured in the United States of America

10 9 8 7 6 5 4 3 2 1

WILEY

About the Author

John Walkenbach is author of more than 50 spreadsheet books and lives in southern Arizona. Visit his Web site: `http://spreadsheetpage.com`.

Publisher's Acknowledgments

We're proud of this book; please send us your comments at http://dummies.custhelp.com. For other comments, please contact our Customer Care Department within the U.S. at 877-762-2974, outside the U.S. at 317-572-3993, or fax 317-572-4002.

Some of the people who helped bring this book to market include the following:

Acquisitions, Editorial, and Media Development

Project Editor: Kelly Ewing

Acquisitions Editor: Katie Mohr

Technical Editor: Todd Meister

Editorial Manager: Jodi Jensen

Media Development Project Manager:
Laura Moss-Hollister

Media Development Assistant Project Manager:
Jenny Swisher

Media Development Associate Producer:
Douglas Kuhn

Media Development Quality Assurance:
Marilyn Hummel

Editorial Assistant: Leslie Saxman

Sr. Editorial Assistant: Cherie Case

Composition Services

Project Coordinator: Kristie Rees

Layout and Graphics: Samantha K. Cherolis, Julie Trippetti

Proofreader: Laura Bowman

Indexer: Potomac Indexing, LLC

Publishing and Editorial for Technology Dummies

Richard Swadley, Vice President and Executive Group Publisher

Andy Cummings, Vice President and Publisher

Mary Bednarek, Executive Acquisitions Director

Mary C. Corder, Editorial Director

Publishing for Consumer Dummies

Diane Graves Steele, Vice President and Publisher

Composition Services

Debbie Stailey, Director of Composition Services

▶ Contents at a Glance

Table of Contents

Part II: Data Entry

Part III: Formatting

Part IV: Basic Formulas and Functions

Part V: Useful Formula Examples

Part VI: Conversions and Mathematical Calculations

Part VII: Charts and Graphics

Part VIII: Data Analysis and Lists

Part IX: Working with Files

Part X: Printing

INTRODUCTION

Excel is a very popular program. Millions of people throughout the world use it on a regular basis. But it's a safe bet that the vast majority of users have yet to discover some of the amazing things this product can do. If I've done my job, you'll find enough useful information in this book to help you use Excel on a new level.

This is the third edition of this book, and I added many new tips and beefed up many of the old tips based on feedback from readers of the previous editions.

What You Should Know

This book isn't a beginner's guide to Excel. Rather, it's a book for those who already use Excel but realize that they have a lot more to learn. This book is filled with tips and tricks that I've learned over the years, and I'm certain that about 99 percent of all Excel users will find something new and useful in these pages.

If you have absolutely no experience with Excel, this book might not be the best choice for you. To get the most out of this book, you should have some background in using Excel. Specifically, I assume that you know how to accomplish the following tasks with Excel:

> Create workbooks, insert worksheets, save files, and perform other basic tasks.

> Navigate through a workbook.

> Use the Excel Ribbon and dialog boxes.

> Use basic Windows features, such as file management and copy-and-paste techniques.

What You Should Have

To use this book, you need a copy of Microsoft Excel 2010 for Windows. If you use an older version of Excel, you should get one of the previous editions of this book.

As far as hardware goes for the computer you use to run Excel, the faster, the better. And, of course, the more memory in your system, the happier you'll be.

Conventions Used in This Book

Take a minute to skim this section and learn some of the typographic conventions used throughout this book.

Formula listings

Formulas usually appear on a separate line in `monospace font`. For example, I might list the following formula:

```
=VLOOKUP(StockNumber,PriceList,2,False)
```

Excel supports a special type of formula known as an *array formula*. When you enter an array formula, press Ctrl+Shift+Enter (not just Enter). Excel encloses an array formula in curly braces to remind you that it's an array formula.

Note

Do not type the curly braces for an array formula. Excel puts them in automatically.

VBA code listings

This book also contains examples of VBA code. Each listing appears in a `monospace font`; each line of code occupies a separate line. To make the code easier to read, I usually use indentation on specific lines. Although indentation is optional, it helps to delineate statements that go together.

If a line of code doesn't fit on a single line in this book, I use the standard VBA line continuation sequence, a space followed by an underscore character, to indicate that the line of code extends to the next line. For example, the following two lines comprise a single VBA statement:

```
If Right(cell.Value, 1) = "!" Then cell.Value _
    = Left(cell.Value, Len(cell.Value) - 1)
```

You can enter this code either exactly as shown, on two lines, or on a single line without the trailing underscore character.

Key names

Names of keys on the keyboard appear in normal type: for example Alt, Home, PgDn, and Ctrl. When you should press two or more keys simultaneously, the keys are connected with a plus sign: "Press Ctrl+G to display the Go To dialog box."

The Ribbon

Excel 2010 features the Ribbon user interface, which was introduced in Excel 2007.

When you need to select a command by using the Ribbon, I describe the command by using the tab name, the group name, and the command name: for example, "Choose Home➜Alignment➜ Wrap Text." This command translates to "Click the Home tab, locate the Alignment group, and then click the Wrap Text button."

Some commands use a drop-down Ribbon control. For example: Home➜Styles➜Conditional Formatting➜New Rule. In this case, you need to click the down-pointing arrow on the Conditional Formatting control in order to access the New Rule command.

Many commands begin with the word File. Clicking the File tab takes you to the new Backstage View.

Functions, procedures, and named ranges

The names of the Excel worksheet functions appear in all uppercase, like so: "Use the SUM function to add the values in column A."

Macro and VBA procedure names appear in normal type: "Execute the InsertTotals procedure." I often use mixed upper- and lowercase to make these names easier to read.

Unless you're dealing with text inside quotation marks, Excel isn't sensitive to case. In other words, both the following formulas produce the same result:

```
=SUM(A1:A50)
=sum(a1:a50)
```

Excel, however, converts the characters in the second formula to uppercase.

Mouse conventions

The mouse terminology in this book is all standard fare: pointing, clicking, right-clicking, dragging, and so on. You know the drill.

What the icons mean

Throughout this book, icons appear in the left margin to call your attention to points that are particularly important.

Note

I use Note icons to tell you that something is important — perhaps a concept that can help you master the task at hand or something fundamental for understanding subsequent material.

Caution

I use Caution icons when the operation I'm describing can cause problems if you're not careful.

Cross-Ref

I use the Cross-Reference icon to refer you to other tips that have more to say on a particular topic.

New Feature

This icon indicates a feature new to Excel 2010.

Entering VBA Code

Some of these tips and tricks involve *Visual Basic for Applications (VBA)*, a programming language built into Excel. You use the following basic procedure to enter a VBA procedure into a workbook:

1. Press Alt+F11 to activate the VBA editor window.

2. Click your workbook's name in the Project window.

   If the Project window isn't visible, press Ctrl+R to display it.

3. Choose Insert➡Module to add a VBA module to the project.

   A code window appears.

4. Type the code in the code window.

When your workbook contains VBA code, you must save it as a macro-enabled workbook. These workbooks have the *.xlsm extension.

When a workbook contains VBA code, you might receive a warning when you open the workbook. This warning depends on your security settings. To view or change your security settings, display the Trust Center dialog box:

1. Choose File➡Options.

2. In the Excel Options dialog box, click the Trust Center tab.

3. Click the Trust Center Settings button.

4. In the Trust Center dialog box, click the Macro Settings tab.

I recommend the default setting: Disable All Macros with Notification. When this setting is in effect, you have the option to enable or disable macros in every workbook you open. The exception is when the workbook is opened from a trusted location. Specify trusted locations on the Trusted Locations tab of the Trust Center dialog box.

How This Book Is Organized

To provide some semblance of order, I grouped these tips and tricks into 12 parts:

- ➤ Part I: Basic Excel Usage
- ➤ Part II: Data Entry
- ➤ Part III: Formatting
- ➤ Part IV: Basic Formulas and Functions
- ➤ Part V: Useful Formula Examples
- ➤ Part VI: Conversions and Mathematical Calculations
- ➤ Part VII: Charts and Graphics
- ➤ Part VIII: Data Analysis and Lists
- ➤ Part IX: Working with Files
- ➤ Part X: Printing
- ➤ Part XI: Spotting, Fixing, and Preventing Errors
- ➤ Part XII: Basic VBA and Macros

How to Use This Book

This book really isn't intended to be read from cover to cover, as you would read a novel — but I'm sure that some people will do so. More likely, you'll want to use it as a reference book and consult it when necessary. If you're faced with a challenging task, you might want to check the index first, to see whether the book specifically addresses your problem. The order of the parts and tips is arbitrary. Most readers will probably skip around and pick up useful tidbits here and there.

About the Power Utility Pak Offer

Toward the back of this book is a coupon that you can redeem for a discounted copy of my award-winning Power Utility Pak — a collection of useful Excel utilities, plus many new worksheet functions.

You can also use this coupon to purchase the complete VBA source code for a nominal fee. Studying the code is an excellent way to pick up some useful programming techniques. You can take the product for a test drive by downloading the trial version from my Web site at `http://spreadsheetpage.com`.

Note **Power Utility Pak version 7 requires Excel 2007 for Windows or Excel 2010 for Windows.**

Reach Out

I'm always interested in getting feedback on my books. The best way to provide this feedback is by e-mail. Send your comments and suggestions to john@j-walk.com.

Unfortunately, I cannot reply to specific questions. Posting your question to one of the Excel newsgroups is, by far, the best way to get assistance.

Also, when you're out surfing the Web, don't overlook my Web site (The Spreadsheet Page) at `http://spreadsheetpage.com`.

Now, without further ado, it's time to turn the page and expand your horizons.

## PART I

Basic Excel Usage

In this part, you'll find tips and tricks covering some of the fundamental uses of Excel, from selecting cells and navigating sheets in a workbook to hiding rows and columns, as well as working with the Quick Access toolbar and changing Excel's color scheme.

Tips and Where to Find Them

Understanding Excel Versions

If you're reading this book, you should be using Excel 2010 — which is part of Microsoft Office 2010, released in 2010.

I've found that many users don't even know which version of Excel they use. The easiest way to find out is to press F1, which brings up the Help window. The Help window identifies the version of Excel — but you might have to look for it. If the version number isn't displayed in the main Help window, just search for *version,* and you'll find it. A more surefire method for Excel 2010 is to choose File→Help. Then you'll see complete details about the Excel version.

So, who cares which version of Excel you use? Most of the time, nobody cares. As long as your version does what you want it to do, the version makes no difference. But if you share your workbooks with other users, the version may be very important.

Suppose that you use Excel 2010 and you give a coworker who uses Excel 2002 a copy of a workbook. If you happened to use a feature that was introduced in Excel 2003, Excel 2007, or Excel 2010, your coworker may not be able to work with your file in the way you intended. In fact, if you saved the file in one of the newer Excel file formats, she may not even be able to *open* the file.

Note

Microsoft provides the free add-on Office Compatibility Pack. This download gives previous versions of Office support for the new Office file formats introduced in Office 2007. Therefore, you can share Excel 2007 and Excel 2010 files with users of Excel 2000, Excel 2002, and Excel 2003. Note, however, that this add-on doesn't endow the older versions with any new features. It just allows the software to open and save the files.

For the record, the following table shows the major version numbers of Excel.

Version	Released	Comments
1	1985	The first version of Excel was for the Apple Macintosh.
2	1987	The first Windows version was labeled 2 to correspond to the Macintosh version. Because Windows was not widely used, this version included a runtime version of Windows.
3	1990	This version included toolbars, drawing capabilities, outlining, add-in support, 3D charts, and many more new features.
4	1992	The first "popular" version of Excel. It included quite a few usability features.
5	1993	Excel 5, a major upgrade, included multisheet workbooks and support for VBA.
7*	1995	This version, known as Excel 95, was the first major 32-bit version of Excel. Feature-wise, it was similar to Excel 5.

continued

Version	Released	Comments
8	1997	This version, known as Excel 97, was the first version to support conditional formatting and data validation. It also incorporated new menus and toolbars. VBA programmers found quite a few enhancements, including a completely new VBA editor, UserForms, class modules, and more.
9	1999	This version, known as Excel 2000, could use HTML as a native file format and (for the first time) supported COM add-ins. It also featured a self-repair capability, an enhanced Clipboard, and pivot charts. VBA programmers could use modeless UserForms, and several new VBA functions were introduced.
10	2001	Known as Excel 2002 (or Excel XP), this version is part of Office XP. It has a long list of new features, but most of them are of little value to the majority of users. Perhaps this version's most significant feature is its ability to recover your work when Excel crashes.
11	2003	Officially known as Microsoft Office Excel 2003, this version's new features are improved support for XML, a new list range feature, Smart Tag enhancements, and corrected statistical functions.
12	2007	This version is officially known as Microsoft Office Excel 2007. This version introduced many new features, including new file formats, a revamped user interface, support for much larger worksheets, a handy page layout view, document themes, new conditional formatting options, much better-looking charts, a new table feature, a few new worksheet functions, and much more.
14**	2010	I used this version when I wrote this book. Microsoft Office Excel 2010 includes a fair number of new features, including Sparkline graphics, a new Backstage View for document-related operations, new worksheet functions, end-user Ribbon customization, PivotTable Slicers, an Equation Editor, and even image-editing enhancements.

Excel 6 doesn't exist. Beginning with Excel 7, the version numbering was changed so that all Microsoft Office applications had the same version number.
**Apparently, Microsoft is a bit superstitious. They skipped Office 13.*

If you must share a workbook with someone using a version before Excel 2007, save the file as an XLS file by choosing the Excel 97–2003 Workbook option in the Save As dialog box. *Pay attention* to the results of the Compatibility Checker, which appears automatically whenever you save your file in this older format. This useful dialog box, shown in Figure 1-1, identifies potential problems when your workbook is used by someone who has an Excel version earlier than Excel 2007.

Figure 1-1: The Compatibility Checker helps identify potential compatibility problems.

You can display the Compatibility Checker dialog box at any time by choosing File➔Info➔Check For Issues➔Check Compatibility.

Maximizing Ribbon Efficiency

Beginning with Excel 2007, Microsoft made some very significant changes to the user interface in its Office products. Since the beginning of time, all Windows programs have had a similar user interface that consists of menus and toolbars. The Office 2007 designers went out on a limb and came up with a radically different user interface: the Ribbon.

The words along the top (Home, Insert, and Page Layout, for example) are known as *tabs*. Click a tab, and the Ribbon changes to display a new set of commands, arranged in groups. (For example, the Home tab has groups labeled Clipboard, Font, Alignment, and more.)

Using the Ribbon is straightforward enough. Somewhat ironically, new users will adapt much more quickly to the Ribbon than experienced users will. Long-time Excel users will spend a considerable amount of time scratching their heads and trying to figure out where their favorite commands now live.

The following tips help you get the most out of the Ribbon user interface:

> ➤ Don't be afraid to click on the stuff you find on the Ribbon. This advice applies especially if you're an experienced user who is trying to adapt to the new user interface. You can undo just about everything you do by clicking Undo (located on the Quick Access toolbar, which is on the left side of the Excel title bar by default). Or, use the Ctrl+Z shortcut key to undo your work.

> ➤ To get more screen real estate, enter Hide the Ribbon mode. You can hide the Ribbon by double-clicking any of the tabs. When you need to access a command, just click the tab, and the Ribbon comes back to life. The Ribbon disappears again when you finish. To leave this mode and return to normal, just double-click a tab. You can also enable and disable Hide the Ribbon mode by pressing Ctrl+F1 or clicking the icon next to the Help icon, to the right of the tabs.

> ➤ Access the Ribbon from the keyboard. Although the Ribbon appears to be mouse-centric, it's quite functional from the keyboard. See Tip 13 for some keyboard access tips.

> ➤ Note that the appearance of the commands on the Ribbon varies, depending on the width of the Excel window. When the window is too narrow to display the entire Ribbon, the commands adapt and may seem to be missing. But the commands are still available. Figure 2-1 shows the Home tab of the Ribbon when the Excel window is at three different widths. In the first view, all controls are fully visible. When the Excel window is made narrower, some descriptive text disappears, but the icons remain. When the window is made very narrow, some groups display a single icon. However, if you click the icon, all the group commands are available to you.

Figure 2-1: The look of the Ribbon varies, depending on the width of the Excel window.

➤ Take advantage of contextual tabs on the Ribbon. In some cases, the Ribbon displays new, *contextual* tabs. For example, when you select a chart, you see three new tabs: Design, Layout, and Format. Notice that these new tabs contain a description on the Excel title bar (when a chart is selected, the description reads Chart Tools). Selecting any of the following elements also results in the display of contextual tabs: a table, a PivotTable, a PivotTable Slicer, a drawing (a shape or WordArt), a picture (a photo or clip art), a header or footer (in Page Layout view), a SmartArt diagram, or an equation. You can, of course, continue to use all the other tabs when a contextual tab is displayed.

➤ When the mouse pointer is within the Ribbon arrow, use the mouse's scroll wheel to scroll through the tabs.

➤ Right-click just about anything on-screen to get a context-sensitive shortcut menu. Shortcut menus are one part of the old user interface that's still in place. And, if you're trying to decrease your mouse dependence, you can also press Shift+F10 to display the shortcut menu for the selected item (cell, range, or chart element, for example).

➤ Some of the tab groups contain a small icon, to the right of the group name. These icons are known as dialog box launchers. Click one, and you get a dialog box relevant to the commands in the group. For example, click the dialog box launcher in the Number group of the Home tab, and you get the Format Cells dialog box, with the Number tab selected. You can use this dialog box to specify number formats that aren't available directly from the Ribbon.

➤ Right-click certain items in Excel to take advantage of the Mini Toolbar, displayed above the shortcut menu (see Figure 2-2). This toolbar contains formatting tools that may save you a trip to the Ribbon. When I started using Excel 2007, I just ignored the Mini Toolbar, but I soon realized that it's a very handy tool.

Figure 2-2: The Mini Toolbar is easy to ignore, but it can save lots of trips to the Ribbon.

➤ Don't ignore the Quick Access toolbar. This is where you put commands that you use frequently. The Quick Access toolbar is always visible, no matter which tab is displayed. Check out Tip 11 to find out how easy it is to customize it.

➤ Finally, keep in mind that Excel has additional commands that aren't even on the Ribbon. If you come up empty-handed after performing an exhaustive Ribbon search for the old text-to-speech commands, for example, don't despair: You need to add those commands yourself, by customizing the Quick Access Toolbar (see Tip 11) or by customizing the Ribbon (see Tip 12).

Understanding Protected View

One of the new features in Excel 2010 is called Protected View. Although it may seem like Excel is trying to keep you from opening your own files, Protected View is all about protecting you from malware.

Malware refers to something that can harm your system. Hackers have figured out several ways to manipulate Excel files so that harmful code can execute. Protected View essentially prevents these types of attacks by opening a file in a protected environment (sometimes called a *sandbox*).

If you use Excel 2010 to open an Excel workbook that you downloaded from the Web, you'll see a colorful message above the Formula bar (see Figure 3-1). In addition, Excel's title bar displays the text *[Protected View]*.

Figure 3-1: This message tells you the workbook was opened in Protected View.

If you are certain that the file is safe, click Enable Editing. If you don't enable editing, you'll be able to view the contents of the workbook, but you won't be able to make any changes to it.

If the workbook contains macros, you'll see another message after you enable editing: *Security Warning. Macros have been disabled*. If you're sure that the macros are harmless, click Enable Content.

Protected View kicks in for the following:

> ➤ Files downloaded from the Internet

> ➤ Attachments opened from Outlook 2010

> ➤ Files opened from potentially unsafe locations, such as your Temporary Internet Files folder

> ➤ File that are blocked by File Block Policy (a feature that allows administrators to define potentially dangerous files)

> ➤ Files that were digitally signed, but the signature has expired

In addition, you can specifically request that a file be opened in Protected View in the File Open dialog box: Click the Open button and choose Open in Protected View.

In some situations, you don't care about working with the document. You just want to print it. Fortunately, printing is allowed for documents opened in Protected View. Choose File➜Print and then click the Enable Printing button.

It would be nice if copying were allowed in Protected View — but it's not. The only way to copy information from a workbook in Protected View is to enable editing.

If you would like to explicitly open a file in Protected View, choose File➜Open to display the Open dialog box. Select your file and then click the arrow to the right of the Open button. One of the options displayed is Open In Protected View.

You have some control over how Protected View works. To change the settings, choose File➜ Options and click Trust Center. Then click the Trust Center Settings button and click the Protected View tab in the Trust Center dialog box. Figure 3-2 shows the options. By default, all four options are checked.

Figure 3-2: Change the Protected View settings in the Trust Center dialog box.

Selecting Cells Efficiently

Many Excel users think that the only way to select a range of cells is to drag over the cells with the mouse. Although selecting cells with a mouse works, it's rarely the most *efficient* way to accomplish the task. A better way is to use your keyboard to select ranges.

Selecting a range by using the shift and arrow keys

The simplest way to select a range is to press (and hold) Shift and then use the arrow keys to highlight the cells. For larger selections, you can use PgDn or PgUp while pressing Shift to move in larger increments.

You can also use the End key to quickly extend a selection to the last non-empty cell in a row or column. To select the range B3:B8 (see Figure 4-1) by using the keyboard, move the cell pointer to B3 and then press the Shift key while you press End followed by the down arrow key. Similarly, to select B3:D3, press the Shift key while you press End, followed by the right-arrow key.

	A	B	C	D	E	F	G
1							
2							
3		200	138	206			
4		86	162	96			
5		77	104	177			
6		175	156	199			
7		95	130	205			
8		96	132	152			
9							
10							
11							
12							

Figure 4-1: A range of cells.

Selecting the current region

Often, you need to select a large rectangular selection of cells — the *current region*. To select the entire block of cells, move the cell pointer anywhere within the range and press Ctrl+A.

Selecting a range by Shift+clicking

When you're selecting a very large range, using the mouse may be the most efficient method — but dragging is not required. Select the upper left cell in the range. Then scroll to the lower right corner of the range, press Shift, and click the lower right cell.

Selecting noncontiguous ranges

Most of the time, your range selections are probably simple rectangular ranges. In some cases, you may need to make a *multiple selection* — a selection that includes nonadjacent cells or ranges. For example, you may want to apply formatting to cells in different areas of your worksheet. If you make a multiple selection, you can apply the formatting in one step to all selected ranges. Figure 4-2 shows an example of a multiple selection.

	A	B	C	D	E	F	G
1							
2							
3		200	138	206			
4		86	162	96			
5		77	104	177			
6		175	156	199			
7		95	130	205			
8		96	132	152			
9							
10							
11							
12							

Figure 4-2: A multiple selection that consists of noncontiguous ranges.

You can select a noncontiguous range by using either the mouse or the keyboard.

Press Ctrl as you click and drag the mouse to highlight individual cells or ranges.

From the keyboard, select a range as described previously (by using the Shift key). Then press Shift+F8 to select another range without canceling the previous range selection. Repeat this action as many times as needed.

Selecting entire rows

To select a single row, click a row number along the left of the worksheet. Or, select any cell in the row and press Shift+spacebar.

To select multiple adjacent rows, click and drag in the row number area. Or, select any cell in the first (or last) row, and press Shift+spacebar to select one row. Then press Shift and use the arrow keys to extend the row selection down (or up).

To select multiple nonadjacent rows, press Ctrl while you click the row numbers for the rows you want to include.

Selecting entire columns

To select a single column, click a column letter along the top of the worksheet. Or, select any cell in the column and press Ctrl+spacebar.

To select multiple adjacent columns, click and drag in the column letter section. Or, select any cell in the first (or last) column, and press Ctrl+spacebar to select one column. Then press Shift and use the arrow keys to extend the selection to the right (or left).

To select multiple nonadjacent columns, press Ctrl while you click the column letters for the columns you want to include.

Selecting multisheet ranges

In addition to two-dimensional ranges on a single worksheet, ranges can extend across multiple worksheets to be three-dimensional ranges.

Figure 4-3 shows a simple example of a multisheet workbook. The workbook has four sheets, named Totals, Marketing, Operations, and Manufacturing. The sheets are laid out identically.

	A	B	C	D	E	F	G
1	Budget Summary						
2							
3		Q1	Q2	Q3	Q4	Year Total	
4	Salaries	286,500.00	286,500.00	286,500.00	290,500.00	1,150,000.00	
5	Travel	40,500.00	42,525.00	44,651.25	46,883.81	174,560.06	
6	Supplies	59,500.00	62,475.00	65,598.75	68,878.69	256,452.44	
7	Facility	144,000.00	144,000.00	144,000.00	144,000.00	576,000.00	
8	Total	530,500.00	535,500.00	540,750.00	550,262.50	2,157,012.50	
9							
10							
11							
12							
13							

Totals / Marketing / Operations / Manufacturing

Figure 4-3: Each worksheet in this workbook is laid out identically.

Assume that you want to apply the same formatting to all sheets — for example, you want to make the column headings bold with background shading. Selecting a multisheet range is the best approach. When the ranges are selected, the formatting is applied to all sheets.

In general, selecting a multisheet range is a simple two-step process:

1. Select the range in one sheet.

2. Select the worksheets to include in the range.

Note

To select a group of contiguous worksheets, press Shift and click the sheet tab of the last worksheet that you want to include in the selection. To select individual worksheets, press Ctrl and click the sheet tab of each worksheet that you want to select. When you make the selection, the sheet tabs of the selected sheets appear with a white background, and Excel displays [Group] on the title bar.

When you finish working with the multisheet range, click any sheet tab to leave Group mode.

Making "Special" Range Selections

In some cases, you want to locate specific types of cells in your worksheets. For example, wouldn't it be handy to be able to locate every cell that contains a formula, or perhaps all cells whose values depend on the current cell?

Excel provides an easy way to locate these and many other special types of cells.

The key to many types of special selections is the Go To Special dialog box. Choose Home→Find & Select→Go To Special to display the Go To Special dialog box, as shown in Figure 5-1. Another way to open the Go To Special dialog box is to press F5 and then click the Special button in the Go To dialog box.

Figure 5-1: Use the Go To Special dialog box to select specific types of cells.

After you make your choice in the Go To Special dialog box, Excel selects the qualifying subset of cells in the current selection. Usually, this results in a multiple selection. If no cells qualify, Excel lets you know with the message No cells were found.

Note   **If you bring up the Go To Special dialog box when only one cell is selected, Excel bases its selection on the entire active area of the worksheet. Otherwise, the selection is based on the selected range.**

Table 5-1 summarizes the options available in the Go To Special dialog box.

Table 5-1: Go To Special Options

Option	What It Selects
Comments	Only the cells that contain cell comments.
Constants	All non-empty cells that don't contain formulas. This option is useful if you have a model set up and you want to clear out all input cells (so you can enter new values), but keep the formulas intact. Use the check boxes under the Formulas option to choose which cells to include.
Formulas	Cells that contain formulas. Qualify this choice by selecting the check box for the type of result: Numbers, Text, Logicals (the logical values TRUE or FALSE), or Errors.
Blanks	All empty cells.
Current Region	A rectangular range of cells around the active cell. This range is determined by surrounding blank rows and columns. You can also use the Ctrl+A shortcut key combination.
Current Array	The entire array (used for multicell array formulas).
Objects	All graphical objects on the worksheet. This is useful if you want to delete all objects.
Row Differences	If one row is selected, cells that are different from the active cell. If more than one row is selected, the same comparison is done, but the comparison cell for each row is the cell in the same column as the active cell.
Column Differences	If one column is selected, cells that are different from the active cell. If more than one column is selected, the same comparison is done, but the comparison cell for each column is the cell in the same rows as the active cell.
Precedents	Cells that are referred to in the formulas in the active cell or selection (limited to the active sheet). You can select either direct precedents or precedents at any level.
Dependents	Cells with formulas that refer to the active cell or selection (limited to the active sheet). You can select either direct dependents or dependents at any level.
Last Cell	The lower right cell in the worksheet that contains data or formatting.
Visible Cells Only	Only visible cells in the selection. This option is useful when dealing with outlines or a filtered list.
Conditional Formats	Cells that have a conditional format applied (by using the Home→Styles→ Conditional Formatting command).
Data Validation	Cells that are set up for data entry validation (by using the Data→Data Tools→ Data Validation command). The All option selects all cells of this type. The Same option selects only the cells that have the same validation rules as the active cell.

Note

When you select an option in the Go To Special dialog box, be sure to note which suboptions become available. For example, when you select the Constants or Formulas option, the four suboptions become available to help you further refine the results. Likewise, the Dependents suboptions also apply to Precedents, and the Data Validation suboptions also apply to Conditional formats.

Undoing, Redoing, and Repeating

This tip describes three operations that help you recover from mistakes and improve your editing efficiency.

Undoing

You can reverse just about every command in Excel by using the Undo command, located on the Quick Access toolbar. The Quick Access toolbar is normally displayed on the left side of the Excel title bar. You can also press Ctrl+Z to undo your actions.

Choose Undo after issuing a command in error, and it's as though you never issued the command. You can reverse the effects of the last 100 commands that you executed by selecting Undo multiple times.

You can't reverse some actions, however. Anything that you do by using the File button — for example, saving a workbook — is not undoable.

If you click the arrow on the right side of the Undo button, you see a description of the recent commands that you can reverse (see Figure 6-1). You can highlight a series of these commands to undo several actions with one click. In the figure, seven actions are highlighted, beginning with the command that inserted a chart.

Figure 6-1: The Undo button displays a list of recent actions that can be undone.

 Note   Keep in mind that you can't undo the effect of executing a macro. In fact, running a macro that changes a worksheet wipes out all the Undo information. This serious weakness in Excel isn't present in Microsoft Word.

Redoing

The Redo button (located to the right of the Undo button on the Quick Access toolbar) essentially undoes the Undo command. If you undo too much, you can click the Redo button (or press Ctrl+Y or F4) to repeat commands that have been undone.

Repeating

You can repeat many Excel operations by pressing Ctrl+Y or F4. This command simply repeats the last action — unless the last operation was an Undo operation. In this case, the Undo is undone (as described in the previous section).

Repeating a command can be a great timesaver. Here's an example of how useful the Repeat command can be. You may apply lots of formatting (for example, font size, bold formatting, background color, and borders) to a cell by using the Format Cells dialog box. After you close the dialog box, it's a snap to apply that same formatting to other cells or ranges by pressing Ctrl+Y. Or, you may need to insert blank rows at certain locations in your worksheet. Issue the Home→Cells→Insert→Insert Sheet Rows command one time. Then move the cell pointer to the next row to be inserted and press Ctrl+Y to repeat the row insertion command.

Excel also has a Repeat button, but it's not normally available. You can, however, add this button to your Quick Access toolbar:

1. Right-click the Quick Access toolbar and choose Customize Quick Access Toolbar to display the Quick Access Toolbar tab of the Excel Options dialog box.

2. In the Excel Options dialog box, select Popular Commands from the drop-down list on the left.

3. In the list of commands, select Repeat.

4. Click Add to add the selected command to the Quick Access toolbar.

5. Click OK to close the Excel Options dialog box.

Why add the Repeat button to your Quick Access toolbar, when pressing Ctrl+Y is so easy? One reason is that you can hover your mouse pointer over the button and Excel displays a description of what will be repeated (see Figure 6-2). Another reason is that the Repeat button is disabled if you can't repeat the most recent command — a visual cue that may prevent you from trying to repeat something that can't be repeated.

Figure 6-2: After you add the Repeat button to the Quick Access toolbar, a ToolTip describes the task (if any) that will be repeated.

Note

Unfortunately, repeating an operation is not perfectly reliable. In fact, it's seriously broken. In some situations, you may find that pressing Ctrl+Y has no effect (when it should have an effect). At other times, you may find that pressing Ctrl+Y repeats the command that you issued _before_ the previous command.

Discovering Some Useful Shortcut Keys

Excel has no shortage of shortcut keys. Your productivity is sure to increase if you take the time to learn the shortcut keys for commands that you use frequently. In the following table, I list some of the most useful shortcut keys. This list is certainly not an exhaustive one — it describes just the commands that I find most useful.

Shortcut	What You Can Do with It
F11	Create a new chart on a separate chart sheet (of the default chart type) by using data in the selected range.
Alt+F1	Create a new, embedded chart (of the default chart type) by using the data in the selected range.
F5	Display the Go To dialog box.
Alt	Display the keytips for the Ribbon commands so that you can access the commands by using letters on the keyboard.
F2	Edit the active cell.
Shift+F2	Edit the comment in the active cell or insert a comment if the cell doesn't have one.
Ctrl+Shift+_	Remove all borders from the selected cells.
Shift+F10	Display the shortcut menu for the selected item.
Ctrl+F6	Activate the next window.
Ctrl+PgUp	Activate the previous sheet in the workbook.
Ctrl+PgDn	Activate the next sheet in the workbook.
Alt+Ctrl+V	Display the Paste Special dialog box.
Alt+=	Perform the equivalent of clicking the AutoSum button.
Ctrl+B	Make the selected cells bold.
Ctrl+C	Copy the selected cells.
Ctrl+D	Copy the top cell in a selected range to the other cells in the selection.
Ctrl+F	Display the Find dialog box.
Ctrl+H	Display the Replace dialog box.
Ctrl+I	Make the selected cells italic.
Ctrl+N	Create a new default workbook.
Ctrl+R	Copy the leftmost cell in a selected range to the other cells in the selection.
Ctrl+S	Save the active workbook.
Ctrl+V	Paste a copied or cut item in the selected cell.
Ctrl+X	Cut the selected cells.
Ctrl+Y	Repeat the last repeatable command. If the last command was Undo, this shortcut reverses the Undo.
Ctrl+Z	Undo the last action.

Navigating Sheets in a Workbook

As you know, a single workbook can contain multiple worksheets. The sheet tabs at the bottom of the Excel window identify the worksheets. Click a sheet tab, and that sheet becomes the active sheet. If the tab for the sheet you want isn't visible, you can use the tab scroll controls to the left of the first sheet tab to scroll the tabs left or right (see Figure 8-1).

Figure 8-1: Use these controls to scroll the sheet tabs to the left or right.

The sheet tabs share space with the horizontal scroll bar. You can reduce the width of the horizontal scroll bar to reveal more sheet tabs. Just click the vertical bar on the left side of the scroll bar and drag it to the right.

Another way to activate a sheet is to right-click the tab scroll controls. This action displays a pop-up list of sheet names (see Figure 8-2). Just click a name, and you're there. If not all the sheet names are listed, click the More Sheets item at the bottom, and a dialog box that lists the sheet names appears. Just double-click a sheet name to activate that sheet.

Figure 8-2: Right-clicking the tab scroll controls displays a list of sheet names.

In many cases, the most efficient way to activate a different sheet is to avoid the mouse and use the keyboard. Surprisingly, many users don't know about two useful keyboard commands:

> ➤ **Ctrl+PgDn:** Activates the next sheet

> ➤ **Ctrl+PgUp:** Activates the previous sheet

I use these keys 90 percent of the time — but then again, I avoid using a mouse whenever I can.

Resetting the Used Area of a Worksheet

When you press Ctrl+End, Excel activates the lower right cell in the used area of the worksheet. In some cases, you find that the lower right cell in the worksheet is an empty cell — not the *real* last cell. In other words, Excel sometimes loses track of the used area of your worksheet. For example, you may find that a workbook's file size seems much too large. It's possible that Excel has misidentified the used area and is storing a large number of empty cells.

First, try saving the workbook. After the workbook is saved, Excel may correctly identify the last cell. If Excel still doesn't identify the last cell, it's probably because you deleted data but left the formatting in the cells. To force Excel to identify the real used area, you need to delete the columns to the right of your data and then delete the rows below your data.

For example, assume that the real last cell in your workbook is G25, but pressing Ctrl+End takes you to some other cell — M50, for example.

To delete those formatted cells, follow these steps:

1. Select all columns to the right of column G.

   To do this, activate any cell in column H; press Ctrl+spacebar, followed by Shift+End, and then press Shift while you press the right-arrow key.

2. Choose Home➔Cells➔Delete➔Delete Sheet Columns (or, right-click any column header and choose Delete).

3. Select all rows below row 25.

   To do this, activate any cell in row 26. Press Shift+spacebar, followed by Shift+End, and then press Shift while you press the down-arrow key.

4. Choose Home➔Cells➔Delete➔Delete Sheet Rows (or, right-click any row header and choose Delete).

5. Save your workbook, and Excel resets the last cell.

After performing these steps, pressing Ctrl+End takes you to the *real* last cell.

By the way, if you can't remember Ctrl+End, you can use the Go To Special dialog box. Choose Home➔Find & Select➔Go To Special. Choose the Last Cell option and click OK.

Understanding Workbooks versus Windows

One of the most common questions asked in the Excel newsgroups is "Why is Excel displaying two copies of my workbook?" Then the Excel users go on to describe the symptoms: The file-name is followed by a colon and a number (for example, `budget.xlsx:2`).

Normally, a workbook is displayed in a single window within Excel. However, you can create multiple windows for a single workbook by using the View➜Window➜New Window command.

Most people who ask this question in the newsgroups have probably issued the New Window command accidentally. What they're really asking for is a way to close the additional window (or windows). That's an easy problem to solve: Just click the X on the title bar of the unwanted windows. Or, use the Ctrl+F4 shortcut to close the window. After you close all extra windows, the title bar no longer displays the window number.

By the way, the multiple window configuration is saved with the workbook, so when you open the file later, the multiple windows are still displayed.

Although many people are confused about multiple windows, there are at least two good reasons why you might want your workbook to display in two or more windows:

> ➤ You can view two worksheets in the same workbook simultaneously. For example, you can display Sheet1 in the first window and Sheet2 in the second window and then tile the two windows so that both are visible. The View➜Window➜Arrange All command is useful for tiling windows. This statement also applies to chart sheets. If you have a chart on a chart sheet, you can arrange the windows so that you can see the chart along with its data.

> ➤ You can view cells and their formulas at the same time. Create a second window and then press Ctrl+` (the key that usually also has the tilde character) to display the formulas. Tile the two windows so that you can view the formulas and their results side by side (see Figure 10-1).

Note

When you need to compare information in two worksheets (or the same worksheet in two windows), try the View➜Window➜View Side by Side command. It makes comparing two worksheets easy because Excel automatically scrolls the second window to keep them synchronized. To use this feature with a single workbook, first create a second window by choosing the View➜Window➜New Window command.

Figure 10-1: Displaying two windows for a workbook lets you view the cells and their formulas.

Customizing the Quick Access Toolbar

If you find that you continually need to switch Ribbon tabs because a frequently used command never seems to be on the Ribbon that's displayed, this tip is for you. The Quick Access toolbar is always visible, regardless of which Ribbon tab is selected. After you customize the Quick Access toolbar, your frequently used commands will always be one click away.

Note

The only situation in which the Quick Access toolbar is not visible is in Full Screen mode, which is enabled by choosing View➜Workbook Views➜Full Screen. To cancel Full Screen mode, right-click any cell and choose Close Full Screen or press Escape.

About the Quick Access toolbar

By default, the Quick Access toolbar is located on the left side of the Excel title bar, and it includes the following three tools:

- ➤ **Save:** Saves the active workbook.
- ➤ **Undo:** Reverses the effect of the last action.
- ➤ **Redo:** Reverses the effect of the last undo.

If you prefer, you can move the Quick Access toolbar below the Ribbon: Right-click the Quick Access toolbar and choose Show Quick Access Toolbar Below The Ribbon. Moving the Quick Access toolbar below the Ribbon eats up additional vertical space on your screen. In other words, you see one or two fewer rows of your worksheet if you move the Quick Access toolbar from its default location.

Commands on the Quick Access toolbar always appear as small icons, with no text. When you hover your mouse pointer over an icon, you see the name of the command and a brief description.

As far as I can tell, the number of commands that you can add to your Quick Access toolbar is limitless. But regardless of the number of icons, the Quick Access toolbar always displays a single line of icons. If the number of icons exceeds the Excel window width, it displays an additional icon at the end: More Controls. Click the More Controls icon, and the hidden Quick Access toolbar icons appear in a pop-up window.

Adding new commands to the Quick Access toolbar

You can add a new command to the Quick Access toolbar in three ways:

- ➤ Click the Quick Access toolbar drop-down control, which is located on the right side of the Quick Access toolbar (see Figure 11-1). The list contains several commonly used commands. Select a command from the list, and Excel adds it to your Quick Access toolbar.

➤ Right-click any control on the Ribbon and choose Add To Quick Access Toolbar. The control is added to your Quick Access toolbar, positioned after the last control.

➤ Use the Quick Access Toolbar tab of the Excel Options dialog box. A quick way to access this dialog box is to right-click any Quick Access toolbar or Ribbon control and choose Customize Quick Access Toolbar.

Figure 11-1: The Quick Access toolbar drop-down menu is one way to add a new command to the Quick Access toolbar.

Figure 11-2 shows the Quick Access Toolbar tab of the Excel Options dialog box. The left side of the dialog box displays a list of Excel commands, and the right side shows the commands that are now on the Quick Access toolbar. Above the command list on the left is a drop-down control that lets you filter the list. Select an item from the drop-down list, and the list displays only the commands for that item.

Some of the items in the drop-down control are described in this list:

➤ **Popular Commands:** Displays commands that Excel users commonly use

➤ **Commands Not In The Ribbon:** Displays a list of commands that you cannot access from the Ribbon

➤ **All Commands:** Displays a complete list of Excel commands

➤ **Macros:** Displays a list of all available macros

➤ **File Tab:** Displays the commands available in the back stage window

➤ **Home Tab:** Displays all commands that are available when the Home tab is active

In addition, the drop-down list contains an item for every other tab.

Figure 11-2: Use the Quick Access Toolbar tab in the Excel Options dialog box to customize the Quick Access toolbar.

Sometimes, you need to do some guessing to find a particular command. For example, if you'd like to add the command that displays the Excel Options dialog box, you'll find it listed as Options, not Excel Options.

Some commands simply aren't available. For example, I'd like the Quick Access toolbar to display the command to toggle the "dashed line" page break display on a worksheet. The only way to issue that command is to display the Advanced tab of the Excel Options dialog box and then scroll down until you find the Show Page Breaks check box. There is no command that can be added to the Quick Access toolbar. To add an item to your Quick Access toolbar, select it from the list on the left and click Add. If you add a macro to your Quick Access toolbar, you can click the Modify button to change the text and choose a different icon for the macro.

Notice the drop-down control above the list on the right. This lets you create a Quick Access toolbar that's specific to a particular workbook. This is most useful when you add macro commands to the Quick Access toolbar. Most of the time, you'll use the setting labeled For All Documents (Default).

The only time you ever need to use the Quick Access Toolbar tab of the Excel Options dialog box is when you want to add a command that's not on the Ribbon or add a command that executes a macro. In all other situations, it's much easier to locate the command on the Ribbon, right-click the command, and choose Add To Quick Access Toolbar.

Only you can decide which commands to put on your Quick Access toolbar. In general, if you find that you use a particular command frequently, it should probably be on your Quick Access toolbar. For example, when I work on a chart, I like to use the Chart Elements control to make it easy to select chart elements. That control is located in the Chart Tools→Format tab and the Chart Tools→Layout tab, but not in the Chart Tools→Design tab. Putting a copy of this control on my Quick Access toolbar saves me many mouse clicks for every chart I work on.

Performing other Quick Access toolbar actions

Here are some other things you can do with your Quick Access toolbar:

> **Rearrange the Quick Access toolbar icons:** If you want to change the order of your Quick Access toolbar icons, you can do so on the Customization tab of the Excel Options dialog box. Select the command and then use the up- and down-arrow buttons on the right to move the icon.

> **Remove Quick Access toolbar icons:** The easiest way to remove an icon from your Quick Access toolbar is to right-click the icon and choose Remove from Quick Access Toolbar. You can also use the Quick Access Toolbar tab of the Excel Options dialog box. Just select the command in the list on the right and click the Remove button.

> **Share your Quick Access toolbar:** Use the Import/Export button to save a file that contains your Quick Access toolbar customization. You can then share this file with others. Unfortunately, this file also contains any Ribbon customizations that you might have made (see Tip 12). In other words, you can't share your Quick Access toolbar without also sharing your Ribbon customizations.

> **Reset the Quick Access toolbar:** If you want to return the Quick Access toolbar to its default state, display the Quick Access Toolbar tab in the Excel Options dialog box and click the Reset button and choose Reset Only Quick Access Toolbar. All your customizations disappear, and the Quick Access toolbar then displays its three default commands.

Customizing the Ribbon

In Excel 2007, user interface modifications were limited to the Quick Access toolbar. But Excel 2010 lets you customize the Ribbon in many ways. Tip 11 describes how to customize the Quick Access toolbar, but some users will prefer to make some changes to the Ribbon itself.

You can customize the Ribbon in these ways:

> ➤ Add a new tab.

> ➤ Add a new group to a tab.

> ➤ Add commands to a group.

> ➤ Remove groups from a tab.

> ➤ Remove commands from custom groups.

> ➤ Change the order of the tabs.

> ➤ Change the order of the groups within a tab.

> ➤ Change the name of a tab.

> ➤ Change the name of a group.

> ➤ Reset the Ribbon to remove all customizations.

That's a fairly comprehensive list of customization options, but there are some actions that you *cannot* do:

> ➤ You cannot remove built-in tabs — but you *can* hide them.

> ➤ You cannot add commands to built-in groups.

> ➤ You cannot remove commands from built-in groups.

> ➤ You cannot change the order of commands in a built-in group.

Note

Unfortunately, you can't customize the Ribbon (or Quick Access toolbar) by using VBA macros. However, developers can write RibbonX code and store it in workbook files. When the file is open, the Ribbon is modified to display new commands. Writing RibbonX is relatively complicated and is the subject of several complete books.

Customizing the Ribbon is done in the Customize Ribbon panel of the Excel Options dialog box (see Figure 12-1). The quickest way to display this dialog box is to right-click anywhere in the Ribbon and choose Customize The Ribbon.

Figure 12-1: The Customize Ribbon tab of the Excel Options dialog box.

Customizing the Ribbon is very similar to customizing the Quick Access toolbar, which is described in Tip 11. The only difference is that you need to decide where to put the command within the Ribbon. The general procedure is

1. Use the drop-down list on the left (labeled Choose Command From) to display various groups of commands.

2. Locate the command in the list box on the left and select it.

3. Use the drop-down list on the right (labeled Customize The Ribbon) to choose a group of tabs.

   Main Tabs refer to the tabs that are always visible; Tool Tabs refer to the contextual tabs that appear when a particular object is selected.

4. In the list box on the right, select the tab and the group where you would like to put the command.

   You'll need to click the "plus sign" controls to expand the hierarchical lists. Remember that you cannot add commands to built-in groups, so you might need to use the New Tab or New Group button to add a tab or group.

5. Click the Add button to add the selected command from the left to the group on the right.

New tabs and groups are given generic names, so you'll probably want to give them more meaningful names. Use the Rename button to rename the selected tab or group. You can also rename built-in tabs and groups.

Tip

Although you cannot remove a built-in tab, you can hide the tab by unchecking the check box next to its name.

Figure 12-2 shows a part of a customized Ribbon. In this case, I added two groups to the View tab: Extra Commands (with four new commands), and Text To Speech (with two new commands). I inserted these new groups between the Zoom and Window groups.

Figure 12-2: The View tab, with two new groups added.

Accessing the Ribbon with Your Keyboard

At first glance, you may think that the Ribbon is completely mouse-centric. After all, none of the commands has the traditional underlined letter to indicate the Alt+keystrokes. In fact, the Ribbon is very keyboard friendly. The trick is to press the Alt key (or forward slash key) to display the pop-up *keytips:* Each Ribbon control has a letter (or series of letters) that you type to issue the command.

By the way, you don't have to hold down the Alt key as you type the keytip letters.

Figure 13-1 shows how the Home tab looks after I press the Alt key to display the keytips. Each tab has a corresponding letter, known as a keytip. If you press one of the keytips, the screen then displays more keytips. For example, to use the keyboard to align the cell contents to the left, press Alt followed by H (for Home) and then AL (for Align Left). If you're a keyboard fan (like I am), after just a few times you memorize the keystrokes required for common commands that you use frequently.

Figure 13-1: Pressing Alt displays the keytips.

After you press Alt, you can also use the left- and right-arrow keys to scroll through the tabs. When you reach the proper tab, press the down-arrow key to enter the Ribbon. Then use the left- and right-arrow keys to scroll through the Ribbon commands. When you reach the command you need, press Enter to execute it. This method isn't as efficient as using keytips, but it's an easy, mouse-free way to take a quick look at the available commands.

Recovering Your Work

If you've used computers for any length of time, you've probably lost some work. You forgot to save a file, or maybe the power went out and your unsaved work was lost. Or maybe you were working on something and didn't think it was important, so you closed it without saving — and later realized that it *was* important. The new Versions feature in Excel 2010 can make these types of "doh!" moments less frequent.

As you work in Excel, your work is periodically saved, automatically. It happens in the background, so you don't even know that it's happening. New in Excel 2010 is the ability to access these autosaved versions of your work. And this ability even applies to workbooks that you never explicitly saved.

The Versions feature consists of two components:

> ➤ Versions of a workbook are saved automatically, and you can view them.

> ➤ Workbooks that you closed without saving are saved as draft versions.

Recovering versions of the current workbook

To see whether any previous versions of the current workbook are available, choose File➜Info. The section labeled Versions lists the available old versions (if any) of the current workbook. Figure 14-1 shows that two autosaved versions of the active workbook are available.

You can open an autosaved version by clicking its name. Remember that opening an autosaved version *won't* automatically replace the current version of your workbook. Therefore, you can decide whether the autosaved version is preferable to the current version. Or, you can just copy some information that may have been accidentally deleted and paste it to your current workbook.

When you close the workbook, the autosaved versions are deleted.

Recovering unsaved work

When you close a workbook without saving your changes, Excel asks whether you're sure. If that unsaved workbook has an autosaved version, the "Are you sure?" dialog box informs you of that fact, as shown in Figure 14-2.

To recover a workbook that you closed without saving, choose File➜Info➜Versions and choose Recover Draft Versions. You see a list of all draft versions of your workbooks. You can open them and (hopefully) recover something that you needed. These drafts are also listed in the recent file list, displayed when you choose File➜Recent.

Remember that draft versions are deleted after four days, or until you edit the file.

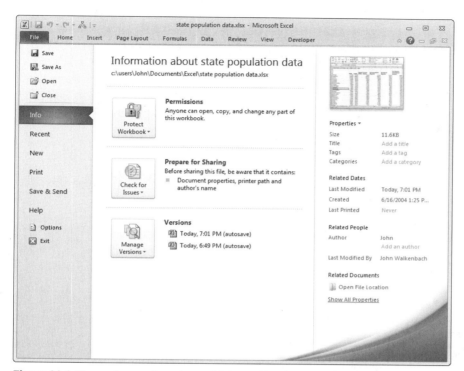

Figure 14-1: Two autosaved versions of this workbook are available.

Note

You can adjust the Versions feature in the Save tab of the Excel Options dialog box. For example, you can change the autosave time interval (the default is 10 minutes), turn off autosave for a particular workbook, or disable this feature for all workbooks.

Figure 14-2: If you close a workbook without saving, Excel tells you whether an autosaved version will be available.

Customizing the Default Workbook

When you create a new Excel workbook, you get a standard default workbook. What if you don't like that workbook? For example, you may prefer a workbook with only one worksheet. Or, maybe you don't like the default font or font size. Perhaps you prefer to have the gridlines hidden in your worksheets. Or, maybe you have a standard header that you always use on printed pages.

As it turns out, Excel gives you quite a bit of control in this area. You can make some changes in the Excel Options dialog box. Other changes require a template.

Changing defaults in the Excel Options dialog box

The General tab of the Excel Options dialog box has four setting that control new workbooks (see Figure 15-1).

Figure 15-1: Use the Excel Options dialog box to change some settings for new workbooks.

You can specify the font, font size, view, and number of worksheets. When you change any of these settings, all new workbooks will use those settings. Changing these settings will not affect workbooks that you've already created.

Creating a book.xltx template

For a new workbook setting that can't be specified in the Excel Options dialog box, you need to create a custom template file named book.xltx and then save that file to the proper location on your hard drive.

To create a new default workbook template, all you need to do is customize a blank workbook exactly as you like it. Here's a list of some of the items you can change:

> ➤ **Number of sheets:** Add or delete sheets as you like. You can also change their names.

> ➤ **Styles:** Use the Style Gallery (Home➜Styles) to customize styles. By default, all cells use the Normal style, so if you want to change the default font in any way (including fill color, number format, font, and borders), modify the Normal style. To change the Normal style, right-click its name in the Style Gallery and choose Modify. Then make the changes in the Style dialog box.

> ➤ **Print settings:** Use the commands on the Page Layout tab to specify print-related settings. For example, you can include header or footer information or adjust the margins.

> ➤ **Column widths:** If you don't like the default column widths, change them.

> ➤ **Graphics:** You can even insert a graphical object or two — for example, your company logo or a picture of your cat.

When the new default workbook is set up to your specifications, choose File➜Save As. In the Save As dialog box, follow these steps:

1. Select Template (`*.xltx`) in the Save As Type drop-down list.

   If your template contains any VBA macros, select Excel Macro-Enabled Template (`*.xltm`).

2. Name the file `book.xltx` (or `book.xltm` if it has macros).

3. Make sure that the file is saved to your XLStart folder.

   Excel proposes that you save the file in your Templates folder, but it must be saved in your XLStart folder.

Note The location of the XLStart folder varies. To find the location of your XLStart folder, press Alt+F11 to activate the VB Editor. Press Ctrl+G to display the Immediate window, and then type this statement and press Enter:

```
? Application.StartupPath
```

After you save the file, you can close it. Now, every time you start Excel, the blank workbook that's displayed will be based on the template you created. In addition, when you press Ctrl+N, the new workbook will be created from your template.

If you ever need to bypass your new default workbook and start with one of the normal Excel default workbooks, choose File➜New and choose the Blank Workbook item.

Using Document Themes

Over the years, I've seen hundreds of Excel workbooks that were created by others. A significant percentage of these workbooks have one thing in common: They are ugly!

In an effort to help users create more professional-looking documents, Microsoft designers (starting with Office 2007) incorporated the concept of Office *document themes.* Using themes is an easy (and almost foolproof) way to specify the colors and fonts and a variety of graphical effects in a document. Best of all, changing the entire look of your document is a breeze. A few mouse clicks is all it takes to apply a different theme and change the look of your workbook.

Importantly, the concept of themes is incorporated into other Office applications. Therefore, a company can now easily create a standard look for all its documents.

Elements within Excel that are controlled by document themes are:

> ➤ Cells and ranges that use theme colors (as opposed to standard colors)
> ➤ Tables
> ➤ Charts
> ➤ Sparkline graphics
> ➤ Pivot tables
> ➤ PivotTable Slicers
> ➤ Shapes
> ➤ SmartArt
> ➤ WordArt
> ➤ Sheet tab colors

Figure 16-1 shows a worksheet that contains various Excel elements. These items all use the default theme, which is known as Office Theme.

Figure 16-2 shows the same worksheet after applying a different document theme. The different theme changes the fonts, colors (which may not be apparent in the figure), and graphical effects for the SmartArt diagram.

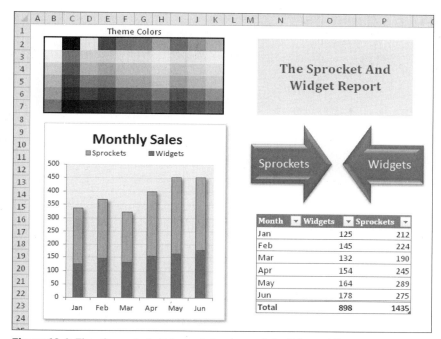

Figure 16-1: The elements in this worksheet use default formatting.

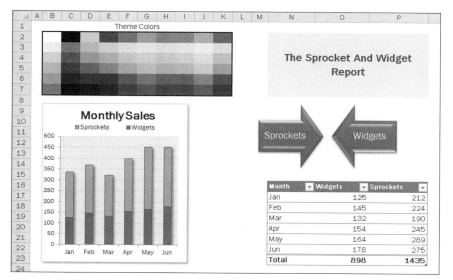

Figure 16-2: The worksheet, after applying a different theme.

Applying a theme

Figure 16-3 shows the theme choices that appear when you choose Page→Layout→Themes. This display is a "live preview" display. As you move your mouse over the theme choices, the active worksheet displays the theme. When you see a theme you like, click it to apply the theme to all worksheets in the workbook.

A theme applies to the entire workbook. You cannot use different themes on different worksheets within a workbook.

Figure 16-3: The built-in Excel theme choices.

When you specify a particular theme, you find that the gallery choices for various elements reflect the new theme. For example, the chart styles that you can choose from vary, depending on which theme is active.

Note

Because themes use different fonts and font sizes, changing to a different theme can affect the layout of your worksheet. For example, after you apply a new theme, a worksheet that printed on a single page may spill over to a second page. Therefore, you may need to make some adjustments after you apply a new theme. For best results, decide on a theme before you do too much work on the file.

Customizing a theme

Office 2010 includes 40 themes. If that's not enough, you can modify them and even create your own themes.

Notice that the Page Layout→Themes group contains three other controls: Colors, Fonts, and Effects. You can use these controls to change just one of the three components of a theme. For example, if you like the Urban theme but prefer different fonts, apply the Urban theme and then specify your preferred font set by using the Page Layout→Themes→Fonts control.

Each theme uses two fonts (one for headers and one for the body), and in some cases, these two fonts are the same. If none of the theme choices is suitable, choose Page Layout→Themes→ Fonts→Create New Theme Fonts to specify the two fonts you prefer (see Figure 16-4). When you use the Home→Fonts→Font control, the two fonts from the current theme are listed first in the drop-down list.

Figure 16-4: Use this dialog box to specify two fonts for a theme.

Use the Page Layout→Themes→Colors control to select a different set of colors. And, if you're so inclined, you can even create a custom set of colors by choosing Page Layout→Themes→Colors→ Create Theme Colors. This command displays the dialog box shown in Figure 16-5. Note that each theme consists of 12 colors. Four of the colors are for text and backgrounds, six are for accents, and two are for hyperlinks. The first ten are the colors that appear in theme color selector controls. As you specify different colors, the Preview panel in the dialog box is updated.

Theme effects operate on graphical elements, such as SmartArt, shapes, and charts. You can't customize theme effects.

If you customize a theme by using different fonts or colors, you can save the new theme by choosing Page Layout→Themes→Save Current Theme. Your customized themes appear in the theme list in the Custom category. Other Office applications, such as Word and PowerPoint, can use these theme files.

Figure 16-5: If you're feeling creative, you can specify a set of custom colors for a theme.

Hiding User Interface Elements

Excel has various options that enable you to hide elements in order to customize your workspace. In some cases, you can change the display options in more than one place. For each of the elements listed in this section, I show you the easiest Hide method possible.

From the Ribbon

Change the following settings by using controls on the Ribbon:

> **Ruler:** When your worksheet is in Page Layout view, use View➜Show➜Ruler to toggle the display of the rulers at the top and left side of the window. Turning off the rulers gives you slightly more screen real estate.

> **Gridlines:** When View➜Show➜Gridlines is not checked, cell gridlines are not displayed. If you format ranges by using cell borders, turning off the gridlines makes the borders more prominent.

> **Formula Bar:** The Formula bar, located just below the Ribbon, displays the contents of the selected cell. To see more of your worksheet, turn it off by choosing View➜Show➜ Formula Bar.

> **Row & Column Headers:** If this setting is turned off (by choosing View➜Show➜ Headings), you don't see the row (numbers) and column (letters) headers.

From the keyboard

Modify the items below by using the keyboard:

> **The Ribbon:** Press Ctrl+F1 to turn the Ribbon display off or on. The tabs remain visible, and the Ribbon appears (temporarily) when you click a tab.

> **Outline symbols:** This option is relevant only if you added a worksheet outline (by using the Data➜Outline➜Group command). If you don't like seeing the Outline symbols, you can turn them off. Or, you can press Ctrl+8 to toggle the display of the Outline symbols.

From the Excel Options dialog box

You change the following settings from the Advanced tab in the Excel Options dialog box. To display this dialog box, choose File➜Options and then click the Advanced tab. Scroll down, and you see three groups of options, as shown in Figure 17-1.

Figure 17-1: Display options available in the Advanced tab of the Excel Options dialog box.

Following are some of the more useful display options:

> **Show All Windows in Taskbar:** When this option is turned on, each workbook appears as a separate icon on the Windows taskbar. It's too much clutter for my taste, so I keep it turned off.

> **For Cells With Comments Show:** This determines how cell comments appear. I prefer the Indicators Only, And Comments On Hover option. You can find choices to override this setting on the Review➔Comments tab.

> **Page Breaks:** After you print or preview a document, Excel displays dotted-line page breaks in the worksheet. You can turn them off, if you like. Use the Show Page Breaks

check box in the Display Options for This Worksheet section of the Advanced tab in the Excel Options dialog box.

> **Zero Values:** Sometimes, you may prefer to hide all zero cells and show a blank cell instead. Control this option by using the Show a Zero in Cells That Have Zero Value check box in the Display Options For This Worksheet section of the Advanced tab in the Excel Options dialog box.

> **Scroll Bars:** You can hide the horizontal and vertical scroll bars for a workbook. Go to the Display Options for This Workbook section on the Advanced tab of the Excel Options dialog box and use the two check boxes labeled Show Horizontal Scroll Bar and Show Vertical Scroll Bar.

> **Sheet Tabs:** To hide the sheet tab, go to the Display Options for This Workbook section on the Advanced tab of the Excel Options dialog box and remove the checkmark from the Show Sheet Tabs check box. With no sheet tabs, you can use Ctrl+PgUp and Ctrl+PgDn to activate a different sheet.

A setting that requires a macro

Turning off the display of one user interface element requires a macro.

The status bar, at the bottom of the Excel window, displays a variety of information. In versions prior to Excel 2007, the user could turn the status bar display on or off. Now, a VBA macro is required to toggle the status bar display:

```
Sub ToggleStatusBar()
  With Application
     .DisplayStatusBar = Not .DisplayStatusBar
  End With
End Sub
```

Hiding Columns or Rows

If you have data in a column or row that you don't want to see, you can hide the column or row. Doing this is often useful if you have formulas that provide intermediate calculations and you don't want them to appear in a report. Or, you may just want to hide unused rows and columns so that you can focus only on the used area of the sheet.

Note

Formulas that refer to data in hidden rows columns continue to function normally. An exception is the SUBTOTAL function. If the first argument for SUBTOTAL is greater than 100, the SUBTOTAL function ignores the data in the hidden rows or columns resulting from filtering or outlines. In addition, the new AGGREGATE function has an option to ignore hidden data in rows, even if the rows are hidden manually. Refer to the Help system for information about these functions — which do a lot more than just add numbers.

Hiding

To hide one or more columns, use any of these techniques:

> ➤ Select a cell in the column (or columns) to be hidden. Then choose Home➜Cells➜ Format➜Hide & Unhide➜Hide Columns.

> ➤ Select entire columns and then right-click and choose Hide from the shortcut menu.

> ➤ Select a cell in the column (or columns) to hide and press Ctrl+0 (that's a zero).

To hide one or more rows, use any of these methods:

> ➤ Select a cell in the row (or rows) to be hidden. Then choose Home➜Cells➜Format➜Hide & Unhide➜Hide Rows.

> ➤ Select entire rows and then right-click and choose Hide from the shortcut menu.

> ➤ Select a cell in the row (or rows) to be hidden and press Ctrl+9.

Unhiding

That which is hidden also needs to be unhidden.

To unhide one or more hidden columns, use any of these techniques. Note that it's a bit tricky because you can't select hidden rows or columns directly.

> ➤ Select a range that consists of cells to the left and to the right of the hidden columns. Then choose Home➜Cells➜Format➜Hide & Unhide➜Unhide Columns.

➤ Select entire columns to the left and to the right of the hidden columns, and then right-click and choose Unhide from the shortcut menu.

To unhide one or more hidden rows, use any of these methods:

➤ Select a range that consists of cells above and below the hidden rows. Then choose Home➜Cells➜Format➜Hide & Unhide➜Unhide Rows.

➤ Select entire rows above and below the hidden rows, and then right-click and choose Unhide from the shortcut menu.

➤ Select a range that consists of cells above and below the hidden rows and press Ctrl+Shift+9.

Hiding Cell Contents

Excel doesn't provide a direct way to hide the contents of cells (without hiding entire rows and columns), but you can fake it in a few ways:

> ➤ Use a special custom number format. Select the cell or cells to be hidden, press Ctrl+1 and click the Number tab in the Format Cells dialog box. Select Custom from the Category list, and then, in the Type field, enter ;;; (three semicolons).

> ➤ Make the font color the same as the cell's background color.

> ➤ Add a shape to your worksheet and position it over the cell or cells to be hidden. You should make the shape the same color as the cell background and (probably) remove the borders.

All these methods have problems: The cell's contents are still displayed on the formula bar when the cell is selected. If you don't want to see the cell contents on the formula bar after you use one of those methods, you can either hide the Formula bar or perform these additional steps:

1. Select the cells.

2. Press Ctrl+1 and then click the Protection tab in the Format Cells dialog box.

3. Select the Hidden check box and click OK.

4. Choose Review➜Changes➜Protect Sheet.

5. In the Protect Sheet dialog box, add a password, if desired, and click OK.

Keep in mind that when a sheet is protected, you can't change any cells unless they are not locked. By default, all cells *are* locked. You change the locked status of a cell by using the Protection tab in the Format Cells dialog box.

Taking Pictures of Ranges

Excel makes it easy to convert a range of cells into a picture. The picture can either be a *dead* image (it doesn't change if the original range changes) or a *live* picture (which reflects changes in the original range). The range can even contain objects, such as charts or shapes.

Creating a static image of a range

To create a snapshot of a range, start by selecting a range of cells and then press Ctrl+C to copy the range to the Clipboard. Then choose Home➜Clipboard➜Paste➜Other Paste Options➜Picture (U). The result is a graphic image of the original range, pasted on top of the original range. Just click and drag to move the picture to another location. When you select this image, Excel displays its Picture Tools contextual menu — which means that you can apply some additional formatting to the picture.

Figure 20-1 shows a range of cells (B2:E9), along with a picture of the range after I applied one of the built-in styles from the Picture Tools➜Format➜Picture Styles gallery. It's a static picture, so changes made within the range B2:E9 are not shown in the picture.

Figure 20-1: A picture of a range, after applying some picture formatting.

Creating a live image of a range

To create an image that's linked to the original range of cells, select the cells and press Ctrl+C to copy the range to the Clipboard. Then choose Home➔Clipboard➔Paste➔Other Paste Options➔ Linked Picture (I). Excel pastes a picture of the original range, and the picture is linked — if you make changes to the original, those changes are shown in the linked picture.

Notice that when you select the linked picture, the Formula bar displays the address of the original range. You can edit this range reference to change the cells that are displayed in the picture. To "de-link" the picture, just delete the formula on the Formula bar.

As with an unlinked picture, you can use Excel's Picture Tools contextual menu to modify the appearance of the linked picture.

You can also cut and paste this picture to a different worksheet, if you like. That makes it easy to refer to information on a different sheet.

Figure 20-2 shows a linked picture of a range placed on top of a shape, which has lots of interesting formatting capabilities. Placing a linked picture on top of a shape is a good way to make a particular range stand out.

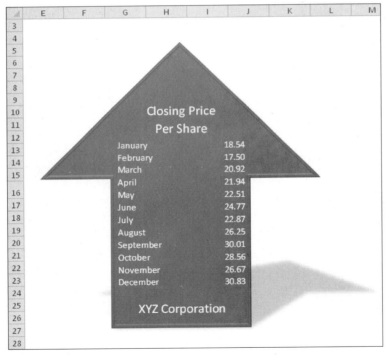

Figure 20-2: A linked picture of a range, placed on top of a shape.

Performing Inexact Searches

If you have a large worksheet with lots of data, locating what you're looking for can be difficult. The Excel Find and Replace dialog box is a useful tool for locating information, and it has a few features that many users overlook.

Access the Find and Replace dialog box by choosing Home➜Editing➜Find & Select➜Find (or pressing Ctrl+F). If you're replacing information, you can use Home➜Editing➜Find & Select➜ Replace (or Ctrl+H). The only difference is which of the two tabs is displayed in the dialog box. Figure 21-1 shows the Find and Replace dialog box after clicking the Options button, which expands the dialog box to show additional options.

Figure 21-1: The Find and Replace dialog box, with the Find tab selected.

In many cases, you want to locate "approximate" text. For example, you may be trying to find data for a customer named Stephen R. Rosencrantz. You can, of course, search for the exact text: *Stephen R. Rosencrantz.* However, there's a reasonably good chance that the search will fail. The name may have been entered differently, as Steve Rosencrantz or S.R. Rosencrantz, for example. It may have even been misspelled as Rosentcrantz.

The most efficient search for this name is to use a wildcard character and search for `st*rosen*` and then click the Find All button. In addition to reducing the amount of text that you enter, this search is practically guaranteed to locate the customer, if the record is in your worksheet. The search may also find some records that you aren't looking for, but that's better than not finding anything.

The Find and Replace dialog box supports two wildcard characters:

➤ ? matches any single character.

➤ * matches any number of characters.

Wildcard characters also work with values. For example, searching for `3*` locates all cells that contain a value that begins with 3. Searching for `1?9` locates all three-digit entries that begin with 1 and end with 9.

Note

> To search for a question mark or an asterisk, precede the character with a tilde character (~). For example, the following search string finds the text *NONE*:

```
~*NONE~*
```

If you need to search for the tilde character, use two tildes.

If your searches don't seem to be working correctly, double-check these three options (which sometimes have a way of changing on their own):

> ➤ **Match Case:** If this check box is selected, the case of the text must match exactly. For example, searching for smith does not locate Smith.

> ➤ **Match Entire Cell Contents:** If this check box is selected, a match occurs if the cell contains only the search string (and nothing else). For example, searching for Excel doesn't locate a cell that contains Microsoft Excel.

> ➤ **Look In:** This drop-down list has three options: Values, Formulas, and Comments. If, for example, Values is selected, searching for 900 doesn't find a cell that contains 900 if that value is generated by a formula.

Remember that searching operates on the selected range of cells. If you want to search the entire worksheet, select only one cell before you begin your search.

Also, remember that searches do not include numeric formatting. For example, if you have a value that uses currency formatting so that it appears as $54.00, searching for $5* doesn't locate that value.

Working with dates can be a bit tricky because Excel offers many ways to format dates. If you search for a date by using the default date format, Excel locates the dates even if they're formatted differently. For example, if your system uses the m/d/y date format, the search string 10/*/2010 finds all dates in October 2010, regardless of how the dates are formatted.

You can also use an empty Replace With field. For example, to quickly delete all asterisks from your worksheet, enter ~* in the Find What field and leave the Replace With field blank. When you click the Replace All button, Excel finds all the asterisks and replaces them with nothing.

Replacing Formatting

A useful, but often overlooked, Excel feature is the ability to search for (and replace) cell formatting. For example, if you have cells that use the 14-point Calibri font, it's a simple matter to change the formatting in all those cells to something else.

The process isn't as intuitive as it could be, so I walk you through the steps. Assume that your worksheet contains many cells that are formatted with a yellow background and in 14-point Calibri in bold. Furthermore, assume that these cells are scattered throughout the workbook. The goal is to change all those cells so that they're displayed with 16-point Cambria in bold, with white text on a black background.

To change the formatting by searching and replacing, follow these steps:

1. Click any single cell and choose Home➜Editing➜Find & Select➜Replace (or press Ctrl+H) to display the Find and Replace dialog box.

   If you want to limit the searching to a particular range, select the range rather than a single cell.

2. In the Find and Replace dialog box, make sure that the Find What and Replace With fields are blank.

3. Click the upper Format button (the one beside the Find What field) to display the Find Format dialog box.

   If these fields aren't visible, click the Options button to expand the dialog box.

4. You can use the Find Format dialog box to specify the formatting you're looking for, but it's much easier to click the arrow on the Format button, click Choose Format from Cell, and then click a cell that already has the formatting you want to replace.

5. Click the lower Format button (the one beside the Replace With field) to display the Replace Format dialog box.

6. You can use the Choose Format from Cell option and specify a cell that contains the replacement formatting, or you can use the tabs in the Find Format dialog box to specify the desired formatting.

   In this example, click the Font tab and select Cambria, size 16, bold style, and white color. On the Patterns tab, choose black as the cell shading color. At this point, the Find And Replace dialog box should resemble Figure 22-1.

7. In the Find and Replace dialog box, click the Replace All button.

Figure 22-1: The Replace tab in the Find and Replace dialog box.

Note

If you use the Choose Format from Cell option in Step 4, you may find that not all occurrences of the formatting are replaced — usually because one or more aspects of the formatting do not match. For example, if you click a cell that has General number formatting, it doesn't replace cells that have Date number formatting. The solution is to click the Format button to display the Find Format dialog box and then click the Clear button in each dialog box tab in which the formatting is not relevant.

In some cases, you may prefer to simply *select* the cells with a particular format. To do so, perform Steps 1 through 4 in the preceding step list. Then click the Find All button. The dialog box expands to display information about the qualifying cells (see Figure 22-2). Click the bottom part of the dialog box and then press Ctrl+A to select all qualifying cells.

Book	Sheet	Name	Cell	Value	Formula
data2011.xlsx	Sheet3		$A$1	209	
data2011.xlsx	Sheet3		$C$5	32	
data2011.xlsx	Sheet3		$M$9	123	
data2011.xlsx	Sheet3		$F$15	0	=F13+F13
data2011.xlsx	Sheet3		$L$18	3	
data2011.xlsx	Sheet3		$M$18	3332	
data2011.xlsx	Sheet3		$L$19		
data2011.xlsx	Sheet3		$M$19		
data2011.xlsx	Sheet3		$L$20		
data2011.xlsx	Sheet3		$M$20	January	
data2011.xlsx	Sheet3		$L$21		
data2011.xlsx	Sheet3		$M$21	February	

42 cell(s) found

Figure 22-2: The Find and Replace dialog box expands to display a list of all matching cells.

When these cells are selected, you can then format them any way you like. Note that you can widen the columns in the list of found cells (by dragging a column border), and you can also sort the list by clicking a column header.

Note

Conspicuously absent from the Find and Replace dialog box is the ability to search for cells by their styles. Despite the fact that (beginning with Excel 2007) Microsoft places increased emphasis on cell styles, it's not possible to find all cells that use a particular style and apply a different style to those cells. You can find and replace the formatting, but the cell *style* does not change.

Changing the Excel Color Scheme

One of the features introduced in Office 2007 was the ability to change the color scheme of the applications. You do this in the Excel Options dialog box. Choose File→Options and then click the General tab. Use the Color Scheme drop-down list to select your color choice: Blue, Sliver, or Black (see Figure 23-1). When you change the color scheme, your choice affects all other Microsoft Office applications.

Figure 23-1: Selecting a new color scheme for Excel.

You may find that a particular color scheme is easier on the eyes. Or, you may just want an occasional change of scenery. Unfortunately, the three choices are all there is — what you see is what you get. You cannot customize the color schemes in any way, and (as far as I know) third-party developers cannot even create new color schemes.

Cross-Ref

Don't confuse color schemes with document themes. The document theme feature is an entirely different concept, and these two features are not related. See Tip 16 for more about document themes.

Limiting the Usable Area in a Worksheet

Have you ever wanted to restrict access to a certain range within a worksheet? For example, you may want to set up a worksheet so that only cells in a particular range can be activated or modified. This tip describes two ways to accomplish this task: by using the `ScrollArea` property and by using worksheet protection.

Setting the ScrollArea property

A worksheet's `ScrollArea` property determines which range is visible. The instructions that follow describe how to restrict the usable area of the worksheet to a specific range.

Here's how to do it:

1. Make sure that the Developer tab of the Ribbon is displayed.

   By default, this tab is not displayed. To turn on the Developer tab, access the Excel Options dialog box (choose File➜ Options), click the Customize Ribbon tab, and place a checkmark next to Developer, in the listbox on the right.

2. Choose Developer➜Controls➜Properties to display the Properties window (see Figure 24-1).

3. In the Properties window, enter the range address in the `ScrollArea` field and press Enter.

   In the figure, the range is C6:F13. You can't point to the range; you must enter the range address manually.

Figure 24-1: Use the Properties window to set the scroll area for the worksheet.

After performing these steps, you cannot activate any cell outside the specified range. Also, some commands no longer work. For example, you cannot select entire rows and columns. Note that the scroll area is limited to a single contiguous range of cells.

There's a problem: The ScrollArea property isn't persistent. In other words, if you save your file, close it, and then open it again, the ScrollArea is reset, and you're free to select any cell you like. One solution is to write a simple VBA macro that is executed when the workbook is opened. To add this type of macro, follow these instructions:

1. Make sure that the workbook window is not maximized.

    One way to do this is to press Ctrl+F5.

2. Right-click the workbook's title bar and choose View Code from the shortcut menu.

    This action displays the ThisWorkbook code module for the workbook.

3. Enter the following VBA code in the ThisWorkbook code module (adjusting the sheet name and range address, of course):

```
Private Sub Workbook_Open()
    Worksheets("Sheet1").ScrollArea = "C6:F13"
End Sub
```

4. Press Alt+F11 to return to Excel.

5. Save the workbook, close it, and reopen it.

    If your workbook has an XLSX extension, you need to save it as a macro-enabled workbook (with an XLSM extension).

When the workbook is opened, the Workbook_Open procedure is executed automatically, and the ScrollArea property is set.

Caution

This method is by no means a foolproof way to prevent users from accessing parts of a workbook. Nothing can prevent a savvy user from using the Properties window to delete the contents of the ScrollArea field. Or, when the workbook is open, the user can choose to disable macros for the workbook. Another way to bypass the Workbook_Open macro is to press Shift while the file opens.

Using worksheet protection

The second method of limiting the usable area of a worksheet relies on unlocking cells and protecting the workbook:

1. Select all cells that you want to be accessible.

    They can be single cells or any number of ranges.

2. Press Ctrl+1 to display the Format Cells dialog box.

3. In the Format Cells dialog box, click the Protection tab and remove the checkmark from the Locked check box.

4. Choose Review→Changes→Protect Sheet to display the Protect Sheet dialog box.

5. In the Protect Sheet dialog box, remove the checkmark from the Select Locked Cells check box (see Figure 24-2).

6. If desired, specify a password that will be required in order to unprotect the sheet and then click OK.

Figure 24-2: Use the Protect Sheet dialog box to prevent the user from selecting locked cells.

After you perform these steps, only the unlocked cells (those you selected in Step 1) are accessible.

Worksheet passwords are not at all secure. In fact, it's a trivial matter to crack such a password. Therefore, worksheet protection is more of a convenience feature than a
Caution **security feature.**

Using an Alternative to Cell Comments

As you probably know, you can attach a comment to any cell by using the Review➔Comments➔ New Comment button (or by right-clicking the cell and choosing Insert Comment from the short-cut menu). Use Review➔Comments➔Show All Comments to toggle the display of comments. The Excel Options dialog box has additional comment viewing options, found in the Display section of the Advanced tab. A user can choose to hide all comments and comment indicators — which means that your comments will probably never be seen.

This tip describes how to use Excel's Data Validation feature to display a pop-up message whenever a cell is activated. It's a good way to ensure that your comment will always be seen, regardless of the user's comment viewing setting.

Follow these steps to add a message to a cell:

1. Activate the cell that you want to display the pop-up message.

2. Choose Data➔Data Tools➔Data Validation to display the Data Validation dialog box.

3. In the Data Validation dialog box, click the Input Message tab.

4. (Optional) In the Title field, enter a title for your message.

5. Enter the message itself in the Input Message box.

6. Click OK to close the Data Validation dialog box.

After you perform these steps, the message appears whenever the cell is activated (see Figure 25-1 for an example). You can also click and drag the message to a different location, if it's in your way.

⊿	A	B	C	D	E	F
1	Name:	Paul P. Paulson				
2	Department:	Production				
3	User Code:	P-764				
4			IMPORTANT!			
5			Please enter a valid			
6			User Code, as			
7			defined in the 24- May-2006 revision of			
8			the TPS Report.			
9						
10						
11						

Figure 25-1: This pop-up message was created by using Excel's Data Validation feature.

Understanding the Excel Help System

Along with Office 2007 came a new type of Help system. The new Help system (officially known as the Help Viewer) is also part of Office 2010.

One component of the Office Help system is its Supertip feature. When you hover your mouse over a command on the Ribbon, you see a pop-up description of what that command does. Figure 26-1 shows an example of a Supertip.

Figure 26-1: A pop-up Supertip describes each Ribbon command.

But the real Help content is found in the Help Viewer window. The following notes help familiarize you with the Excel Help system:

> ➤ The Excel Help system has a single entry point. To display Excel Help, press F1 or click the round question mark icon below the Excel title bar.

> ➤ The Help content resides in two places: on your hard drive and on a Microsoft Web server. The lower right corner of the Help window displays the status in a button: either Offline (shows content only from your computer) or Connected to Office.com (shows content from the Web). You can change the status by clicking the button and making your choice. In some cases, using the Online option gives you more up-to-date information.

> ➤ Connecting to Office.com displays additional content that's not available when you choose the Offline option. Specifically, you can search for templates or training materials, and also access information for developers. Figure 26-2 shows the option in the drop-down Search button list.

Figure 26-2: Specifying where to search for help.

➤ When you're connected to Office.com, you can identify the URL for the Help topic and send it to someone else. To do so, right-click the current Help topic and choose Properties. The Properties dialog box displays the URL of the Help topic. Select the URL text with your mouse and press Ctrl+C to copy it. The URL can be opened with any Web browser.

➤ It took me a long time to figure this one out: You can determine which buttons appear on the toolbar in the Help window. Click the tiny icon on the right side of the toolbar and select Add or Remove buttons. You see the list shown in Figure 26-3. Items with a check-mark are displayed in the Help window toolbar.

Figure 26-3: Configuring the Help window toolbar.

➤ When a Help topic is displayed, you can copy some or all of the text. Just highlight the text, and press Ctrl+C. Or, right-click and choose Copy.

➤ Context-sensitive help is spotty. For example, if an Excel dialog box is displayed, pressing F1 (or clicking the question mark icon on the dialog box title bar) displays the Help window. In some cases, the Help information relates to what you're doing. In other cases, you're presented with the opening screen of the Excel Help system. In the latter case, you can use the Search box to find the information that should have been displayed for you automatically.

➤ You have no way to display the Office Help window if an Office application is not running. In versions prior to Office 2007, you could double-click a *.CHM help file, and the help file would be displayed. That's no longer possible in Office 2007 or Office 2010 because of the new Help system technology that's used.

Making a Worksheet "Very Hidden"

You probably already know how to hide a worksheet: Just right-click the sheet tab and choose Hide Sheet from the shortcut menu. And, of course, it's just as easy to *unhide* a sheet: Right-click any sheet tab and choose Unhide from the shortcut menu. (You see a list of all hidden sheets.)

To make it more difficult for the casual user to unhide a hidden sheet, make the worksheet "very hidden." Here's how to do it:

1. Make sure that the Developer tab of the Ribbon is displayed.

   By default, this tab is not displayed. To turn on the Developer tab, access the Excel Options dialog box (choose File➜Options), click the Customize Ribbon tab, and place a checkmark next to Developer, in the listbox on the right.

2. Activate the sheet you want to hide.

3. Click Developer➜Controls➜Properties to display the Properties window (see Figure 27-1).

4. In the Properties window, click the `Visible` property to display a down-arrow button; click the button to display a drop-down list and select `2 -xlSheetVeryHidden`.

Figure 27-1: Use the Properties window to make a worksheet very hidden.

After performing these steps, you find that you cannot unhide the sheet by using any Excel command. In fact, you cannot even unhide the sheet by using the Properties window. The Properties window shows the properties of the active sheet. When a sheet is hidden, it's never the active sheet.

Is the sheet hidden forever? Nope. To make the very hidden sheet visible again, you use a simple VBA macro. The macro listed here unhides `Sheet2` of the active workbook (change the sheet name as appropriate):

```
Sub UnhideSheet()
    Worksheets("Sheet2").Visible = True
End Sub
```

Caution

Making a worksheet very hidden is not a security feature. Anyone who *really* wants to know what resides on a very hidden sheet can easily find out by using a macro such as the one listed here.

Working with the Backstage View

Perhaps one of the most significant new features in Excel 2010 is the Backstage View. I'm not sure why they use that name for it, but it's the window that you see when you click the File tab. Basically, the Backstage View is where you go when you want to do something with your workbook: save it, print it, convert it to a PDF file, share it with others, or just check it for some basic information. Commands you issue in the Backstage View generally don't affect the content of your document.

In the Backstage View, the commands are arranged along the left side. Click a command and the window changes. Figure 28-1 shows the Backstage View when the Info command is selected (which is the default, when you click the File tab).

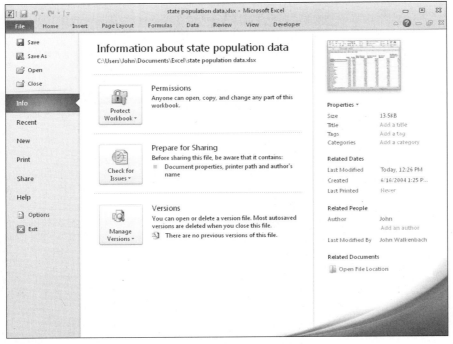

Figure 28-1: The Info view in the Backstage View.

There's a lot more that meets the eye. For example, each of those square boxes contains additional commands. I could list every possible thing that you can do in Backstage View, but that would be some very dull reading. The best way to get familiar with this view is to do some clicking and see what you find.

To get out of Backstage View, just click any Ribbon tab along the top. Contrary to what you might think, clicking the Exit command at the bottom of the command list does not exit Backstage View — it closes Excel.

## PART II

Data Entry

In this part, you'll find tips related to entering data into an Excel workbook. Entering data into an Excel worksheet is easy, but there's an excellent chance that the tips here will improve your overall efficiency.

Tips and Where to Find Them

Understanding the Types of Data

When you type something into a cell in a worksheet, Excel goes to work and makes one of the following decisions regarding the type of data you entered:

➤ You entered a value.

➤ You entered a date or time.

➤ You entered some text.

➤ You entered a formula.

If you understand how Excel interprets the data you enter into a cell, you can save yourself a bit of frustration when Excel's decision about what you entered doesn't correspond to what you had in mind.

Entering values

Any cell entry that consists of numerical digits is considered a *value.* Values can also include a few special characters:

➤ **Negative sign:** If a negative sign (–) precedes the value, Excel interprets it as a negative number.

➤ **Plus sign:** If a plus sign (+) precedes the value, Excel interprets it as a positive number (and does not display the plus sign).

➤ **Parentheses:** If a positive number is enclosed in parentheses, Excel interprets it as a negative value.

➤ **Percent sign:** If a percent sign (%) follows the numbers, Excel interprets the value as a percentage and automatically applies percent numeric formatting.

➤ **Currency symbol:** If your system's currency symbol (for example, a dollar sign) precedes the numbers, Excel interprets the entry as a monetary value and automatically formats it as currency.

➤ **Thousands separator:** If the number includes one or more of your system's thousands separators (for example, a comma), Excel interprets the entry as a number and also applies numeric formatting to display the thousands separator symbol. Note that the thousands separator must be in the appropriate position. For example, if the comma is your system's thousands separator, Excel interprets 4,500 as a value but does not interpret 45,00 as a value.

➤ **Scientific notation:** If the value contains the letter *E,* Excel attempts to interpret it as scientific notation. For example, 3.2E5 is interpreted as 3.2×10^5.

Entering dates and times

Excel treats dates and times as special types of numeric values. Typically, these values are formatted so that they appear as dates or times because humans find it much easier to understand these values if they appear in the correct format.

Excel handles dates by using a serial number system. The earliest date that Excel understands is January 1, 1900. This date has a serial number of 1. January 2, 1900, has a serial number of 2, and so on. This system makes it easy to deal with dates in formulas. For example, you can enter a formula to calculate the number of days between two dates.

Note

The date examples in this book use the U.S. English system. Depending on your regional settings, entering a date in a format such as June 1, 2010, might be interpreted as text rather than as a date. In this case, you need to enter the date in a format that corresponds to your regional date settings — for example, 1 June, 2010.

The following table provides a sampling of the date formats that Excel recognizes. After entering a date, you can format it to appear in a different date format by using the Number tab of the Format Cells dialog box.

Date Entered in Cell	Excel's Interpretation (U.S. Settings)
6-26-10	June 26, 2010
6-26-2010	June 26, 2010
6/26/10	June 26, 2010
6/26/2010	June 26, 2010
6-26/10	June 26, 2010
June 26, 2010	June 26, 2010
Jun 26	June 26 of the current year
June 26	June 26 of the current year
6/26	June 26 of the current year
6-26	June 26 of the current year

Excel is smart, but not perfect, about recognizing dates you enter. For example, Excel does not recognize any of the following entries as dates: June 1 1010, Jun-1 2010, and Jun-1/2010. Rather, it interprets these entries as text. If you plan to use references to dates in formulas, make sure that the date you enter is recognized as a date; otherwise, your formulas will produce incorrect results.

A common problem is that Excel interprets your entry as a date when you intended to enter a fraction. For example, if you enter the fraction 1/5, Excel interprets it as January 5 of the current year. The solution is to precede the fraction with an equal sign.

When you work with times, Excel simply extends its date serial number system to include decimals. In other words, Excel works with times by using fractional days. For example, the date serial number for June 1, 2010, is 40330. Noon on June 1, 2010 (halfway through the day), is represented internally as 40330.5 because the time fraction is added to the date serial number to get the full date-and-time serial number.

Again, you normally don't have to be concerned about these serial numbers (or fractional serial numbers, for times). Just enter the time into a cell in a recognized format.

The following table shows some examples of time formats that Excel recognizes.

Entered into a Cell	Excel's Interpretation
11:30:00 am	11:30 AM
11:30:00 AM	11:30 AM
11:30 pm	11:30 PM
11:30	11:30 AM
13:30	1:30 PM

These examples don't have days associated with them, so they're represented internally as values less than 1. In other words, Excel is using the nonexistent date January 0, 1900. You also can combine dates and times, however, as shown in the following table.

Entered into a Cell	Excel's Interpretation
6/26/10 11:30	11:30 AM on June 26, 2010
6/26/10 12:00	Noon on June 26, 2010
6/26/2010 0:00	Midnight on June 26, 2010

When you enter a time that exceeds 24 hours, the associated date for the time increments accordingly. For example, if you enter the following time into a cell, it's interpreted as 1:00 AM on January 1, 1900:

```
25:00:00
```

The day section of the entry increments because the time exceeds 24 hours. Keep in mind that a time value without a date uses January 0, 1900, as the date.

Entering text

If Excel can't interpret your cell entry as a value, a date, a time, or a formula, it goes into the catchall category of text.

A single cell can hold a massive amount of text — about 32,000 characters. However, you'll see that Excel has lots of limitations when you use large amounts of text in a cell. In fact, it can't even display all the characters. If you need to display a large amount of text in a worksheet, consider putting it in a text box (use Insert→Text→Text Box).

Entering formulas

Normally, you signal that you're entering a formula by beginning the cell entry with an equal sign (=). However, Excel also accepts a plus sign or a minus sign. And (to accommodate old Lotus 1-2-3 users), if your formula begins with a worksheet function, Excel also accepts an ampersand (@). However, as soon as you press Enter, the ampersand is replaced with an equal sign.

Formulas can contain these elements:

> ➤ Mathematical operators, such as + (for addition) and * (for multiplication)

> ➤ Parentheses

> ➤ Cell references (including named cells and ranges)

> ➤ Values or text

> ➤ Worksheet functions (such as SUM or AVERAGE)

If the formula you entered isn't syntactically correct, Excel might propose a correction. Keep in mind that the suggested Excel correction might be syntactically correct, but it isn't always what you had in mind.

Moving the Cell Pointer after Entering Data

By default, Excel automatically moves the cell pointer to the next cell down when you press Enter after entering data into a cell. To change this setting, use the Excel Options dialog box (choose File➔Options). The setting you're looking for is on the Advanced tab of the Excel Options dialog box, in the Editing Options section (see Figure 30-1).

The check box that controls this behavior is labeled After Pressing Enter, Move Selection. When that check box is enabled, you can also specify the direction in which the cell pointer moves (down, left, up, or right).

Figure 30-1: Use the Advanced tab in the Excel Options dialog box to specify where to move the cell pointer after you press Enter.

Your choice is completely a matter of personal preference. I prefer to keep this option turned off and use the arrow keys rather than press Enter. Not surprisingly, the arrow keys send the cell pointer in the direction that you indicate. For example, if you're entering data in a row, press the right-arrow key rather than Enter. The other arrow keys work as expected, and you can even use the PgUp and PgDn keys.

Selecting a Range of Input Cells before Entering Data

Here's a tip that most Excel users don't know about: When a range of cells is selected, Excel automatically moves the cell pointer to the next cell in the range when you press Enter.

The next cell is determined by the Direction setting on the Advanced tab of the Excel Options dialog box (see Tip 30).

For example, if the Direction setting is Down (or if the Move Selection option isn't enabled), it works like this: If the selection consists of multiple rows, Excel moves down the column; when Excel reaches the end of the selection in the column, it moves to the first selected cell in the next column. To skip a cell, just press Enter without entering anything. To go backward, press Shift+Enter. If you prefer to enter the data by rows rather than by columns, press Tab rather than Enter.

Using AutoComplete to Automate Data Entry

Excel's AutoComplete feature makes it easy to enter the same text into multiple cells. With AutoComplete, you type the first few letters of a text entry into a cell and Excel automatically completes the entry, based on other entries that you already made in the column. In addition to reducing typing, this feature ensures that your entries are spelled correctly and are consistent.

Here's how it works. Suppose that you're entering product information in a column. One product is named Sugar-Free Snaphylytes. The first time that you enter Sugar-Free Snaphylytes into a cell, Excel remembers it. Later, when you start typing the words Sugar-Free Snaphylytes into that column, Excel recognizes the word by the first few letters and finishes typing it for you. Just press Enter, and you're done.

AutoComplete also changes the case of letters for you automatically. If you start entering sugar (with a lowercase *s*) in the second entry, Excel makes the *s* uppercase, to be consistent with the previous entry in the column.

If the column contains multiple entries that match on the first few characters, Excel doesn't display a suggestion until your entry matches one of them uniquely. For example, if the column also contains a product named Sugar-Free Marpinettes, AutoComplete doesn't kick in until you type either the first letter of Snaphylytes or the first letter of Marpinettes.

Note

You also can access a mouse-oriented version of AutoComplete by right-clicking the cell and choosing Pick from Drop-Down List from the shortcut menu. Excel then displays a drop-down list that has all the entries in the current column, and you just click the one you want. See Figure 32-1.

You can even access the drop-down list from the keyboard: Press Shift+F10 to display the shortcut menu, and then press k (the hotkey for Pick from List). Use the arrow keys to make your selection and then press Enter.

Keep in mind that AutoComplete works only within a contiguous column of cells. If you have a blank row, for example, AutoComplete looks only at the cell contents below the blank row.

If you find the AutoComplete feature distracting, you can turn it off, on the Advanced tab of the Excel Options dialog box (choose File→Options). The setting, labeled Enable AutoComplete for Cell Values, is in the Editing Options section.

	A	B	C	D
1	Month	Product	Sales	
2	January	Sugar-Free Snaphylytes	154,982	
3	January	Sweet & Sour Crunchies	198	
4	January	Sugar-Free Marpinettes	125,930	
5	January	Snaphylytes Original	9,823	
6	January	Marpinettes With Basil	18,982	
7	January	Extra Sweet Sugar Crunchies	598,012	
8	January	Oregano Flavored Sugar Crunchies	76,332	
9	February			
10	February	Extra Sweet Sugar Crunchies		
11	February	Marpinettes With Basil		
12	February	Oregano Flavored Sugar Crunchies		
13	February	Snaphylytes Original		
14	February	Sugar-Free Marpinettes		
15	February	Sugar-Free Snaphylytes		
16		Sweet & Sour Crunchies		
17				
18				

Figure 32-1: Right-clicking a cell and choosing Pick From List from the shortcut menu displays a list of column entries.

Removing Duplicate Rows

A longstanding item on the Excel wish list is the ability to automatically delete duplicate rows in a worksheet. Beginning with Excel 2007, Microsoft has made that particular wish come true. Figure 33-1 shows a range of data after it was converted to a table using Insert➜Tables➜Table. Notice that this table has some duplicate rows.

	A	B	C	D
1	Name	Birthday	Region	
2	Amy Foster	July 3	Central	
3	Gregory Hanson	August 26	Central	
4	Joseph Adkins	January 5	Central	
5	Lynn Boyd	December 12	Central	
6	Elizabeth Gregory	August 25	Central	
7	Patricia Anderson	September 28	Central	
8	Joseph Adkins	January 5	Central	
9	Amber Murray	March 12	Eastern	
10	Mark Walker	February 16	Central	
11	Tony Patrick	June 3	Eastern	
12	Brenda Brooks	December 1	Eastern	
13	Amber Murray	March 12	Eastern	
14	Irma Scott	September 15	Eastern	
15	Isaac Jones	December 1	Eastern	
16	Susan Burch	March 18	Western	
17	Berry Hernandez	April 21	Western	
18	Shonda Rogers	June 9	Western	
19	Joan O. Johnson	July 12	Western	
20	Connie Mcdonald	November 30	Western	
21	Jessica Davis	December 2	Western	
22	Berry Hernandez	April 21	Western	
23				

Figure 33-1: The goal is to remove all duplicate rows from this table.

Start by selecting any cell in your table. Then choose Table Tools➜Design➜Tools➜Remove Duplicates. Excel responds with the dialog box shown in Figure 33-2. The dialog box lists all columns in your table. Select the check boxes for the columns that you want to be included in the duplicate search. Most of the time, you select all the columns — which means that a duplicate is defined as having the same data in *every* column.

Click OK, and Excel weeds out the duplicate rows and displays a message that tells you how many duplicates it removed (see Figure 33-3).

Remove Duplicates

To delete duplicate values, select one or more columns that contain duplicates.

[Select All]   [Unselect All]   ☑ My data has headers

Columns
☑ Name
☑ Birthday
☑ Region

[OK]   [Cancel]

Figure 33-2: Removing duplicate rows is easy.

Note

If your data is not in a table, use the Data➜Data Tools➜Remove Duplicates command to display the Remove Duplicates dialog box.

Caution

Understand that duplicate values are determined by the value *displayed* in the cell — not necessarily by the value *stored* in the cell. Assume that two cells contain the same date: One date is formatted to display as 5/15/2010, and the other is formatted to display as May 15, 2010. When removing duplicates, Excel considers these dates to be different.

	A	B	C	D
1	**Name**	**Birthday**	**Region**	
2	Amy Foster	July 3	Central	
3	Gregory Hanson	August 26	Central	
4	Joseph Adkins	January 5	Central	
5	Lynn Boyd	December 12	Central	
6	Elizabeth Gregory	August 25	Central	
7	Patricia Anderson	September 28	Central	
8	Amber Murray	March 12	Eastern	
9	Mark Walker	February 16	Central	
10	Tony P			
11	Brenda			
12	Irma S			
13	Isaac Jo			
14	Susan			
15	Berry Hernandez	April 21	Western	
16	Shonda Rogers	June 9	Western	
17	Joan O. Johnson	July 12	Western	
18	Connie Mcdonald	November 30	Western	
19	Jessica Davis	December 2	Western	
20				
21				
22				
23				

Microsoft Excel

ℹ 3 duplicate values found and removed; 18 unique values remain.

[OK]

Figure 33-3: Excel tells you the result of deleting duplicate rows.

Keeping Titles in View

A common type of worksheet contains a table of data with descriptive headings in the first row. But, as you scroll down the worksheet, the first row scrolls off the screen so you can no longer see the column descriptions.

A feature introduced in Excel 2007 eliminated this age-old spreadsheet problem — but only if your data is in the form of a table (created with Insert➜Tables➜Table). Figure 34-1 shows a table that has been scrolled down. Normally, the column headers are scrolled out of view. But, when you're working with a table, Excel displays the column headers where the column letters normally appear.

Agent	Date Listed	Area	List Price	Bedrooms	Baths	SqFt	Type	Pool	Sold
88 Randolph	8/11/2009	Central	$389,900	4	2.5	2,284	Single Family	FALSE	TRUE
89 Randolph	4/20/2009	N. County	$259,900	3	2.5	2,122	Condo	FALSE	TRUE
90 Randolph	4/23/2009	N. County	$405,000	2	3	2,444	Single Family	TRUE	TRUE
91 Randolph	7/11/2009	S. County	$205,500	4	2.5	1,751	Single Family	FALSE	FALSE
92 Robinson	9/3/2009	Central	$239,900	4	3	2,278	Single Family	FALSE	FALSE
93 Robinson	7/31/2009	Central	$338,876	4	3	2,483	Single Family	TRUE	FALSE
94 Robinson	11/24/2009	Central	$375,000	4	3	2,368	Single Family	TRUE	TRUE
95 Robinson	5/13/2009	N. County	$359,900	3	3	1,839	Condo	FALSE	TRUE
96 Robinson	3/29/2009	N. County	$379,000	4	3	3,000	Single Family	FALSE	TRUE
97 Robinson	3/25/2009	S. County	$215,000	1	2	1,552	Condo	FALSE	TRUE
98 Robinson	8/27/2009	S. County	$300,000	4	3	2,650	Condo	FALSE	FALSE
99 Robinson	7/19/2009	S. County	$349,000	4	3	1,838	Single Family	FALSE	FALSE
100 Romero	3/15/2009	Central	$235,910	4	3	2,285	Single Family	TRUE	TRUE
101 Romero	4/30/2009	Central	$250,000	3	2	2,066	Single Family	FALSE	FALSE
102 Romero	7/28/2009	N. County	$215,000	4	2.5	1,640	Condo	TRUE	FALSE
103 Romero	8/2/2009	N. County	$359,900	3	2	2,198	Condo	TRUE	FALSE
104 Romero	11/27/2009	N. County	$369,900	4	3	1,988	Condo	FALSE	TRUE
105 Romero	4/3/2009	N. County	$799,000	6	5	4,800	Single Family	FALSE	FALSE
106 Romero	8/25/2009	S. County	$229,500	3	2	1,694	Single Family	FALSE	FALSE

Figure 34-1: The column headers for this table are displayed where the column letters normally appear.

Note that the column headers are visible only when a cell within the table is selected.

If your data isn't in the form of a table, you have to resort to the old-fashioned method: freeze panes. This method keeps the headings visible while you're scrolling through the worksheet.

To freeze the first row, choose View➜Window➜Freeze Panes➜Freeze Top Row. Excel inserts a dark horizontal line to indicate the frozen row. To freeze the first column, choose View➜ Window➜Freeze Panes➜Freeze First Column.

If you want to freeze more than one column or one row, move the cell pointer to the cell below and to the right of where you want the freeze to occur. Then choose View➜Window➜Freeze Panes➜Freeze Panes. For example, if you want to freeze the first two rows and the first column, move the cell pointer to cell B3 before you issue the command. To freeze the first three rows (but not any columns), select cell A4 before you issue the Freeze Panes command.

Some navigation keys operate as though the frozen rows or columns don't exist. For example, if you press Ctrl+Home while the worksheet has frozen panes, the cell selector moves to the upper left unfrozen cell. Similarly, the Home key moves to the first unfrozen cell in the current row. You can move into the frozen rows or columns by using the direction keys or your mouse.

To remove the frozen panes, choose View➜Window➜Freeze Panes➜Unfreeze Panes.

Automatically Filling a Range with a Series

If you need to fill a range with a series of values, one approach is to enter the first value, write a formula to calculate the next value, and copy the formula. For example, Figure 35-1 shows a series of consecutive numbers in column A. Cell A1 contains the value 1, and cell A2 contains this formula, which was copied down the column:

```
=A1+1
```

⊿	A	B	C	D	E	F
1	1					
2	2					
3	3					
4	4					
5	5					
6	6					
7	7					
8	8					
9	9					
10	10					
11	11					
12	12					
13	13					
14	14					
15						

Figure 35-1: Excel offers an easy way to generate a series of values like these.

Another approach is to let Excel do the work by using the handy Autofill feature:

1. Enter 1 into cell A1.

2. Enter 2 into cell A2.

3. Select A1:A2.

4. Move the mouse cursor to the lower right corner of cell A2 (the cell's *fill handle*) and when the mouse pointer turns into a black plus sign, drag down the column to fill in the cells.

Note You can turn this behavior on and off. If cells don't have a fill handle, choose File➔ Options and click the Advanced tab in the Excel Options dialog box. Select the check box labeled Enable Fill Handle and Cell Drag-And-Drop.

The data entered in Steps 1 and 2 provide Excel with the information it needs to determine which type of series to use. If you entered 3 into cell A2, the series would then consist of odd integers: 1, 3, 5, 7, and so on.

Here's another Autofill trick: If the data you start with is irregular, Excel completes the Autofill action by doing a linear regression and fills in the predicted values. Figure 35-2 shows a worksheet with monthly sales values for January through July. If you use Autofill after selecting C2:C8,

Excel extends the best fit linear sales trend and fills in the missing values. Figure 35-3 shows the predicted values, along with a chart.

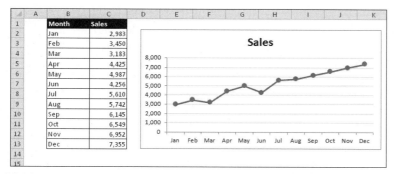

Figure 35-2: Use Autofill to perform a linear regression and predict sales values for August through December.

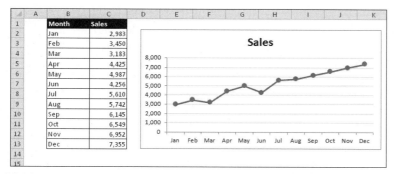

Figure 35-3: The sales figures, after using Autofill to predict the last five months.

Autofill also works with dates and even a few text items — day names and month names. The following table lists a few examples of the types of data that can be Autofilled.

First Value	Autofilled Values
Sunday	Monday, Tuesday, Wednesday, and so on
Quarter-1	Quarter-2, Quarter-3, Quarter-4, Quarter-1, and so on
Jan	Feb, Mar, Apr, and so on
January	February, March, April, and so on
Month 1	Month 2, Month 3, Month 4, and so on

You can also create your own lists of items to be Autofilled. To do so, open the Excel Options dialog box and click the Advanced tab. Then scroll down and click the Edit Custom Lists button to display the Custom Lists dialog box. Enter your items in the List Entries box (each on a new line). Then click the Add button to create the list. Figure 35-4 shows a custom list of region names that use Roman numerals.

Figure 35-4: These region names work with the Excel Autofill feature.

For more control over what happens when using Autofill, use the right mouse button to click and drag the fill handle. When you release the button, you see a shortcut menu with some options (see Figure 35-5). The items that are available on the shortcut menu depend on the type of data selected. For example, if the first cell in the series contains a date, the date-related options are enabled.

Figure 35-5: The shortcut menu for Autofill.

Working with Fractions

Although most users work with decimal values, some types of data are normally displayed as fractions, not as decimals. This tip describes how to enter noninteger values as fractions.

To enter a whole number and a fraction into a cell, leave a space between the whole number and the fractional part. For example, to display 6⅞, type 6 7/8 and then press Enter. When you select the cell, 6.875 appears on the Formula bar, and the cell entry appears as a fraction.

If you have only a fraction (for example, ⅛), you must enter a zero first, like this: 0 1/8 — otherwise, Excel likely assumes that you're entering a date. When you select the cell and look at the Formula bar, you see 0.125. In the cell, you see 1/8.

If the numerator is larger than the denominator, Excel converts it to a whole number and a fraction. For example, if you enter 0 65/8, Excel converts it to 8 1/8.

After you enter a fraction, bring up the Format Cells dialog box and take a look at the number format for the cell. You see that Excel automatically applied one of its Fraction number formats (see Figure 36-1).

Figure 36-1: A list of the Excel built-in Fraction number formats.

Figure 36-2 shows a worksheet that displays fractional data. The values in column C are expressed in 4ths, 8ths, and 16ths, and the values in column D are all in 16ths.

If none of the built-in Fraction number formats meets your needs, you might be able to create a custom number format. Press Ctrl+1, and in the Format Cells dialog box, click the Number tab. In the Category list, click Custom and then enter a number format string in the Type field. For example, enter the following Number format string in the Type field to display a value in 32nds:

```
# ??/32
```

	A	B	C	D	E
1					
2					
3		**Closing Price Per Share**			
4		January	14 1/8	14 2/16	
5		February	15 3/8	15 6/16	
6		March	16 1/4	16 4/16	
7		April	14 3/16	14 3/16	
8		May	11 1/4	11 4/16	
9		June	10	10	
10		July	12 1/8	12 2/16	
11		August	13 3/8	13 6/16	
12		September	15 5/16	15 5/16	
13		October	15 3/8	15 6/16	
14		November	18 7/8	18 14/16	
15		December	20 3/4	20 12/16	
16					

Figure 36-2: Displaying values as fractions.

The following number format string displays a value in terms of fractional dollars. For example, the value 154.87 is displayed as 154 and 87/100 Dollars.

```
0 "and "??/100 "Dollars"
```

The following example displays the value in 16ths, with a quotation mark appended to the right. This format string is useful when you deal with inches (for example, 3/16").

```
# ??/16\"
```

Resizing the Formula Bar

In earlier versions of Excel, editing a cell that contains a lengthy formula or lots of text often obscures the worksheet. Figure 37-1 shows Excel 2003 when a cell that contains lengthy text is selected. Notice that many of the cells are covered up by the expanded Formula bar. Beginning with Excel 2007, this problem is fixed thanks to a resizable Formula bar.

Figure 37-1: In previous versions, editing a lengthy formula or a cell that contains lots of text often obscures the worksheet.

The Excel 2010 (and Excel 2007) Formula bar displays a small vertical scroller on the right, but it might not be obvious that you can drag the bottom border of the Formula bar to change its height. Figure 37-2 shows an example of the resized Formula bar. As you can see, increasing the height of the Formula bar doesn't obscure the information in the worksheet.

The ability to change the height of the Formula bar is a relatively minor change, but it can be very helpful — if you know that it exists.

Figure 37-2: Changing the height of the formula bar makes it much easier to edit lengthy formulas, and you can still view all cells in your worksheet.

Also useful is a shortcut key combination: Ctrl+Shift+U. Pressing this key combination toggles the height of the Formula bar to show either one row or the previous size.

Proofing Your Data with Audio

Excel 2002 introduced a handy feature: text-to-speech. In other words, Excel is capable of speaking to you. You can have this feature read back a specific range of cells, or you can set it up so that it reads the data as you enter it.

For some reason, this feature appears to be missing in action, beginning with Excel 2007. You can search the Ribbon all day and not find a trace of the text-to-speech feature. Fortunately, the feature is still available — you just need to spend a few minutes to make it available.

Adding speech commands to the Ribbon

Following are instructions to add these commands to a new group in the Review tab of the Ribbon:

1. Right-click the Ribbon and then choose Customize the Ribbon from the shortcut menu.

   Excel displays the Customize Ribbon tab of the Excel Options dialog box.

2. In the list box on the right, select Review and click New Group.

3. Click Rename and give the group a name, such as Speech.

4. Click the drop-down list on the left and choose Commands Not in the Ribbon.

5. Scroll down the list, and you find five items that begin with the word *Speak;* select each one and then click Add.

   They're added to the newly created group.

6. Click OK to close the Excel Options dialog box.

After you perform these steps, the Review tab displays a new group with five new icons (see Figure 38-1).

Figure 38-1: Speech commands added to the Ribbon.

Using the speech commands

To read a range of cells, select the range first and then click the Speak Cells button. You can also specify the orientation (By Rows or By Columns). To read the data as it's entered, click the Speak On Enter button.

Some people (myself included) find the voice in this "love it or hate it" feature much too annoying to use for any extended period. And, if you enter the data at a relatively rapid clip, the voice simply cannot keep up with you.

You have a small bit of control over the voice used in the Excel text-to-speech feature. To adjust the voice, open the Windows Control Panel and display the Speech Properties dialog box (see Figure 38-2). You can choose a different voice and also adjust the speed. Click the Preview Voice button to help make your choices.

Figure 38-2: Use the Speech Properties dialog box to adjust the voice.

Controlling Automatic Hyperlinks

One of the most common Excel questions is "How can I prevent Excel from creating automatic hyperlinks?"

Normally, Excel watches you type, and if it looks at all like you're typing an e-mail address or a Web URL, the entry is converted into a hyperlink. Sometimes that capability is helpful, but sometimes it's not.

Overriding an automatic hyperlink

To override a single automatic hyperlink, just click Undo (or press Ctrl+Z) after you enter the text. The hyperlink disappears, but the text you entered remains intact. Another option is to precede the entry with an apostrophe so that it's evaluated as plain text.

Turning off automatic hyperlinks

If you never want to create automatic hyperlinks, here's how to turn off this feature (it's not exactly intuitive):

1. Choose File➜Options to display the Excel Options dialog box.

2. Click the Proofing tab.

3. Click the AutoCorrect Options button to display the AutoCorrect dialog box.

4. Click the AutoFormat As You Type tab and deselect the Internet and Network Paths with Hyperlinks check box (see Figure 39-1).

Figure 39-1: Use the AutoCorrect dialog box to turn off automatic hyperlinks.

Removing existing hyperlinks

To remove a hyperlink from a cell (but keep the cell's contents), right-click the cell and choose Remove Hyperlink from the shortcut menu.

In previous versions of Excel, you were forced to delete hyperlinks one at a time. Excel 2010 finally gets it right and lets you remove multiple hyperlinks with a single action. Just select the range, right-click, and choose Remove Hyperlinks. This command works even if the selection includes cells that don't contain a hyperlink. To remove all hyperlinks on a worksheet, press Ctrl+A to select all cells. Then right-click any cell and choose Remove Hyperlinks. Depending on the location of the cell pointer, you may need to press Ctrl+A twice to select all cells.

Entering Credit Card Numbers

If you've ever tried to enter a 16-digit credit card number into a cell, you might have discovered that Excel always changes the last digit to a zero. Why? The reason is that Excel can handle only 15 digits of numerical accuracy.

If you need to store credit card numbers in a worksheet, you have two options:

> ➤ **Precede the credit card number with an apostrophe.** Excel then interprets the data as a text string rather than as a number.

> ➤ **Preformat the cell or range by using the Text number format.** Select the range, choose Home➜Number, and then select Text from the Number Format drop-down control.

This tip, of course, also applies to other long numbers (such as part numbers) that aren't used in numeric calculations.

Using the Excel Built-In Data Entry Form

When entering data into an Excel list, some people prefer to use Excel's data entry form — a dialog box that adjusts to your data. Before you can use this form, you have to set up the column headers in your worksheet. Alternatively, you can designate the data range as a table, by choosing Insert➜Tables➜Table.

The Data Form command doesn't appear on the Ribbon, so you need to do a bit of prep work. Here's how to add the command to the Quick Access toolbar:

1. Right-click the Quick Access toolbar and choose Customize Quick Access Toolbar from the shortcut menu.

   Excel displays the Quick Access Toolbar tab of the Excel Options dialog box.

2. In the drop-down list on the left, choose Commands Not in the Ribbon.

3. In the list box on the left, choose Form and then click the Add button.

4. Click OK to close the Excel Options dialog box.

After you perform these steps, your Quick Access toolbar includes a new icon that, when clicked, displays the data entry form.

Activate any cell within your list and choose the Form command from your Quick Access toolbar. You see a dialog box like the one shown in Figure 41-1. (The fields shown in the dialog box vary, depending on your column headers.)

Real Estate Listings		
Agent:	Jenkins	47 of 125
Date Listed:	4/8/2009	New
Area:	N. County	Delete
List Price:	248500	Restore
Bedrooms:	4	
Baths:	2.5	Find Prev
SqFt:	2101	Find Next
Type:	Single Family	Criteria
Pool:	TRUE	
Sold:	TRUE	Close

Figure 41-1: The Excel data entry form.

Note

If the number of columns in your list exceeds the limit of your display, the dialog box contains two columns of field names. If your list consists of more than 32 columns, however, the Form command doesn't work. You must forgo this method of data entry and enter the information directly into the cells.

When the Data Form dialog box appears, the first record (if any) in the list is displayed. Notice the indicator in the upper right corner of the dialog box; this indicator tells you which record is selected and the total number of records in the list.

To enter a new record, click the New button to clear the fields. Then you can enter the new information into the appropriate fields. Press Tab or Shift+Tab to move among the fields. When you click the New (or Close) button, the data that you entered is appended to the bottom of the list. You also can press Enter, which is equivalent to clicking the New button. If your list contains any formulas, they're also entered automatically into the new record in the list for you.

Note

If your list is named Database, Excel automatically extends the range definition to include the new row or rows that you add to the list by using the Data Form dialog box. Note that this method works only if the list has the name Database; no other name works. Use the Formulas➜Defined Names➜Define Name command to name the range. If your list is in a table (created using Insert➜Tables➜Table), there's no need to name the range. The table will be expanded automatically when you add new data.

You can use the Data Form dialog box for more than just data entry. You can edit existing data in the list, view data one record at a time, delete records, and display records that meet certain criteria.

The dialog box contains a number of additional buttons:

➤ **Delete:** Deletes the displayed record.

➤ **Restore:** Restores any information that you edited. You must click this button before you click the New button.

➤ **Find Prev:** Displays the previous record in the list. If you entered a criterion, this button displays the previous record that matches the criterion.

➤ **Find Next:** Displays the next record in the list. If you entered a criterion, this button displays the next record that matches the criterion.

➤ **Criteria:** Clears the fields and lets you enter a criterion on which to search for records. For example, to locate records that have a List Price less than $200,000, enter **<200000** into the List Price field. Then you can use the Find Next and Find Prev buttons to display the qualifying records.

➤ **Close:** Closes the dialog box (and enters any data that you were entering).

Note

If you like the idea of using a data entry dialog box — but don't care much for the Excel implementation — try out my Enhanced Data Form. This add-in, which provides a much more versatile data entry form, is available for downloading at my Web site:

```
http://spreadsheetpage.com
```

Customizing and Sharing AutoCorrect Entries

Most users have encountered the Excel AutoCorrect feature — often accidentally. For example, if you enter (c) into a cell, Excel automatically "corrects" it by substituting a copyright symbol ©. Excel also corrects some spelling errors and other common mistakes, such as starting a word with two initial uppercase letters.

Note

To override an AutoCorrection, press Ctrl+Z while you're entering information into the cell. For example, if you need to enter (c) rather than a copyright symbol, type a space after the (c). Excel makes the autocorrection, but you can override it by pressing Ctrl+Z. If you press Ctrl+Z after you make the cell entry, the entire contents of the cell are deleted.

Fortunately, the AutoCorrect feature is highly customizable, and you can turn it off completely if you find it annoying. You might find it worth the effort to spend some time configuring AutoCorrect so that it works best for you. Figure 42-1 shows the AutoCorrect dialog box. To display this dialog box, choose File➔Options. Click the Proofing tab and then click the AutoCorrect Options button. Or, just press Alt+T,A.

Figure 42-1: Use the AutoCorrect dialog box to customize the Excel AutoCorrect settings.

To add an AutoCorrect shortcut, type the shortcut text in the Replace field (for example, **msft**), and type the text that it will expand to in the With field (for example, **Microsoft Corporation**). To remove an existing shortcut, locate it in the list and click the Delete button.

Excel 2010 introduces a new twist: Math AutoCorrect. This feature lets you define shortcuts for use with the Equation editor (accessible by choosing Insert➔Symbols➔Equation). View or adjust these settings in the Math AutoCorrect tab of the AutoCorrect dialog box.

The AutoCorrect shortcuts that you create in Excel are used in other Microsoft Office applications (and vice versa). The shortcut definitions are stored in the file named `*.acl`. Its exact name depends on the language version of Office. If you use the U.S. English language version of Office, the file is named `mso1033.acl`. The location also varies, so you'll need to search your hard drive to find it.

If you create some custom AutoCorrect shortcuts that you want to share with a colleague, you just make a copy of your `*.acl` file and place it in her directory. Be aware that replacing the `*.acl` file wipes out any custom AutoCorrect shortcuts that your colleague might have created. You have no way to merge two `*.acl` files.

Restricting Cursor Movement to Input Cells

A common type of worksheet uses two types of cells: input cells and formula cells. The user enters data into the input cells, and the formulas calculate and display the results.

Figure 43-1 shows a simple example. The input cells are in the range C4:C7. These cells are used by the formulas in C10:C13. To prevent the user from accidentally typing over formula cells, it's useful to limit the cursor movement so that the formula cells can't even be selected.

	A	B	C	D	E	F
1		Mortgage Loan Worksheet				
2						
3		Input Cells				
4		Purchase Price:	$409,000			
5		Down Payment:	20%			
6		Loan Term (Months):	360			
7		Interest Rate (APR):	6.50%			
8						
9		Result Cells				
10		Loan Amount:	$327,200			
11		Monthly Payment:	$2,068			
12		Total Payments:	$744,526			
13		Total Interest:	$417,326			
14						
15						

Figure 43-1: This worksheet has input cells at the top and formula cells below.

Setting up this sort of arrangement is a two-step process: Unlock the input cells and then protect the sheet. The following specific instructions are for the example shown in Figure 43-1:

1. Select C4:C7.

2. Press Ctrl+1 to display the Format Cells dialog box.

3. In the Format Cells dialog box, click the Protection tab, deselect the Locked check box, and click OK.

   By default, all cells are locked.

4. Choose Review→Changes→Protect Sheet.

5. In the Protect Sheet dialog box, deselect the Select Locked Cells check box and make sure that the Select Unlocked Cells check box is selected.

6. (Optional) Specify a password that will be required to unprotect the sheet.

7. Click OK.

After you perform these steps, only the unlocked cells can be selected. If you need to make any changes to your worksheet, you need to unprotect the sheet first, by choosing Review→Changes→Unprotect Sheet.

Although this example used a contiguous range of cells for the input, that isn't necessary for the steps to work. The input cells can be scattered throughout your worksheet.

Note

Protecting a worksheet with a password isn't a security feature. This type of password is easily cracked.

Controlling the Office Clipboard

You're undoubtedly familiar with the Windows Clipboard. When you copy (or cut) something (such as text or an image), the information is stored on the Clipboard. Then you can paste the information somewhere else.

In Office 2000, Microsoft introduced the Office Clipboard. Why another Clipboard? The simple answer is because the Office Clipboard is more versatile than the Windows Clipboard. It enables you to store as many as 24 copied items. The Windows Clipboard, on the other hand, can hold only a single item. When you copy or cut something, the previous Windows Clipboard contents are wiped out. The downside to the Office Clipboard is that it works only in Microsoft Office applications (Word, Excel, PowerPoint, Access, and Outlook).

If the Office Clipboard doesn't seem to be working, you can display it by clicking the dialog box launcher in the Home➔Clipboard group. The dialog box launcher is the smaller icon to the right of the Clipboard group name. Clicking this dialog box launcher toggles the display of the Office Clipboard.

Every time you copy (or cut) something, the Office Clipboard displays a portion of the information (see Figure 44-1). After you stored 24 items, newly added items replace older items. To paste the information, just select the paste location and click the item in the Office Clipboard.

Caution

For Excel users, the Office Clipboard has a serious limitation that makes it almost worthless: It cannot hold formulas! If you copy a range of formulas to the Office Clipboard and then paste the data elsewhere, you find that the formula results (not the formulas themselves) are pasted. In a few situations, this behavior can be advantageous. In the vast majority of cases, you want to copy and paste formulas, not their values.

Although the Office Clipboard can be useful, a significant number of users find it annoying. To control some aspects of the Office Clipboard, click the Options button at the bottom of the Clipboard task pane (see Figure 44-2). Normally, the Office Clipboard is displayed automatically whenever you copy two pieces of information. To prevent this from happening, deselect the Show Office Clipboard Automatically check box.

5 of 24 - Clipboard

Paste All   Clear All

Click an item to paste:

- 19 34 20 61 36 94 43 60 33 99 84 22 80 36 24 91 72 100 66 97 42 63 95 58 91 14 35 25 69 21 20 27 37 8 16 12 36 26 6 33 33 63 48 59 ...

- You're undoubtedly familiar with the Windows Clipboard.

- 60 27 89 39 23

- 14 47 26 41 34 36

- 72 51 74 62 52 88 38 85

Options ▼

Figure 44-1: The Office Clipboard, displaying five copied items.

6 of 24 - Clipboard

Paste All   Clear All

Click an item to paste:

- 19 34 20 61 36 94 43 60 33 99 84 22 80 36 24 91 72 100 66 97 42 63 95 58 91 14 35 25 69 21 20 27 37 8 16 12 36 26 6 33 33 63 48 59 51 59 35 31 20 30 32 84 45 93 5 31 59 60 ...

- 19 34 20 61 36 94 43 60 33 99 84 22 80 36 24 91 72 100 66 97 42 63 95 58 91 14 35 25 69 21 20 27 37 8 16 12 36 26 6 33 33 63 48 59 51 59 35 31 20 30 32 84 45 93 5 31 59 60 ...

- You're undoubtedly familiar with the Windows Clipboard.

- 60 27 89 39 23

- 14 47 26 41 34 36

Options ▼

	Show Office Clipboard Automatically
	Show Office Clipboard When Ctrl+C Pressed Twice
	Collect Without Showing Office Clipboard
✓	Show Office Clipboard Icon on Taskbar
✓	Show Status Near Taskbar When Copying

Figure 44-2: Options available for the Office Clipboard.

Creating a Drop-Down List in a Cell

Most Excel users probably believe that a VBA macro is required in order to display a drop-down list in a cell. But it's not. You can easily display a drop-down list in a cell — no macros required.

Figure 45-1 shows an example. Cell B2, when selected, displays a down arrow. Click the arrow, and you get a list of items (in this case, month names). Click an item, and it appears in the cell. The drop-down list can contain text, numeric values, or dates. Your formulas, of course, can refer to cells that contain a drop-down list. The formulas always use the value that's currently displayed.

◢	A	B	C	D	E	F
1					January	
2		March			February	
3		March			March	
4		April			April	
5		May			May	
6		June			June	
7		July			July	
8		August			August	
9		September			September	
10		October			October	
11					November	
12					December	
13						
14						

Figure 45-1: Creating a drop-down list in a cell is easy and doesn't require macros.

The trick to setting up a drop-down list is to use the data validation feature. The following steps describe how to create a drop-down list of items in a cell:

1. Enter the list of items in a range.

   In this example, the month names are in the range E1:E12.

2. Select the cell that will contain the drop-down list (cell B2, in this example).

3. Choose Data➜Data Tools➜Data Validation.

4. In the Data Validation dialog box, click the Settings tab.

5. In the Allow drop-down list, select List.

6. In the Source box, specify the range that contains the items.

   In this example, the range is E1:E12.

7. Make sure that the In-Cell Dropdown option is checked (see Figure 45-2) and click OK.

If your list is short, you can avoid Step 1. Rather, just type your list items (separated by commas) in the Source box in the Data Validation dialog box.

In previous versions, the list of items were required to be on the same worksheet as the cell that contains the drop-down list. With Excel 2010, that's no longer the case.

If you plan to share your workbook with others who use an older version of Excel, make sure that the list is on the same sheet as the drop-down list. Alternatively, you can put the list on any sheet, as long as it's a named range. For example, you can choose Formulas➜Defined Names➜ Define Name to define the name `MonthNames` for E1:E12. Then, in the Data Validation dialog box, enter **=MonthNames** in the Source box.

Figure 45-2: Using the Data Validation dialog box to create a drop-down list.

## PART III

Formatting

Excel has lots of formatting options to make your work look good. In this part, you'll find tips that cover formatting numbers, dates, times, text, and many other aspects of Excel.

Tips and Where to Find Them

Using the Mini Toolbar

Excel 2007 introduced a new user interface element known as the *Mini Toolbar.* This little pop-up toolbar appears whenever you right-click an object (a range of cells, a chart legend, or a shape, for example). The Mini Toolbar appears above the shortcut menu and contains icons that are normally found on the Home tab. Figure 46-1 shows the Mini Toolbar that appears when I right-click a chart title. Using the Mini Toolbar is especially useful if you need to apply some formatting and the Home tab isn't selected.

Figure 46-1: A Mini Toolbar appears above the shortcut menu whenever you right-click an object.

The icons displayed on the Mini Toolbar vary a bit, depending on the element that's selected. In Word, the Mini Toolbar is available when you make a selection (right-click not required) and is semitransparent, becoming less transparent when you move your mouse toward it. This type of behavior doesn't occur in Excel.

The main problem with the Mini Toolbar is remembering to use it. When I first started using Excel 2007, I tended to just ignore the Mini Toolbar. But after I got in the habit of using it, I realized that it really is a convenient feature. If you disagree and want to prevent the Mini Toolbar from appearing, you need to use VBA. Execute this statement to turn off the Mini Toolbar:

```
Application.ShowMenuFloaties = True
```

That's not a typo. To turn off the Mini Toolbar, you set the property to True, not False. And, a bit of trivia: When Office 2007 was being developed, the original term for Mini Toolbars was *floaties.* That term still survives in the Excel object model.

You may have noticed an option in the General tab of the Excel Options dialog box: Show Mini Toolbar on Selection. That option determines whether the Mini Toolbar appears when you select text while editing a cell.

And finally, you cannot customize the Mini Toolbar. What you see is what you get.

Indenting Cell Contents

The contents of a cell can be left-aligned, right-aligned, or centered. By default, numbers are right-aligned, and text is left-aligned. Figure 47-1 shows a table of data that uses the default alignment. As you can see, entries in the Sales and Region columns appear right next to each other, making it difficult to read.

	A	B	C	D	E
1					
2	State	Sales	Region		
3	California	198,093	Western		
4	Arizona	87,926	Western		
5	Washington	106,653	Western		
6	New York	174,610	Eastern		
7	New Jersey	65,023	Eastern		
8	Pennsylvania	93,801	Eastern		
9					
10					
11					

Figure 47-1: Default cell alignment can make information difficult to read.

One solution is to change the alignment of the Region column. By making the text centered or right-aligned, the text wouldn't be next to the numbers in the Sales column. Another option is to indent the Region text.

To indent, start by selecting the cell or range. Then press Ctrl+1 to display the Format Cells dialog box. Click the Alignment tab and specify a nonzero value for the Indent setting (see Figure 47-2). The direction of the indentation depends on the Horizontal alignment choice (Left or Right).

Figure 47-2: Choosing an Indent value for the selected range.

Figure 47-3 shows the original table after indenting the Region names one space. Alternatively, you can indent the values in the Sales column to provide a space after each number. Either choice improves the legibility.

	A	B	C	D
1				
2	State	Sales	Region	
3	California	198,093	Western	
4	Arizona	87,926	Western	
5	Washington	106,653	Western	
6	New York	174,610	Eastern	
7	New Jersey	65,023	Eastern	
8	Pennsylvania	93,801	Eastern	
9				
10				

Figure 47-3: Legibility is improved by indenting the Region names.

Quick Number Formatting

As you probably know, a value in a cell can be displayed in many different ways. Excel provides a few common number-formatting options in the Home➜Number group of the Ribbon. For complete control over number formatting, press Ctrl+1 to display the Format Cells dialog box and then click the Number tab.

Some common number formats can be applied without using the Format Cells dialog box. If you use any of these number formats regularly, you can save some time by using the keyboard shortcuts shown in Table 48-1. Note that, on most keyboards, the third key in these Ctrl+Shift shortcuts is located on the top row of your keyboard.

Table 48-1: Shortcut Keys to Apply Number Formatting

Shortcut Keys	Format That the Shortcut Applies
Ctrl+Shift+` (the accent/ tilde key above Tab)	General number format (removes any other number formatting)
Ctrl+Shift+1	Number format with two decimal places, thousands separator, and minus sign (–) for negative values
Ctrl+Shift+2	Time format with the hour and minute and AM or PM
Ctrl+Shift+3	Date format with the day, month, and year
Ctrl+Shift+4	Currency format with two decimal places (and negative numbers displayed in parentheses)
Ctrl+Shift+5	Percentage format with no decimal places
Ctrl+Shift+6	Exponential Number format with two decimal places

Creating Custom Number Formats

Although Excel provides a good variety of built-in number formats, you may find that none of them suits your needs. In such a case, you can probably create a custom number format. You do this on the Number tab of the Format Cells dialog box (see Figure 49-1). The easiest way to display this dialog box is to press Ctrl+1. Or, click the dialog box launcher in the Home➜Number group. (The dialog box launcher is the small icon to the right of the word *Number*.)

Figure 49-1: Create custom number formats on the Number tab of the Format Cells dialog box.

Many Excel users — even advanced users — avoid creating custom number formats because they think that the process is too complicated. In reality, custom number formats tend to *look* more complex than they are.

You construct a number format by specifying a series of codes as a number format string. To enter a custom number format, follow these steps:

1. Press Ctrl+1 to display the Format Cells dialog box.

2. Click the Number tab and select the Custom category.

3. Enter your custom number format in the Type field.

   See Tables 49-1 and 49-2 for examples of codes you can use to create your own, custom number formats.

4. Click OK to close the Format Cells dialog box.

Parts of a number format string

A custom format string enables you to specify different format codes for four categories of values: positive numbers, negative numbers, zero values, and text. You do so by separating the codes for each category with a semicolon. The codes are arranged in four sections, separated by semicolons:

```
Positive format; Negative format; Zero format; Text format
```

The following general guidelines determine how many of these four sections you need to specify:

> If your custom format string uses only one section, the format string applies to all values.

> If you use two sections, the first section applies to positive values and zeros, and the second section applies to negative values.

> If you use three sections, the first section applies to positive values, the second section applies to negative values, and the third section applies to zeros.

> If you use all four sections, the last section applies to text stored in the cell.

The following example of a custom number format specifies a different format for each of these types:

```
[Green]General;[Red]-General;[Black]General;[Blue]General
```

This example takes advantage of the fact that colors have special codes. A cell formatted with this custom number format displays its contents in a different color, depending on the value. When a cell is formatted with this custom number format, a positive number is green, a negative number is red, a zero is black, and text is blue. By the way, using the Excel conditional formatting feature is a much better way to apply color to cells based on their content.

Note

When you create a custom number format, don't overlook the Sample box in the Number tab of the Format Cells dialog box. This box displays the value in the active cell by using the format string in the Type field. Be sure to test your custom number formats by using the following data: a positive value, a negative value, a zero value, and text. Often, creating a custom number format takes several attempts. Each time you edit a format string, it's added to the list. When you finally get the correct format string, open the Format Cells dialog box one more time and delete your previous attempts.

Custom number format codes

Table 49-1 briefly describes the formatting codes available for custom formats.

Table 49-1: Codes Used to Create Custom Number Formats

Code	What It Does
General	Displays the number in General format
#	Serves as a digit placeholder that displays only significant digits and does not display insignificant zeros
0 (zero)	Serves as a digit placeholder that displays insignificant zeros if a number has fewer digits than there are zeros in the format
?	Serves as a digit placeholder that adds spaces for insignificant zeros on either side of the decimal point so that decimal points align when formatted with a fixed-width font; also used for fractions that have varying numbers of digits
.	Displays the decimal point
%	Displays a percentage
,	Displays the thousands separator
E- E+ e- e+	Displays scientific notation
$ – + / ( ) : space	Displays this character
\	Displays the next character in the format
*	Repeats the next character to fill the column width
_ (underscore)	Leaves a space equal to the width of the next character
"text"	Displays the text inside the double quotation marks
@	Serves as a text placeholder
[color]	Displays the characters in the specified color and can be any of the following text strings (not case sensitive): Black, Blue, Cyan, Green, Magenta, Red, White, or Yellow
[COLOR n]	Displays the corresponding color in the color palette, where n is a number from 0 to 56
[condition value]	Enables you to set your own criteria for each section of a number format

Table 49-2 describes the codes used to create custom formats for dates and times.

Table 49-2: Codes Used in Creating Custom Formats for Dates and Times

Code	What It Displays
m	The month as a number without leading zeros (1–12)
mm	The month as a number with leading zeros (01–12)
mmm	The month as an abbreviation (Jan–Dec)
mmmm	The month as a full name (January–December)
mmmmm	The first letter of the month (J–D)
d	The day as a number without leading zeros (1–31)
dd	The day as a number with leading zeros (01–31)
ddd	The day as an abbreviation (Sun–Sat)
dddd	The day as a full name (Sunday–Saturday)
yy or yyyy	The year as a two-digit number (00–99) or as a four-digit number (1900–9999)
h or hh	The hour as a number without leading zeros (0–23) or as a number with leading zeros (00–23)
m or mm	The minute as a number without leading zeros (0–59) or as a number with leading zeros (00–59)
s or ss	The second as a number without leading zeros (0–59) or as a number with leading zeros (00–59)
[ ]	Hours greater than 24 or minutes or seconds greater than 60
AM/PM	The hour using a 12-hour clock, or no AM/PM indicator if the hour uses a 24-hour clock

Cross-Ref

For more tips that deal with custom number formatting, see Tip 50, Tip 51, and Tip 52.

Using Custom Number Formats to Scale Values

If you work with large numbers, you may prefer to display them scaled to thousands or millions rather than display the entire number. For example, you may want to display a number like 132,432,145 in millions: 132.4.

The way to display scaled numbers is to use a custom number format. The actual unscaled number, of course, will be used in calculations that involve that cell. The formatting affects only how the number is displayed. To enter a custom number format, press Ctrl+1 to display the Format Cells dialog box. Then click the Number tab and select the Custom category. Put your custom number format in the Type field.

Table 50-1 shows examples of number formats that scale values in millions.

Table 50-1: Examples of Displaying Values in Millions

Value	Number Format	Display
123456789	#,###,,	123
1.23457E+11	#,###,,	123,457
1000000	#,###,,	1
5000000	#,###,,	5
–5000000	#,###,,	–5
0	#,###,,	(blank)
123456789	#,###.00,,	123.46
1.23457E+11	#,###.00,,	123,457.00
1000000	#,###.00,,	1.00
5000000	#,###.00,,	5.00
–5000000	#,###.00,,	–5.00
0	#,###.00,,	.00
123456789	#,###,,"M"	123M
1.23457E+11	#,###,,"M"	123,457M
1000000	#,###,,"M"	1M
–5000000	#,###,,"M"	–5M
123456789	#,###.0,,"M"_);(#,###.0,,"M)";0.0"M"_)	123.5M
1000000	#,###.0,,"M"_);(#,###.0,,"M)";0.0"M"_)	1.0M
–5000000	#,###.0,,"M"_);(#,###.0,,"M)";0.0"M"_)	(5.0M)
0	#,###.0,,"M"_);(#,###.0,,"M)";0.0"M"_)	0.0M

Table 50-2 shows examples of number formats that scale values in thousands.

Table 50-2: Examples of Displaying Values in Thousands

Value	Number Format	Display
123456	#,###,	123
1234565	#,###,	1,235
−323434	#,###,	−323
123123.123	#,###,	123
499	#,###,	(blank)
500	#,###,	1
500	#,###.00,	.50

Table 50-3 shows examples of number formats that display values in hundreds.

Table 50-3: Examples of Displaying Values in Hundreds

Value	Number Format	Display
546	0"."00	5.46
100	0"."00	1.00
9890	0"."00	98.90
500	0"."00	5.00
−500	0"."00	−5.00
0	0"."00	0.00

Using Custom Date and Time Formatting

When you enter a date into a cell, Excel formats the date by using the system short-date format. You can change this format by opening the Windows Control Panel and selecting Regional Settings.

Excel provides many useful built-in date and time formats, accessible in the Date and Time categories on the Number tab of the Format Cells dialog box. Table 51-1 shows some other date and time formats that you might find useful. The Value column in the table shows the date-and-time serial number.

Table 51-1: Examples of Time and Date Number Formats

Value	Number Format	Display
40328	mmmm d, yyyy (dddd)	May 30, 2010 (Sunday)
40328	"It's" dddd!	It's Sunday!
40328	dddd, mm/dd/yyyy	Sunday, 05/30/2010
40328	"Month: "mmm	Month: May
40328	General (m/d/yyyy)	40328 (5/30/2010)
0.345	h "Hours"	8 Hours
0.345	h:mm o'clock	8:16 o'clock
0.345	h:mm a/p"m"	8:16 am
0.345	h "hours and" m "minutes"	8 hours and 16 minutes
0.78	h:mm a/p".m."	6:43 p.m.

Examining Some Useful Custom Number Formats

This tip provides some useful examples of custom number formats.

Cross-Ref

See Tip 49 for the steps to enter a custom number format in the Format Cells dialog box as well as a list of the number format codes.

Hiding zeros

In the following number format string, the third element of the string is empty, which causes zero-value cells to be displayed as blank:

```
General;General;;@
```

This format string uses the General format for positive and negative values. You can, of course, substitute any other format codes.

Displaying leading zeros

To display leading zeros, create a custom number format that uses the 0 character. For example, if you want all numbers to be displayed with ten digits, use the following number format string; values with fewer than ten digits are displayed with leading zeros:

```
0000000000
```

In the following example, the format string uses the repeat-character code (an asterisk) to apply leading zeros to fill the entire width of the cell:

```
*00
```

Two zeros are required because the first one represents the character to be repeated, and the second one represents the value to be displayed.

Formatting percentages

Using a percent symbol (%) in a format string displays the cell in Percentage format. Note that the percent sign also appears on the formula bar.

The following format string formats values less than or equal to 1 in Percentage format (values greater than 1 and text are formatted using the General format):

```
[<=1]0.00%;General
```

When you mix cells with Percentage and General formatting in a column, you might prefer to see the nonpercent values indented from the right so that the values line up properly. To do so, apply the following number format to nonpercent cells. This format string uses an underscore followed by the percent symbol. The result is a space equal to the width of the percent symbol:

```
#.00_%
```

Displaying fractions

Excel supports quite a few built-in fraction number formats. (Select the Fraction category from the Number tab of the Format Cells dialog box to see available formats.) For example, to display the value .125 as a fraction with 8 as the denominator, select As Eighths (⅛) from the Type list.

You can use a custom format string to create other fraction formats. For example, the following format string displays the fractional part of a value in 50ths:

```
# ??/50
```

The following format string displays a value in terms of fractional dollars. For example, the value 154.87 is displayed as 154 and 87/100 Dollars:

```
0 "and "??/100 "Dollars"
```

The following example displays the value in sixteenths, with a quotation mark appended to the right. This format string is useful when you deal with inches (for example, ¾₆").

```
# ??/16\"
```

Repeating text

The number format string displays the contents of the cell three times. For example, if the cell contains the text *Budget,* the cell displays Budget Budget Budget:

```
;;;@ @ @
```

Displaying a negative sign on the right

The following format string displays negative values with the negative sign to the right of the number. Positive values have an additional space on the right, so both positive and negative numbers align properly on the right:

```
0.00_-;0.00-
```

Suppressing certain types of entries

You can use number formatting to hide certain types of entries. For example, the following format string displays text but not values:

```
;;
```

This format string displays values (with one decimal place) but not text or zeros:

```
0.0;-0.0;;
```

This format string displays everything except zeros (values are displayed with one decimal place):

```
0.0;-0.0;;@
```

You can use the following format string to completely hide the contents of a cell:

```
;;;
```

Note that when the cell is activated, however, the cell's contents are visible on the Formula bar.

Updating Old Fonts

When you install Microsoft Office, several new fonts are added to your system, and these new fonts are used when you create a new workbook. The exact fonts that are used as defaults vary, depending on which document theme is in effect.

 See Tip 16 for more information about using document themes.
Cross-Ref

If you use the default Office theme, a newly created Excel workbook uses two new fonts: Cambria (for headings) and Calibri (for body text). When you open a workbook that was saved in a version prior to Excel 2007, the old fonts are not updated. The difference in appearance between a worksheet that uses the old fonts and a worksheet that uses the new fonts is dramatic. When you compare an Excel 2003 worksheet with an Excel 2010 worksheet, the latter is much more readable and seems less cramped.

To update the fonts in a workbook that was created in a previous version of Excel, follow these steps:

1. Press Ctrl+N to create a new, blank workbook.

2. Activate the workbook that uses the fonts to be updated.

3. Choose Home➜Styles and click the bottom arrow of the scroller on the right side of the Style Gallery.

4. When the gallery expands, choose Merge Styles.

5. In the Merge Styles dialog box, select the workbook that you created in Step 1 and click OK.

    Excel asks whether you want to merge styles that have the same names.

6. Reply by clicking the Yes button.

This procedure updates the fonts used in all cells except those that have additional formatting, such as a different font size, bold, italic, colored text, or a shaded background. To change the font in these cells, follow these steps:

1. Select any single cell.

2. Choose Home➜Editing➜Find & Select➜Replace to display the Find and Replace dialog box.

    Or, press Ctrl+H.

3. Make sure that the Find What and Replace With boxes are empty.

   If these boxes aren't visible, click the Options button to expand the dialog box.

4. Click the upper Format button to display the Find Format dialog box.

5. Click the Font tab.

6. In the Font list, select the name of the font that you're replacing (probably Arial, the old default font) and then click OK to close the Find Format dialog box.

7. Click the lower Format button to display the Replace Format dialog box.

8. Click the Font tab.

9. In the Font list, select the name of the font that will replace the old font (probably Calibri) and then click OK to close the Replace Format dialog box.

10. In the Find and Replace dialog box, click Replace All to replace the old font with the new font.

Understanding Conditional Formatting Visualization

Conditional formatting enables you to apply cell formatting selectively and automatically, based on the contents of the cells. For example, you can specify that all negative values in a range have a light yellow background color. When you enter or change a value in the range, Excel examines the value and checks the conditional formatting rules for the cell. If the value is negative, the background is shaded. If not, no formatting is applied.

Beginning with Excel 2007, Microsoft significantly enhanced conditional formatting to include several visualization features: data bars, color scales, and icon sets. This tip describes these features, which you access by using the Home➜Styles➜Conditional Formatting drop-down control.

Data bars

Using the data bars conditional formatting can sometimes serve as a quick alternative to creating a chart. Figure 54-1 shows results from a survey, using data bars to visualize the responses. Data bars conditional formatting is much improved in Excel 2010. For example, you can now use solid bars (rather than gradients), you can specify minimum and maximum scale values, and negative numbers are handled correctly.

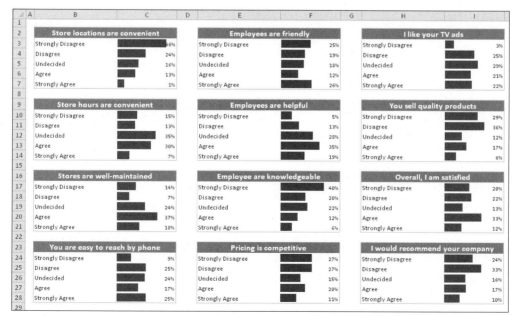

Figure 54-1: These tables use data bars conditional formatting.

Color scales

The color scale conditional formatting option varies the background color of a cell based on the cell's value, relative to other cells in the range. Figure 54-2 shows a range of cells that use color scale conditional formatting. The figure depicts the number of employees on each day of the year. This 3-color scale uses red for the lowest value, yellow for the midpoint, and green for the highest value. Values between those ranges are displayed by using a color within the gradient. The grayscale figure doesn't do justice to this example. The effect is much more impressive when you view it in color.

Daily Staffing Level

	1	2	3	4	5	6	7	8	9	10	11	12	13	14	15	16	17	18	19	20	21	22	23	24	25	26	27	28	29	30	31
January	80	80	80	80	80	80	80	79	79	79	79	79	79	80	82	82	82	82	82	82	82	82	82	82	82	84	84	84	84	84	84
February	84	84	84	84	84	84	84	84	83	83	83	82	82	82	82	82	82	82	82	82	82	82	82	82	85	85	85				
March	85	85	85	85	85	85	85	85	85	85	85	85	86	86	86	86	86	86	86	86	86	86	86	86	86	86	86	86	86	86	86
April	88	88	88	88	88	88	88	88	88	88	88	88	88	88	89	89	89	89	89	88	88	88	88	88	88	88	88	88	88	88	
May	88	88	88	88	88	88	88	88	88	88	89	89	89	89	89	89	89	89	89	89	89	89	89	89	92	92	92	92	92	92	92
June	92	92	92	92	92	92	92	92	92	92	92	92	91	91	91	91	91	91	91	91	91	91	92	92	92	92	92	92	92	92	
July	92	92	92	92	92	92	92	92	92	92	92	93	95	95	95	95	96	98	98	98	96	94	94	94	94	94	92	92	92	92	92
August	92	92	92	92	91	90	90	90	90	91	92	92	92	92	92	92	92	92	92	92	92	92	92	92	92	92	92	92	92	92	92
September	92	93	93	93	93	93	93	93	93	93	93	93	93	93	93	94	94	94	94	94	94	94	94	94	94	95	95	95			
October	95	95	95	95	95	95	94	94	94	94	94	95	95	95	95	95	95	96	96	96	96	96	96	96	96	96	96	97	97	97	97
November	97	97	97	97	97	97	97	96	96	96	96	97	97	97	99	99	99	99	99	99	99	99	99	99	99	99	99	99	99	99	
December	101	101	101	101	101	101	101	102	102	102	102	102	102	102	102	102	101	101	101	101	101	101	101	101	101	101	101	101	101	101	101

Figure 54-2: This range uses color scale conditional formatting.

Icon sets

The third conditional formatting visualization option displays an icon in the cell. Which icon is displayed depends on the value of the cell, relative to other cells. Excel 2010 provides 20 icon sets to choose from (and you mix and match icons from different sets). The number of icons in the sets ranges from three to five.

Figure 54-3 shows an example that uses the icon set named 3 Arrows (although only two of the arrows are used). The symbols graphically depict the change between two test scores. If the change is greater than or equal to five, a green up arrow is displayed. If the change is less than –5, a red down arrow is displayed. All other change values are depicted by no icon.

Student	Test 1	Test 2	Change	Trend
Amy	59	65	6	⬆
Bob	82	78	-4	
Calvind	98	92	-6	⬇
Doug	56	69	13	⬆
Ephraim	98	89	-9	⬇
Frank	67	75	8	⬆
Gretta	78	87	9	⬆
Harold	87	92	5	⬆
Inez	56	85	29	⬆
June	87	72	-15	⬇
Kenny	87	88	1	
Lance	92	92	0	
Marvin	82	73	-9	⬇
Noel	98	100	2	
Opie	84	73	-11	⬇
Paul	94	93	-1	
Quinton	68	92	24	⬆
Rasmus	91	90	-1	
Sam	85	86	1	
Ted	72	92	20	⬆
Ursie	80	75	-5	⬇
Valerie	77	65	-12	⬇
Wally	64	45	-19	⬇
Xerxes	59	63	4	
Yolanda	89	99	10	⬆
Zippy	85	82	-3	

Figure 54-3: In this example, the icons graphically depict the change between two test scores.

Showing Text and a Value in a Cell

If you need to display a number and text in a single cell, Excel provides three options:

- ➤ Concatenation
- ➤ The TEXT function
- ➤ A custom number format

Assume that cell A1 contains a value, and in a cell somewhere else in your worksheet you want to display the word *Total:* along with that value. It looks something like this:

```
Total: 594.34
```

You could, of course, put the word *Total* in the cell to the left. This section describes the three methods for accomplishing this task using a single cell.

Using concatenation

The following formula concatenates the text *Total:* with the value in cell A1:

```
="Total: "&A1
```

This solution is the simplest, but it has a problem. The result of the formula is text so that cell cannot be used in a numeric formula.

Using the TEXT function

Another solution uses the TEXT function, which displays a value by using a specified number format:

```
=TEXT(A1,"""Total: ""0.00")
```

The second argument for the TEXT function is a number format string — the same type of string that you use when you create a custom number format. Besides being a bit unwieldy (because of the extra quotation marks), this formula suffers from the same problem mentioned in the previous section: The result is not numeric.

Using a custom number format

If you want to display text and a value — and still be able to use that value in a numeric formula — the solution is to use a custom number format.

To add text, just create the number format string as usual and put the text within quotation marks. For this example, the following custom number format does the job:

```
"Total: "0.00
```

Even though the cell displays text, Excel still considers the cell contents to be a numeric value.

Merging Cells

Merging cells is a simple concept: Join two or more cells to create a larger single cell. To merge cells, just select them and choose Home→Alignment→Merge & Center. Excel combines the selected cells and displays the contents of the upper left cell, centered.

Merging cells is usually done as a way to enhance the appearance of a worksheet. Figure 56-1, for example, shows a worksheet with four sets of merged cells: C2:I2, J2:P2, B4:B8, and B9:B13. The merged cells in column B also use vertical text.

			Week 1								Week 2			
		1	2	3	4	5	6	7	8	9	10	11	12	13	14
Group 1	33	44	92	12	91	54	93	56	30	95	73	78	31	25
	0	43	78	61	62	31	86	66	15	59	45	1	89	39
	31	18	89	90	49	1	2	88	60	3	96	17	24	64
	94	26	78	24	47	12	30	92	69	8	8	29	74	35
	3	67	43	67	56	40	68	62	59	3	93	27	29	44
Group 2	15	59	24	67	12	48	26	6	26	75	51	33	30	93
	10	32	12	63	42	34	69	40	5	4	93	20	67	21
	36	73	6	1	31	96	75	22	61	76	55	69	10	23
	12	47	0	43	69	51	20	64	85	38	34	29	89	43
	88	21	75	59	32	36	39	26	35	92	27	33	62	86

Figure 56-1: This worksheet has four sets of merged cells.

Remember that merged cells can contain only one piece of information: a single value, text, or a formula. If you attempt to merge a range of cells that contains more than one non-empty cell, Excel prompts you with a warning that only the data in the upper leftmost cell will be retained.

To unmerge cells, just select the merged area and click the Merge and Center button again.

Notice that the Merge and Center button is a drop-down menu. If you click the arrow, you see three additional commands:

> **Merge Across:** Lets you select a range and then creates multiple merged cells — one for each row in the selection.

> **Merge Cells:** Works just like Merge and Center, except that the content of the upper left cell is not centered. (It retains its original horizontal alignment.)

> **Unmerge Cells:** Unmerges the selected merged cell.

Formatting Individual Characters in a Cell

Excel cell formatting isn't an all-or-none proposition. In some cases, you might find it helpful to be able to format individual characters within a cell.

Note

This technique is limited to cells that contain text. It doesn't work if the cell contains a value or a formula.

To apply formatting to characters within a text string, select those characters first. You can select them by clicking and dragging your mouse on the Formula bar. Or, double-click the cell and then click and drag the mouse to select specific characters directly in the cell. A more efficient way to select individual characters is to press F2 first and then use the arrow keys to move between characters and use the Shift+arrow keys to select characters.

When the characters are selected, use formatting controls to change the formatting. For example, you can make the selected text bold, italic, or a different color or even apply a different font. If you right-click, the Mini Toolbar appears, and you can use those controls to change the formatting of the selected characters.

Figure 57-1 shows a few examples of cells that contain individual character formatting.

Unfortunately, two useful formatting attributes are not available on the Ribbon or on the Mini Toolbar: superscript and subscript formatting. If you want to apply superscripts or subscripts, open the Font tab in the Format Cells dialog box. Just press Ctrl+1 after you select the text to format.

Note

My Power Utility Pak add-in includes a handy tool that simplifies individual character formatting, including superscript and subscript formatting. You can use the coupon in the back of this book to order a discounted copy.

	A	B	C	D	E	F	G
1							
2		This is the *final* notice					
3							
4							
5		$z = x^2 + y^2$					
6							
7							
8		This is the ~~unapproved~~ final budget					
9							
10		SALES ARE INCREASING					
11							

Figure 57-1: Examples of individual character formatting.

Displaying Times That Exceed 24 Hours

There's nothing really special about a time value. An Excel time value is a normal number that is formatted to display as a time. For example, 0 represents 12:00 a.m., 0.50 represents noon (half-way through the day), and 0.75 represents 6:00 p.m.

Because time values are numbers, you can add them together. Figure 58-1 shows a worksheet that sums several time values. The formula in cell B8 is a simple SUM formula:

```
=SUM(B3:B7)
```

	A	B	C	D
1				
2	Date	Hours Worked		
3	15-Jan	8:30		
4	16-Jan	4:00		
5	17-Jan	8:00		
6	18-Jan	6:30		
7	19-Jan	4:00		
8	Total	7:00		
9				

Figure 58-1: Summing time values might not display the correct result.

As you can see, the formula is returning an incorrect result. Because a day has only 24 hours, Excel normally ignores hours that exceed 24 hours. To force Excel to display times that exceed 24 hours, you modify the number formatting in the Number tab of the Format Cells dialog box.

In this example, Excel uses the following number format:

```
h:mm
```

To display the correct value, edit the number format code by placing square brackets around the h:

```
[h]:mm
```

Figure 58-2 shows the worksheet after making this number format change.

⁄	A	B	C	D
1				
2	**Date**	**Hours Worked**		
3	15-Jan	8:30		
4	16-Jan	4:00		
5	17-Jan	8:00		
6	18-Jan	6:30		
7	19-Jan	4:00		
8	Total	31:00		
9				
10				

Figure 58-2: Adjusting the number format causes the cell to display the correct value.

Fixing Non-Numeric Numbers

If you import data from other sources, you may have discovered that Excel sometimes does not import values correctly. Specifically, you might find that Excel is treating your numbers as text. For example, you might sum a range of values and find that the SUM formula returns 0 — even though the range apparently contains numeric values.

Often, Excel will notify you of these "non-numbers" and display a Smart Tag that lets you convert the text to numbers. If that Smart Tag isn't displayed, you can use this technique to force Excel to change these non-numeric numbers to actual values. Follow these steps:

1. Activate any empty cell on your worksheet.

2. Press Ctrl+C to copy the empty cell.

3. Select the range that contains the problematic values.

4. Choose Home➜Clipboard➜Paste➜Paste Special to display the Paste Special dialog box.

5. In the Paste Special dialog box, select the Add operation.

6. Click OK.

Excel adds nothing to these values, but in the process it coerces those cells to be actual values.

Adding a Frame to a Range

Excel 2007 added lots of new graphical formatting effects: shadows, glow, and reflection, for example. These effects apply only to graphical objects, such as pictures, shapes, and charts.

If you need to make a range of cells stand out, you can insert a shape to serve as a frame. The shape must be transparent (or semitransparent), but you can apply effects. Use the Insert➔Illustrations➔Shape command to add a shape to your worksheet.

Figure 60-1 shows an example of a range that has a transparent rectangular shape superimposed on top of it. I applied some bevel effects and a shadow to the shape to make it resemble a matted picture frame that's floating above the worksheet. The shape in the figure uses a thick compound line style, a beveled top, and a shadow.

Sales by Month			
	2007	2008	2009
January	9,734,332	11,848,025	12,990,397
February	10,305,225	11,714,522	13,559,113
March	9,696,617	11,624,473	13,206,066
April	9,729,466	12,352,361	13,294,892
May	9,281,935	11,919,277	13,086,995
June	8,875,914	12,002,639	12,731,185
July	9,698,358	12,157,452	13,461,877
August	10,373,539	11,613,938	13,207,491
September	11,070,755	12,308,689	12,598,263
October	11,611,204	12,923,417	12,130,578
November	11,290,181	12,237,090	11,839,221
December	11,603,642	12,930,643	11,301,935

Figure 60-1: A transparent shape on top of a range.

For maximum flexibility in formatting a shape, use the Format Shape dialog box rather than the Ribbon commands. To display this dialog box, select the shape and press Ctrl+1.

Dealing with Gridlines, Borders, and Underlines

If you need to draw attention to or delineate cells in a worksheet, one way to do it is with lines. Excel provides three options:

➤ Worksheet gridlines

➤ Cell borders

➤ Cell underlining

Worksheet gridlines is an all-or-none setting. Turn gridlines on or off for the active worksheet by using the View➔Show➔Gridlines check box. Normally, worksheet gridlines are not printed, but if you want the gridlines to appear on your printed output, use the Page Layout➔Sheet Options➔ Gridlines Print check box.

Cell borders can be applied to individual cells or to a range of cells. The Borders control in the Home➔Font group provides the most common cell border options, but for complete control, use the Border tab of the Format Cells dialog box, which is shown in Figure 61-1. (Press Ctrl+1 to display the Format Cells dialog box.) This dialog box gives you control over border color, line style, and location (for example, horizontal borders only) and works with the selected cell or range. This dialog box can be a bit confusing, but if you take a few minutes to experiment with the various options, you'll understand how it works. Generally, you choose a style and color and then use the Presets or the Border buttons to make your choice.

Figure 61-1: For optimal control over cell borders, use the Format Cells dialog box.

Cell underlining is completely independent of gridlines and cell borders. Excel provides four different types of underlining:

> ➤ Single

> ➤ Double

> ➤ Single accounting

> ➤ Double accounting

The Underline control in the Home➜Font group lets you choose from single or double underlining. To apply the other two types of underlining, you must select the underline type from the Underline drop-down list on the Font tab of the Format Cells dialog box.

How is the accounting underlining different from normal underlining? The difference is subtle. When accounting underlining is applied to a cell that contains text, the complete width of the cell is underlined. In addition, the underline appears slightly lower in the accounting underline formats, making the underlined data more legible.

Figure 61-2 shows all four types of underlining for text (column A) and for values formatted as currency. Worksheet gridlines are turned off to make the underlining more visible.

	A	B	C	D
1	No Underline		$1,234.56	
2				
3	Single Underline		$1,234.56	
4				
5	Double Underline		$1,234.56	
6				
7	Single Accounting Underline		$1,234.56	
8				
9	Double Accounting Underline		$1,234.56	
10				

Figure 61-2: Examples of four types of underlining.

Inserting a Watermark

A *watermark* is an image (or text) that appears on each printed page. A watermark can be a faint company logo or a word, such as *DRAFT.* Excel doesn't have an official command to print a watermark, but you can add a watermark by inserting a picture in the page header or footer. Here's how to do it:

1. Note the location on your hard drive of the image you want to use for the watermark.

2. Choose View→Workbook Views→Page Layout View to enter Page Layout View.

3. Click the center section of the header.

4. Choose Header & Footer Tools→Header & Footer Elements→Picture to display the Insert Picture dialog box.

5. Using the Insert Picture dialog box, locate and select the image you picked in Step 1 and then click Insert to insert the image.

6. Click outside the header to see your image.

7. To center the image vertically on the page, click the center section of the header and press Enter a few times before the &[Picture] code.

   Experiment to determine the number of extra lines to insert.

8. If you need to adjust the image (for example, to make it lighter), click the center section of the header and then choose Header & Footer Tools→Header & Footer Elements→ Format Picture; use the Image controls on the Picture tab of the Format Picture dialog box to adjust the image.

   You may need to experiment with the settings to make sure that the worksheet text is legible.

Figure 62-1 shows an example of a header image (a graphic of a globe) used as a watermark. You can create a similar effect with plain text in the header (for example, the word DRAFT).

raw data

	A	B	C	D	E	F	G	H	I
1	102.74	617.01	224.15	322.05	14.18	874.59	595.84	857.34	438.33
2	681.80	682.94	581.25	838.23	563.49	33.49	358.44	647.72	26.19
3	686.75	457.64	885.08	769.58	624.07	642.26	107.38	812.17	203.02
4	752.73	611.05	129.41	539.49	191.60	695.11	798.15	160.41	239.67
5	986.61	487.63	923.98	694.43	640.11	129.53	979.75	644.81	557.39
6	878.23	973.23	768.64	799.75	232.00	760.54	600.19	813.14	132.11
7	351.60	219.61	931.96	780.71	326.42	760.56	101.87	583.73	693.00
8	318.87	672.92	274.07	835.80	188.01	291.64	184.62	976.44	326.36
9	839.53	856.22	694.81	855.64	651.50	83.06	426.37	657.55	896.82
10	684.46	91.59	174.18	717.48	67.59	633.74	982.62	491.40	147.79
11	960.12	571.44	342.35	327.00	87.78	332.86	70.32	485.69	671.12
12	876.31	107.91	477.02	311.44	1.02	930.67	896.50	284.13	772.08
13	666.77	762.37	363.82	113.99	543.93	94.94	591.51	524.63	803.23
14	611.83	539.98	228.55	160.68	270.85	387.25	26.73	16.93	641.19
15	378.48	554.73	177.90	648.83	29.19	907.18	479.28	653.13	84.32
16	909.91	494.59	219.35	436.18	134.82	30.00	349.48	462.73	16.05
17	357.67	344.99	246.64	679.83	136.91	103.02	249.31	189.67	132.27
18	232.15	240.62	298.79	154.43	203.24	983.02	593.57	81.28	187.05
19	957.43	513.14	522.62	729.12	386.22	322.43	236.33	70.56	764.27
20	333.77	307.46	190.72	31.73	430.39	790.37	19.67	269.13	546.33
21	663.72	589.18	669.32	614.49	12.82	189.98	706.35	296.72	775.39
22	780.85	457.08	808.50	67.24	546.91	736.89	157.48	356.21	814.24
23	59.57	633.62	206.91	3.77	754.82	349.48	894.98	514.36	302.20
24	520.50	32.74	933.78	373.08	657.36	875.80	531.15	599.60	665.84
25	835.59	593.80	826.69	860.07	12.80	919.57	514.75	146.55	395.26
26	388.95	164.01	168.07	800.58	395.53	129.00	578.84	575.67	318.76
27	723.26	934.31	492.38	993.26	35.42	135.14	863.17	11.17	563.52
28	637.44	475.21	297.40	203.38	245.62	719.40	593.96	618.55	800.36
29	709.81	630.89	339.58	743.25	916.43	695.81	272.83	783.30	244.40
30	517.57	544.73	356.86	495.34	178.90	704.82	783.01	668.67	926.28
31	242.40	934.79	919.46	852.88	995.43	447.03	809.73	556.73	593.02
32	641.81	251.30	189.57	342.47	569.64	483.81	998.52	52.50	848.24
33	692.31	527.22	192.30	918.86	227.44	442.48	359.89	907.15	547.65
34	761.99	42.62	209.74	799.61	200.29	45.11	12.66	91.34	779.00
35	226.89	343.53	174.73	297.12	226.94	105.16	510.48	603.68	207.64
36	969.84	263.19	552.58	634.40	826.84	599.68	42.96	4.78	587.82
37	700.43	41.46	633.50	440.72	13.31	113.47	859.82	681.42	265.37
38	850.19	689.68	367.68	4.09	811.75	224.91	14.76	460.61	305.96
39	44.27	713.83	80.19	982.76	981.92	618.16	512.19	877.15	118.25
40	749.90	170.31	608.62	990.98	234.54	734.43	604.92	410.82	441.63
41	576.72	212.96	159.70	229.18	828.01	839.88	253.51	311.03	536.27
42	104.99	367.41	594.98	346.54	104.15	506.04	224.93	581.09	79.10
43	821.59	223.24	627.82	808.39	573.08	492.93	169.73	897.12	178.67
44	855.69	982.73	299.05	653.83	250.70	919.42	772.22	814.98	700.00
45	876.41	306.68	44.67	838.24	138.92	161.18	50.77	173.76	727.56
46	446.26	597.07	755.36	176.62	691.26	678.56	605.24	13.24	87.89
47	336.60	865.74	132.97	419.38	257.47	472.27	917.80	817.46	743.84

Click to add footer

Figure 62-1: Displaying a watermark on a page.

Adding a Background Image to a Worksheet

Most of the time, simpler is better. But, in some cases, you might want to spiff up a worksheet with something fancy. One way to do that is to apply a background image. A background image in Excel is similar to the wallpaper that you might display on your Windows desktop or an image used as the background for a Web page.

Figure 63-1 shows an example of a worksheet that contains an appropriate background image — money, for a financial services company.

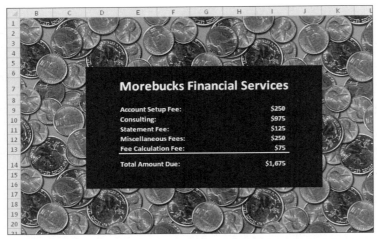

Figure 63-1: You can add almost any image file as a worksheet background image, but some images work better than others.

Note

Before you get too excited about this feature, remember this caveat: The graphical background on a worksheet is for on-screen display only — it isn't printed when you print the worksheet.

To add a background to a worksheet, choose Page Layout➔Page Setup➔Background. Excel displays a dialog box that enables you to select a graphics file. (All common graphics file formats are supported.) When you locate a file, click Insert. Excel tiles the image across your worksheet. Some images are specifically designed to be tiled, such as the one shown in the figure. This type of image is often used for Web page backgrounds, and it creates a seamless background.

You also want to turn off the gridline display because the gridlines show through the image. Some backgrounds make viewing text difficult, so you might want to use a solid background color for cells that contain text. Use the Home➔Font➔Fill Color control to change the background color of cells.

Wrapping Text in a Cell

If you need to enter a lot of text into a cell, you have two choices:

> ➤ Allow the text to spill over into the adjacent cell on the right.

> ➤ Allow the text to wrap so that it's displayed on multiple lines within the cell.

If the cell to the right isn't empty, the text appears to be cut off if you don't wrap it. Figure 64-1 illustrates how different types of wrapped and unwrapped text can look.

	A	B	C	D	E	F	G	H	I
1									
2		This cell contains a lengthy text string, and it appears to spill over into the adjacent cells.							
3									
4		This cell contains a lengtl	14.5						
5									
6		This cell contains a lengthy text string, and is formatted to display on multiple lines by using the Wrap Text command.							
7									
8									

Figure 64-1: Examples of lengthy text in cells.

Cell B2 contains the default formatting. Because the cells to the right are empty, the entire chunk of text is visible.

Cell B4 contains the same text as B2, but the text appears to be cut off because cell C4 isn't empty.

Cell B6 uses the Wrap Text option, which is available in the Home➜Alignment group.

If you change the column width of a cell that uses Wrap Text, you find that the row height doesn't change to compensate. For example, if you reduce the column width, some of the text might not be displayed. If you increase the column width, you see extra white space in the cell. To fix the row height after changing the column width, choose Home➜Cells➜Format➜AutoFit Row Height. Also, remember that you can change the horizontal and vertical alignment of the text. For example, you can center it horizontally and vertically.

To force a line break in a cell, press Alt+Enter. If the cell isn't already formatted with Wrap Text, pressing Alt+Enter applies Wrap Text formatting automatically.

Cross-Ref

You can also merge cells together to hold lengthy text. See Tip 56 for more information.

Another way to handle lengthy text is to put it in a text box (see Figure 64-2). Add a text box by choosing Insert➜Text➜Text Box and then just start typing. A *text box* is just a shape with text, so you can format it any way you like. And, of course, you can position it without respect to cell boundaries. Word wrap is automatic within a text box. To force a line break, press Enter. The text box in the figure uses a drop shadow to make it appear as if it's floating above the worksheet.

Figure 64-2: Using a text box to display lengthy text.

Seeing All Characters in a Font

You probably have dozens of fonts installed on your system. Here's a quick way to view the characters available in any font.

Start with a new worksheet and then follow these steps:

1. Enter this formula into cell A1:

```
=CHAR(ROW())
```

2. Copy cell A1 down the column to cell A255.

3. Click the Column A header to select the entire column.

4. Choose a font from the Font drop-down list in the Home➔Font group.

5. Scroll down the worksheet to see the various characters in the selected font.

6. Repeat Steps 3 and 4 as often as you like.

Figure 65-1 shows a partial view of the characters in the Webdings font. The row number corresponds to the character number. You can enter these characters from the keyboard by using the numeric keypad, but make sure that NumLock is turned on. For example, to enter the character shown in row 120, hold down the Alt key while you type **120** on the numeric keypad. For codes less than 100, enter a leading zero. Make sure that the cell (or character) is formatted using the correct font.

Caution

If you plan to share your workbook with others, be careful about using *nonstandard fonts* (fonts that don't ship with Windows or Microsoft Office). If the font you specified isn't available on your colleague's system, Excel attempts to substitute the closest match. But it's not always successful.

The CHAR function works with only the first 255 characters in the font. Unicode fonts contain many additional characters, which cannot be displayed by using the CHAR function. However, you can create a simple VBA function procedure that mimics the Excel CHAR function, but works with character values greater than 255:

1. Press Alt+F11 to open the Visual Basic Editor window.

2. In the Project window, click the item that corresponds to your workbook.

3. Choose Insert➔Module to insert a VBA module.

4. Type the following lines of code in the VBA module:

```
Function CHAR2(code)
    CHAR2 = ChrW(code)
End Function
```

▲	A	B	C	D	E
111	⚓				
112	🚗				
113	()				
114	✕				
115	?				
116	🏢				
117	🏛				
118	🚌				
119	⚲				
120	⊘				
121	⊖				
122	⊗				
123	✹				
124						
125	✹				
126	⚡				
127	▯				

Figure 65-1: A few characters from the Webdings font.

After performing these steps, you can use the CHAR2 function in your formula. For example, the following formula displays a superscript 5 character:

```
=CHAR2(8309)
```

You can also access these characters (and determine their value) by using the Symbol dialog box. (See Tip 66 for more about using special characters.) The Symbol dialog box displays the code in hexadecimal. The CODE2 function accepts only a decimal argument, so you can convert it using the HEX2DEC function. For example, I learned from the Symbol dialog box that the hexadecimal code for a chessboard pawn character is 265F. To display this character, use this formula:

```
=CHAR2(HEX2DEC("265F"))
```

Note

The character displays correctly in most (but not all) fonts.

Entering Special Characters

The Excel Symbol dialog box is useful for locating and inserting special characters into a cell (see Figure 66-1). You access this dialog box by choosing Insert➜Symbols➜Symbol.

Figure 66-1: Characters in the Miscellaneous Technical subset of the Arial Unicode MS font.

On the Symbols tab, you select a font from the Font drop-down list. For most fonts, you can also select a subset of the font from the Subset drop-down list. Select the character you want and click the Insert button. Insert additional characters if you like, or click Close to close the dialog box.

Note

> If you insert a character from a particular font, Excel continues to display that same character, regardless of the font applied to the cell. For the largest selection of characters, use the Arial Unicode MS font.

If you use a particular character frequently, you might prefer to make it more accessible. You can do this by using Excel's AutoCorrect feature. The following instructions make the "place of interest sign" character (it's selected in Figure 66-1) easy to access:

1. Select an empty cell.
2. Choose Insert➜Symbols➜Symbol, and use the Symbol dialog box to locate the character you want to use.

   In this case, the symbol is character code 2318, located in the Miscellaneous Technical subset of the Arial Unicode MS font.
3. Insert that symbol into the cell by clicking the Insert button.
4. Click Close to close the Symbol dialog box.
5. Press Ctrl+C to copy the character in the active cell.

6. Choose File➜Options to display the Excel Options dialog box, click the Proofing tab, and then click the AutoCorrect Options button to display the AutoCorrect dialog box (or, just press Alt+TA).

7. In the AutoCorrect dialog box, click the AutoCorrect tab.

8. In the Replace field, enter a character sequence, such as (p).

9. Activate the With field and press Ctrl+V to paste the special character.

10. Click OK to close the AutoCorrect dialog box.

After you perform these steps, Excel substitutes the symbol whenever you type (p). When you select a replacement string, choose a character sequence that you don't normally type. Otherwise, you may find that Excel is making the substitution when you don't want it to happen. Remember that you can always press Ctrl+Z to override an AutoCorrect entry. See Tip 42 for more about AutoCorrect.

Using Named Styles

Throughout the years, one of the most underused features in Excel has been named styles. It seems that the Excel designers set out to make this feature more visible. Beginning with Excel 2007, the Style gallery is difficult to miss. (It's on the Home tab.)

Named styles make it very easy to apply a set of predefined formatting options to a cell or range. In addition to saving time, using named styles helps to ensure a consistent look across your worksheets.

A style can consist of settings for up to six different attributes (which correspond to the tabs in the Format Cells dialog box):

- ➤ Number format
- ➤ Alignment (vertical and horizontal)
- ➤ Font (type, size, and color)
- ➤ Borders
- ➤ Fill (background color)
- ➤ Protection (locked and hidden)

The real power of styles is apparent when you change a component of a style. All cells that use that named style automatically incorporate the change. Suppose that you apply a particular style to a dozen cells scattered throughout your worksheet. Later, you realize that these cells should have a font size of 14 points rather than 12 points. Rather than change each cell, simply edit the style definition. All cells with that particular style change automatically.

Using the Style Gallery

Excel comes with dozens of predefined styles, and you apply these styles in the Style gallery (located in the Home➜Styles group). Figure 67-1 shows the predefined styles in the Style gallery. To apply a style to the selected cell or range, just click the style. Notice that this gallery provides a preview. When you hover your mouse over a style, it's temporarily applied to the selection so that you can see the effect. To make it permanent, just click the style.

After you apply a style to a cell, you can apply additional formatting to it by using any formatting method discussed in this chapter. Formatting modifications that you make to the cell don't affect other cells that use the same style.

To maximize the value of styles, it's best to avoid additional formatting. Rather, consider creating a new style (explained later in this tip).

Figure 67-1: Use the Style gallery to work with named styles.

Modifying an existing style

To change an existing style, activate the Style gallery, right-click the style you want to modify, and choose Modify from the shortcut menu. Excel displays the Style dialog box, shown in Figure 67-2. In this example, the Style dialog box shows the settings for the Normal style, which is the default style for all cells. (The style definitions vary, depending on which document theme is active.)

Figure 67-2: Use the Style dialog box to modify named styles.

Cells, by default, use the Normal style. Here's a quick example of how you can use styles to change the default font used throughout your workbook:

1. Choose Home➜Styles➜Cell Styles.

   Excels displays the list of styles for the active workbook.

2. Right-click Normal in the Styles list and choose Modify.

    Excel displays the Style dialog box, with the current settings for the Normal style.

3. Click the Format button.

    Excel displays the Format Cells dialog box.

4. Click the Font tab and choose the font and size that you want as the default.

5. Click OK to return to the Style dialog box.

6. Click OK again to close the Style dialog box.

The font for all cells that use the Normal style changes to the font that you specified. You can change any formatting attributes for any style.

Creating new styles

In addition to using the built-in Excel styles, you can create your own styles. This flexibility can be quite handy because it enables you to apply your favorite formatting options very quickly and consistently.

To create a new style, follow these steps:

1. Select a cell and apply all the formatting that you want to include in the new style.

    You can use any of the formatting that's available in the Format Cells dialog box.

2. After you format the cell to your liking, activate the Style gallery and choose New Cell Style.

    Excel displays its Style dialog box, along with a proposed generic name for the style. Note that Excel displays the words By Example to indicate that it's basing the style on the current cell.

3. Enter a new style name in the Style Name box.

    The check boxes display the current formats for the cell. By default, all check boxes are checked.

4. If you don't want the style to include one or more format categories, remove the check-marks from the appropriate boxes.

5. Click OK to create the style and to close the dialog box.

After you perform these steps, the new custom style is available in the Style gallery. Custom styles are available only in the workbook in which they were created. To copy your custom styles, see the section that follows.

Note

The Protection option in the Styles dialog box controls whether users can modify cells for the selected style. This option is effective only if you also turned on worksheet protection, by choosing Review➜Changes➜Protect Sheet.

Merging styles from other workbooks

It's important to understand that custom styles are stored with the workbook in which they were created. If you created some custom styles, you probably don't want to go through all the work to create copies of those styles in each new Excel workbook. A better approach is to merge the styles from a workbook in which you previously created them.

To merge styles from another workbook, open both the workbook that contains the styles you want to merge and the workbook into which you want to merge styles. From the workbook into which you want to merge styles, activate the Style gallery and choose Merge Styles. Excel displays the Merge Styles dialog box, which shows a list of all open workbooks. Select the workbook that contains the styles you want to merge and click OK. Excel copies styles from the workbook you selected into the active workbook.

You might want to create a master workbook that contains all your custom styles so that you always know which workbook to merge styles from.

Basic Formulas and Functions

The ability to create formulas is what makes a spreadsheet a spreadsheet. In this part, you'll find formula-related tips that can make your workbooks more powerful than ever.

Tips and Where to Find Them

Using Formula AutoComplete

Excel 2007 introduced a useful feature known as Formula AutoComplete. When you type an equal sign and the first letter of a function in a cell, Excel displays a drop-down list box that contains all the functions that begin with that letter. You also see a ScreenTip with a brief description for the function (see Figure 68-1).

	A	B	C	D	E	F	G	H	I
1									
2									
3									
4		=s							
5		*fx* STDEV.P							
6		*fx* STDEV.S							
7		*fx* STDEVA							
8		*fx* STDEVPA							
9		*fx* STEYX							
10		*fx* SUBSTITUTE							
11		*fx* SUBTOTAL							
12		*fx* SUM							
13		*fx* SUMIF	Adds the cells specified by a given condition or criteria						
14		*fx* SUMIFS							
15		*fx* SUMPRODUCT							
		fx SUMSQ							
16									
17									
18									

Figure 68-1: When you begin to enter a function, Excel lists available functions that begin with the typed letters.

When the AutoComplete list is displayed, you can continue typing (to narrow the number of items displayed in the list) or use the arrow keys to select the function from the list. After you select a function, press Tab (or double-click) to insert the function and its opening parenthesis into the cell.

Note

In addition to displaying function names, the Formula AutoComplete feature lists names and table references.

After you press Tab to insert the function, Excel displays another ScreenTip, which shows the arguments for the function (see Figure 68-2). The bold argument is the argument you are currently entering. Arguments shown in brackets are optional. If the ScreenTip gets in your way, you can drag it to a different location.

Tip 68: Using Formula AutoComplete

⊿	A	B	C	D	E	F	G
1							
2							
3							
4		=SUMIF(					
5		SUMIF(**range**, criteria, [sum_range])					
6							
7							
8							
9							

Figure 68-2: A function argument is displayed in a ScreenTip.

Knowing When to Use Absolute References

When you create a formula that refers to another cell or range, the cell or range reference can be relative or absolute. A *relative* cell reference adjusts to its new location when the formula is copied and pasted. An *absolute* cell reference does not change, even when the formula is copied and pasted elsewhere. An absolute reference is specified with two dollar signs; for example:

```
=$A$1
=SUM($A$1:$F$24)
```

A relative reference, on the other hand, does not use dollar signs:

```
=A1
=SUM(A1:F24)
```

The majority of cell and range references you will ever use are relative references. In fact, Excel creates relative cell references in formulas except when the formula includes cells in different worksheets or workbooks. When do you use an absolute reference? The answer is simple: The only time you even need to *think* about using an absolute reference is if you plan to copy the formula.

The easiest way to understand this concept is with an example. Figure 69-1 shows a simple worksheet. The formula in cell D2, which multiplies the quantity by the unit price, is

```
=B2*C2
```

	A	B	C	D	E
1	Item	Quantity	Price	Total	
2	Chair	4	$125.00	$500.00	
3	Desk	4	$695.00		
4	Lamp	3	$39.95		
5					
6					

Figure 69-1: Copying a formula that contains relative references.

This formula uses relative cell references. Therefore, when the formula is copied to the other cells in the column, the references adjust in a relative manner. For example, copy the formula to cell D3, and it becomes

```
=B3*C3
```

What if the cell references in D2 contain absolute references, like this?

```
=$B$2*$C$2
```

In this case, copying the formula to the cells below produces incorrect results. The formula in cell D3 is exactly the same as the formula in cell D2 and returns the total for Chairs, not Desks.

Now extend the example to calculate sales tax. The sales tax rate is stored in cell B7 (see Figure 69-2). In this situation, the formula in cell E2 is

```
=D2*$B$7
```

	A	B	C	D	E	F
1	Item	Quantity	Price	Total	Tax	
2	Chair	4	$125.00	$500.00	$37.50	
3	Desk	4	$695.00	$2,780.00		
4	Lamp	3	$39.95	$119.85		
5						
6						
7	Sales Tax:	7.50%				
8						
9						

Figure 69-2: Formula references to the sales tax cell should be absolute.

The Total is multiplied by the tax rate stored in cell B7. Notice that the reference to B7 is an absolute reference, and this reference will not change when you copy the cell. When the formula in E2 is copied to the cells below, cell E3 contains this formula:

```
=D3*$B$7
```

The reference to cell D2 is adjusted, but the reference to cell B7 is not — which is exactly what you want.

Knowing When to Use Mixed References

In the previous tip, I discuss absolute versus relative cell references. This tip covers an additional type of cell reference: In a *mixed cell reference,* either the column part or the row part of a reference is absolute (and therefore doesn't change when the formula is copied and pasted). Mixed cell references aren't used often, but as you see in this tip, in some situations, using mixed references makes your job much easier.

An absolute cell reference contains two dollar signs. A mixed cell reference contains, by comparison, only one dollar sign. Here are two examples of mixed references:

```
=$A1
=A$1
```

In the first example, the column part of the reference (A) is absolute, and the row part (1) is relative. In the second example, the column part of the reference is relative, and the row part is absolute.

Figure 70-1 shows a worksheet demonstrating a situation in which using mixed references is the best choice.

◢	A	B	C	D	E	F	G
1				Width			
2			1.0	1.5	2.0	2.5	
3		1.0	1.0	1.5	2.0	2.5	
4	Length	1.5	1.5	2.3	3.0	3.8	
5		2.0	2.0	3.0	4.0	5.0	
6		2.5	2.5	3.8	5.0	6.3	
7		3.0	3.0	4.5	6.0	7.5	
8							
9							
10							

Figure 70-1: Using mixed cell references.

The formulas in the table calculate the area for various lengths and widths. Here's the formula in cell C3:

```
=$B3*C$2
```

Notice that both cell references are mixed. The reference to cell B3 uses an absolute reference for the column ($B), and the reference to cell C2 uses an absolute reference for the row ($2). As a result, this formula can be copied down and across, and the calculations are correct. For example, the formula in cell F7 is

```
=$B7*F$2
```

If C3 used either absolute or relative references, copying the formula would produce incorrect results.

Changing the Type of a Cell Reference

In Tips 69 and 70, I discuss absolute, relative, and mixed cell references. This tip describes an easy way to change the type of reference used when creating a formula.

You can enter nonrelative references (absolute or mixed) manually by simply typing dollar signs in the appropriate positions of the cell address. Or, you can use a handy shortcut: the F4 key. After you enter a cell reference when creating a formula, you can press F4 repeatedly to have Excel cycle through all four reference types.

For example, if you enter =A1 to start a formula, pressing F4 converts the cell reference to =$A$1. Pressing F4 again converts it to =A$1. Pressing it again displays =$A1. Pressing it one more time returns to the original =A1. Keep pressing F4 until Excel displays the type of reference you want.

Note

When you name a cell or range, Excel uses (by default) an absolute reference for the name. For example, if you give the name SalesForecast to A1:A12, the Refers To field in the Define Name dialog box lists the reference as $A$1:$A$12, which is almost always what you want. If you copy a cell that has a named reference in its formula, the copied formula contains a reference to the original name.

Converting a Vertical Range to a Table

Often, tabular data is imported into Excel as a single column. Figure 72-1 shows an example. Column A contains name and address information, and each "record" consists of five rows.

⊿	A	B	C	D	E	F
1	Joe Smith					
2	505 Main St.					
3	St. Louis					
4	MO					
5	64333					
6	Sally Jones					
7	3930 Elmer Road					
8	Fuddville					
9	NY					
10	10909					
11	Karen Richardson					
12	PO Box 1092					
13	Tucson					
14	AZ					
15	85763					
16	James R. Tulip					
17	1201 Flower Rd.					
18	Garden City					
19	CA					
20	98222					
21						
22						

Figure 72-1: This vertical range of data needs to be converted to a table.

Excel doesn't provide a direct way to convert such a range to a more usable table. But a few clever formulas will do the job. Insert the following formulas in range C1:G1:

```
C1: =INDIRECT("A" & ROW()*5-4)
D1: =INDIRECT("A" & ROW()*5-3)
E1: =INDIRECT("A" & ROW()*5-2)
F1: =INDIRECT("A" & ROW()*5-1)
G1: =INDIRECT("A" & ROW()*5-0)
```

After you enter the formulas, copy them to the rows below to accommodate the amount of data in column A. Figure 72-2 shows the result.

	A	B	C	D	E	F	G
1	Joe Smith		Joe Smith	505 Main St.	St. Louis	MO	64333
2	505 Main St.		Sally Jones	3930 Elmer Road	Fuddville	NY	10909
3	St. Louis		Karen Richardson	PO Box 1092	Tucson	AZ	85763
4	MO						
5	64333						
6	Sally Jones						
7	3930 Elmer Road						
8	Fuddville						
9	NY						
10	10909						
11	Karen Richardson						
12	PO Box 1092						
13	Tucson						
14	AZ						
15	85763						
16	James R. Tulip						
17	1201 Flower Rd.						
18	Garden City						
19	CA						
20	98222						
21							

Figure 72-2: Five formulas in columns C:G convert the original data into a table.

These formulas assume that the original data begins in cell A1 and that the conversion formulas begin in row 1. In addition, these formulas assume that each record consists of five rows. If your data uses fewer or more rows, you need to use fewer or more formulas — one for each row. In addition, you need to modify the formulas accordingly. For example, if each record consists of only three rows of data, the formulas are

```
C1: =INDIRECT("A" & ROW()*3-2)
D1: =INDIRECT("A" & ROW()*3-1)
E1: =INDIRECT("A" & ROW()*3-0)
```

AutoSum Tricks

Just about every Excel user knows about the AutoSum button. This command is so popular that it's available in two Ribbon locations: in the Home➜Editing group and in the Formulas➜Function Library group.

Just activate a cell and click the button, and Excel analyzes the data surrounding the active cell and proposes a SUM formula. If the proposed range is correct, click the AutoSum button again (or press Enter), and the formula is inserted. If you change your mind, press Esc.

If Excel incorrectly guesses the range to be summed, just select the correct range to be summed and press Enter. It's easy and painless.

Following are some additional tricks related to AutoSum:

> The AutoSum button can insert other types of formulas. Notice the little arrow on the right side of that button? Click it, and you see four other functions: AVERAGE, COUNT, MAX, and MIN. Click one of those items, and the appropriate formula is proposed. You also see a More Functions item, which simply displays the Insert Function dialog box — the same one that appears when you choose Formulas➜Function Library➜Insert Function (or click the fx button to the left of the formula bar).

> If you need to enter a similar SUM formula into a range of cells, select the entire range before you click the AutoSum button. In this case, Excel inserts the functions for you without asking you — one formula in each of the selected cells.

> To sum both across and down a table of numbers, select the range of numbers plus an additional column to the right and an additional row at the bottom. Click the AutoSum button, and Excel inserts the formulas that add the rows and the columns. In Figure 73-1, the range to be summed is D4:G15, so I selected an additional row and column: D4:H16. Clicking the AutoSum buttons puts formulas in row 16 and column H.

> You can also access AutoSum using your keyboard. Pressing Alt+= has exactly the same effect as clicking the AutoSum button.

> If you're working with a table (created by using Insert➜Tables➜Table), using the AutoSum button after selecting the row below the table inserts a Total row for the table and creates formulas that use the SUBTOTAL function rather than the SUM function. The SUBTOTAL function sums only the visible cells in the table, which is useful if you filter the data.

> Unless you applied a different number format to the cell that will hold the SUM formula, AutoSum applies the same number format as the first cell in the range to be summed.

> To create a SUM formula that uses only *some* of the values in a column, select the cells to be summed and then click the AutoSum button. Excel inserts the SUM formula in the first empty cell below the selected range. The selected range must be a contiguous group of cells — a multiple selection isn't allowed.

	Region-1	Region-2	Region-3	Region-4	Total
January	92	113	107	108	
February	118	105	100	107	
March	120	91	108	119	
April	102	103	106	96	
May	99	90	98	112	
June	93	112	107	98	
July	117	107	120	90	
August	103	113	96	105	
September	92	112	112	93	
October	98	112	94	113	
November	90	101	104	117	
December	103	114	116	104	
Total					

Figure 73-1: Using AutoSum to insert SUM formulas for rows and columns.

Using the Status Bar Selection Statistics Feature

I'm always surprised when I encounter Excel users who have never noticed the handy selection statistics field on the status bar. When you select a range that contains values, Excel displays information about the selected range on the status bar, which is at the bottom of the Excel window. As you can see in Figure 74-1, the selected cells have an average value of 198.62, the number of selected cells is 39, and the sum of the values is 7,746.

Figure 74-1: Excel displays information about the selected cells on the status bar.

If you prefer to see some other statistic relating to the selection, right-click the text on the status bar and make your selection from the shortcut menu (see Figure 74-2). Your choices are any or all of the following:

> Average

> Count

> Numerical Count

> Minimum

> Maximum

> Sum

Customize Status Bar

✓	Cell Mo_d_e	Ready
✓	Si_g_natures	Off
✓	_I_nformation Management Policy	Off
✓	_P_ermissions	Off
	Caps Loc_k_	Off
	_N_um Lock	Off
✓	S_c_roll Lock	Off
✓	_F_ixed Decimal	Off
	_O_vertype Mode	
✓	_E_nd Mode	
✓	_M_acro Recording	Not Recording
✓	Se_l_ection Mode	
✓	Pa_g_e Number	
✓	_A_verage	198.6153846
✓	_C_ount	39
	Numerical Coun_t_	
	M_i_nimum	
	Ma_x_imum	
✓	_S_um	7746
✓	_U_pload Status	
✓	_V_iew Shortcuts	
✓	_Z_oom	100%
✓	Zoom Slider	

Figure 74-2: Excel offers a choice of six statistics about the selected range.

If you prefer not to see any selection statistics, just remove the checkmark from all six options.

When using this feature, remember that cells that contain text are ignored, except when the Count option is selected.

Converting Formulas to Values

If you have a range of cells that contain formulas, you can quickly convert these cells to values only (that is, the result of each formula). Beginning with Excel 2007, this common operation is easier than ever. In previous versions, you had to display the Paste Special dialog box, but that's no longer required.

Here's how to convert a range of formulas to their current values:

1. Select the range. It can include formula cells as well as nonformula cells.
2. Press Ctrl+C to copy the range.
3. Choose Home➜Clipboard➜Paste➜Paste Values (V).
4. Press Esc to cancel Copy mode.

Each of the formulas in the selected range is replaced with its current value.

If you want to put the formula results in a different location, just select a different cell before you perform Step 3. The original formulas remain intact, but the new range contains the formula results.

Transforming Data without Using Formulas

Often, you have a range of cells containing data that must be transformed in some way. For example, you might want to increase all values by 5 percent. Or, you might need to divide each value by 2. This tip describes how to perform addition, subtraction, multiplication, and division on a range of values without using any formulas.

The following steps assume that you have values in a range and you want to increase all values by 5 percent. For example, the range can contain a price list and you're raising all prices by 5 percent:

1. Activate any empty cell and enter **1.05**.

    You will multiply the values by this number, which results in an increase of 5 percent.

2. Press Ctrl+C to copy that cell.

3. Select the range to be transformed.

    It can include values, formulas, or text.

4. Choose Home➜Clipboard➜Paste➜Paste Special to display the Paste Special dialog box.

5. In the Paste Special dialog box, click the Multiply option.

6. Click OK.

7. Press Esc to cancel Copy mode.

The values in the range are multiplied by the copied value (1.05). Formulas in the range are modified accordingly. Assume that the range originally contained this formula:

```
=SUM(B18:B22)
```

After you perform the Paste Special operation, the formula is converted to

```
=(SUM(B18:B22))*1.05
```

This technique is limited to the four basic math operations: addition, subtraction, multiplication, and division.

For more versatility, see Tip 77, which describes how to use formulas to transform values.

Transforming Data by Using Temporary Formulas

In Tip 76, I describe how to perform simple mathematical transformations on a range of numeric data. This tip describes the much more versatile method of transforming data (numerical or text), by using temporary formulas.

Figure 77-1 shows a worksheet with names in column A. These names are in all uppercase, and the goal is to convert them to proper case (only the first letter of each name is uppercase).

	A	B	C	D	E	F
1	Name	Current Balance				
2	BARBARA KNIGHT	$1,364.17				
3	BRIDGET RUSSELL	$860.84				
4	IRA GREEN	$874.00				
5	RHONDA FISHER	$1,006.89				
6	AUDRA JOHNSON	$1,100.68				
7	JAMIE STEWART	$1,423.09				
8	CATHY JOHNSON	$384.52				
9	JUANITA ROTH	$688.65				
10	DEBORAH MURPHY	$1,365.84				
11	RHONDA OLSON	$901.14				
12	SHIRLEY JOHNSON	$1,267.23				
13	SARAH ALLEN	$648.73				
14	KAREN JOHNSON	$978.24				
15	JESSICA ROSS	$1,000.33				
16	DOROTHY WILLIS	$352.52				
17	DORIS BROWN	$968.52				
18	RENEE HENRY	$1,547.32				
19	MICHELLE DUNN	$898.13				
20	ALLISON SANCHEZ	$131.33				
21	AMBER BENSON	$1,125.10				

Figure 77-1: The goal is to transform the names in column A to proper case.

Follow these steps to transform the data in column A:

1. Create a temporary formula in an unused column.

   For this example, enter this formula in cell C2:

   ```
   =PROPER(A2)
   ```

2. Copy the formula down the column to accommodate all cells to be transformed.

3. Select the formula cells (in column C).

4. Press Ctrl+C.

5. Select the original data cells (in column A).

6. Choose Home➜Clipboard➜Paste➜Paste Values (V).

   The original data is replaced with the transformed data (see Figure 77-2).

7. Press Esc to cancel Copy mode.

8. When you're satisfied that the transformation happened as you intended, you can delete the temporary formulas in column C.

	A	B	C	D	E
1	Name	Current Balance			
2	Barbara Knight	$1,364.17	Barbara Knight		
3	Bridget Russell	$860.84	Bridget Russell		
4	Ira Green	$874.00	Ira Green		
5	Rhonda Fisher	$1,006.89	Rhonda Fisher		
6	Audra Johnson	$1,100.68	Audra Johnson		
7	Jamie Stewart	$1,423.09	Jamie Stewart		
8	Cathy Johnson	$384.52	Cathy Johnson		
9	Juanita Roth	$688.65	Juanita Roth		
10	Deborah Murphy	$1,365.84	Deborah Murphy		
11	Rhonda Olson	$901.14	Rhonda Olson		
12	Shirley Johnson	$1,267.23	Shirley Johnson		
13	Sarah Allen	$648.73	Sarah Allen		
14	Karen Johnson	$978.24	Karen Johnson		
15	Jessica Ross	$1,000.33	Jessica Ross		
16	Dorothy Willis	$352.52	Dorothy Willis		
17	Doris Brown	$968.52	Doris Brown		
18	Renee Henry	$1,547.32	Renee Henry		
19	Michelle Dunn	$898.13	Michelle Dunn		
20	Allison Sanchez	$131.33	Allison Sanchez		
21	Amber Benson	$1,125.10	Amber Benson		
22		(Ctrl) ▾			
23					

Figure 77-2: The formula results from column C replace the original data in column A.

You can adapt this technique for just about any type of data transformation you need. The key, of course, is constructing the proper transformation formula in Step 1.

Deleting Values While Keeping Formulas

A common type of spreadsheet model contains input cells (which are changed by the user) and formula cells that work with those input cells. If you want to delete all the values in the input cells but keep the formulas intact, here's a simple way to do it:

1. Select the range that you want to work with.

    If you want to delete all nonformula value cells on the worksheet, just select any single cell.

2. Choose Home➜Editing➜Find & Select➜Go To Special.

    This step displays the Go To Special dialog box.

3. In the Go To Special dialog box, select the Constants option and then select Numbers.

4. Click OK, and the nonformula numeric cells are selected.

5. Press Delete to delete the values.

If you need to delete the value cells on a regular basis, you can specify a name for the input cells. After completing Step 4, choose Formula➜Defined Names➜Define Name to display the New Name dialog box. Enter a name for the selected cells — something like InputCells is a good choice. Click OK to close the New Name dialog box and create the name.

After naming the input cells, you can select the named cells directly by using the Name box — the drop-down list to the left of the Formula bar. Then press Del, and they're gone.

Summing Across Sheets

Formulas can work with cells in other worksheets. You just need to precede the cell reference with the sheet name and an exclamation point. For example, the following formula adds 12 to the value in cell C1 on Sheet2:

```
=Sheet2!C1+12
```

What if you need to calculate the sum of all values in C1 on Sheet2 through Sheet6? This formula does the job:

```
=SUM(Sheet2:Sheet6!C1)
```

In this case, the colon separates the first sheet name and the last sheet name. To create such a formula by pointing, follow these steps:

1. Activate the cell that will contain the formula and type **=SUM(**.
2. Click the sheet tab for the first sheet (in this case, Sheet2) and select the cell (in this case, C1).
3. Press Shift and click the sheet tab for the last sheet (in this case, Sheet6).
4. Press Enter, and the formula is entered into the cell.

In Step 2, you can select a multicell range rather than a single cell. For example, this formula returns the sum of C1:F12 on all sheets from Sheet2 through Sheet6:

```
=SUM(Sheet2:Sheet6!C1:F12)
```

And now, I show you an interesting trick that I learned from reading the Excel newsgroups. If you want to sum the same cell on all sheets except the active sheet, just enter a formula like this:

```
=SUM('*'!C1)
```

The asterisk serves as a wildcard character that's interpreted to mean "all sheets except this one." When you press Enter after typing this formula, Excel converts the formula to use the actual sheet names. It even works if the active sheet is in the middle of other sheets. For example, if a workbook has six sheets and you enter the preceding formula in a cell on Sheet3, Excel creates the following formula:

```
=SUM(Sheet1:Sheet2!C1,Sheet4:Sheet6!C1)
```

It gets even better. Enter the following formula to find the sum of cell C1 on all sheets that begin with the characters *Region:*

```
=SUM('Region*'!C1)
```

Excel might convert this formula to something like this:

```
=SUM(Region1:Region4!C1)
```

You can also use the ? wildcard character, which indicates any single character. For example, when you enter the formula that follows, Excel creates a formula that sums the value only on Sheet1 through Sheet9 (sheet names that contain a single numeric digit):

```
=SUM('Sheet?'!C1)
```

This trick isn't limited to the SUM function. It works with other functions, such as AVERAGE, MIN, and MAX.

Dealing with Function Arguments

Excel has dozens of useful functions, and each of them has its own, unique set of arguments. You probably memorize the arguments for functions you use frequently, but what about the other functions?

The best way to insert a function is to use the Insert Function dialog box. Display this dialog box by using any of these methods:

> ➤ Click the Insert Function button, located in the Formulas➜Function Library group.

> ➤ Click the fx button to the left of the Formula bar.

> ➤ Press Shift+F3.

If you don't know the name of the function you need, you can search for it by entering some text in the Search for a Function field and clicking the Go button (see Figure 80-1). After you identify the function, click OK, and you see the Function Arguments dialog box, which guides you through the function's arguments, as shown in Figure 80-2.

Figure 80-1: Use the Insert Function dialog box to help find the function you need.

By the way, if you're entering a function manually (without the assistance of the Insert Function dialog box), you can press Ctrl+A to display the Function Arguments dialog box. This key combination works only if you haven't yet entered any arguments for the function.

Figure 80-2: The Function Arguments dialog box helps you enter arguments for a function.

In some cases, you might want to insert "dummy" arguments for a function — placeholders that will be filled in later. This strategy is useful if you don't yet know the cell references that will be used. To insert argument names as placeholders, press Ctrl+Shift+A after you type the function's name. Excel uses the argument's names as arguments. For example, if you press Ctrl+Shift+A while entering the VLOOKUP function, Excel inserts the following:

```
=VLOOKUP(lookup_value,table_array,col_index_num,range_lookup)
```

The formula, of course, returns an error, so you need to replace the dummy arguments with actual values or cell references.

Annotating a Formula without Using a Comment

The Excel comment feature is a great way to annotate your formulas. Just right-click the cell and choose Insert Comment from the shortcut menu. You can then describe the formula any way you like inside the comment.

This tip describes another, less obtrusive, way to annotate a formula. The trick involves Excel's rarely used N function. (This function is included in Excel primarily for compatibility with old Lotus 1-2-3 files.) The N function takes one argument, and this argument is converted to a value. When the argument is a text string, the N function returns 0. You can take advantage of this and modify the formula so that it uses the N function.

Consider this simple formula:

```
=A4*.275
```

You can modify the formula to contain a comment. Because the N function returns 0, the comment has no effect on the value returned by the formula:

```
=A4*.275+N("27.5% represents the anticipated tax rate")
```

Making an Exact Copy of a Range of Formulas

When you copy a cell that contains a formula, Excel adjusts all the relative cell references. Assume that cell D1 contains this formula:

```
=A1*B1
```

When you copy this cell, the two cell references are changed relative to the destination. If you copy D1 to D12, for example, the copied formula is

```
=A12*B12
```

Sometimes, you might prefer to make an exact copy of a formula. One way is to convert all the cell references to absolute references (for example, change =A1*B1 to =$A$1*$B$1). Another way is to (temporarily) remove the equal sign from the formula, which converts the formula to text. Then you can copy the cell and manually insert the equal sign into the original formula and the copied formula.

What if you have a large range of formulas and you want to make an exact copy of those formulas? Editing each formula is tedious and error-prone. Here's a way to accomplish the task. It uses Windows Notepad, but any text editor (including Microsoft Word) will do.

For the following steps, assume that you want to copy the formulas in A1:D10 on Sheet1 and make an exact copy in A13:D22, also on Sheet1:

1. Put Excel in Formula view mode.

    The easiest way to do this is to press Ctrl+` (that character is a backwards apostrophe and is usually on the same key that has the ~ [tilde]).

2. Select the range to copy.

    In this case, it's A1:D10 on Sheet1.

3. Press Ctrl+C to copy the range.

4. Start Windows Notepad.

5. Press Ctrl+V to paste the copied data into Notepad.

6. In Notepad, press Ctrl+A to select all of the text, followed by Ctrl+C to copy the text.

7. Activate Excel, activate the upper left cell where you want to paste the formulas (in this example, A13 on Sheet2), and make sure that the sheet you're copying to is in Formula view mode.

8. Press Ctrl+V to paste.

9. Press Ctrl+` to toggle out of Formula view mode.

Note

If the paste operation back to Excel doesn't work correctly, chances are that you've used Excel's Text-to-Columns feature recently, and Excel is trying to be helpful by remembering how you last parsed your data. You need to fire up the Convert Text to Columns Wizard. Choose the Delimited option and click Next. Clear all of the Delimiter option checkmarks except Tab.

Monitoring Formula Cells from Any Location

If you have a large spreadsheet model, you might find it helpful to monitor the values in a few key cells as you change various input cells. The Watch Window feature makes this sort of task very simple. Using the Watch Window, you can keep an eye on any number of cells, regardless of which worksheet or workbook is active.

To display the Watch Window, choose Formulas➜Formula Auditing➜Watch Window. To watch a cell, click the Add Watch button in the Watch Window and then specify the cell in the Add Watch dialog box. When the Add Watch dialog box is displayed, you can select a range or press Ctrl and click individual cells.

Figure 83-1 shows the Watch Window, with several cells being monitored.

Book	Sheet	Name	Cell	Value	Formula
investment calculations.xlsx	Compound2		B13	4.53%	=(B11/B4)/B7
investment calculations.xlsx	Compound1		E21	$1,030.42	=FV((B5/12),B6,,-B4)
investment calculations.xlsx	Simple		B8	$1,030.00	=B3+B7

Figure 83-1: Using the Watch Window to monitor the value of formula cells.

You can customize the display in the Watch Window by doing any of the following:

> Click and drag a border to change the size of the window.

> Drag the window to an edge of the Excel window, and it becomes docked rather than free floating.

> Click and drag the borders in the header to change the width of the columns displayed. By dragging a column border all the way to the left, you can hide the column.

> Click and drag any of the header borders to increase or decrease the width of the column.

> Click one of the headers to sort the contents by that column.

Displaying and Printing Formulas

When you enter a formula into a cell, Excel displays the calculated value of the formula. To view a formula, activate the cell; Excel shows the formula on the Formula bar.

To view all your formulas, switch to Formula view. The easiest way to switch to this mode is to press Ctrl+`. (That's the accent character, usually located above the Tab key.) Excel then displays the formulas rather than their results. In addition, you can also see which cells are referenced by the selected formula because Excel displays those cells with a colored border. Figure 84-1 shows a worksheet in Formula view. D8 is the selected cell, and it references cells B8 and C8, which are displayed with a colored border.

	A	B	C	D
1		Last Year	This Year	Difference
2	January	7630	8734	=C2-B2
3	February	8365	8463	=C3-B3
4	March	8498	7948	=C4-B4
5	April	8747	8744	=C5-B5
6	May	8919	8877	=C6-B6
7	June	8521	8604	=C7-B7
8	July	8047	8647	=C8-B8
9	August	7474	7955	=C9-B9
10	September	8112	7715	=C10-B10
11	October	8407	7279	=C11-B11
12	November	8881	7748	=C12-B12
13	December	8386	7773	=C13-B13
14		=SUM(B2:B13)	=SUM(C2:C13)	=SUM(D2:D13)
15				

Figure 84-1: Excel's Formula view displays the formulas rather than their results.

In Formula view, you can use all Excel commands and even modify the formulas.

In practice, you might find that Formula view isn't very useful. Although Excel widens the columns, you can see an entire formula only if it's very short. And, if you print the sheet in Formula view, you usually end up with a meaningless mess.

To document a worksheet by printing its formulas, your best bet is to locate a VBA macro to do the job. This simple no-frills VBA procedure makes a list of all formulas on the active worksheet:

```
Sub ListFormulas()
    Dim FormulaCells As Range
    Dim FormulaSheet As Worksheet
    Dim Row As Long
    Dim Cell As Range
    On Error Resume Next
    Set FormulaCells = Range("A1").SpecialCells(xlFormulas, 23)
    If FormulaCells Is Nothing Then Exit Sub
    Set FormulaSheet = ActiveWorkbook.Worksheets.Add
    Row = 1
    For Each Cell In FormulaCells
        With FormulaSheet
            Cells(Row, 1) = Cell.Address(False, False)
```

```
            Cells(Row, 2) = " " & Cell.Formula
            Cells(Row, 3) = Cell.Value
            Row = Row + 1
        End With
    Next Cell
End Sub
```

To use this macro, press Alt+F11 to activate the Visual Basic Editor. Select your workbook in the Project window and choose Insert→Module to insert a new VBA module. Type the code exactly as it appears. To execute the macro, activate the sheet that has the formulas, press Alt+F8, select ListFormulas from the macro list, and click Run. Figure 84-2 shows an example of the output from this macro. The first column contains the address of the formula, the second column contains the formula, and the third column shows the current result of the formula.

	A	B	C	D
1	D2	=C2-B2	1104	
2	D3	=C3-B3	98	
3	D4	=C4-B4	-550	
4	D5	=C5-B5	-3	
5	D6	=C6-B6	-42	
6	D7	=C7-B7	83	
7	D8	=C8-B8	600	
8	D9	=C9-B9	481	
9	D10	=C10-B10	-397	
10	D11	=C11-B11	-1128	
11	D12	=C12-B12	-1133	
12	D13	=C13-B13	-613	
13	B14	=SUM(B2:B13)	99987	
14	C14	=SUM(C2:C13)	98487	
15	D14	=SUM(D2:D13)	-1500	
16				

Figure 84-2: A list of formulas generated by a VBA macro.

Avoiding Error Displays in Formulas

Sometimes a formula returns an error, such as #REF! or #DIV/0!. Usually, you want to know when a formula error occurs, but in some cases you might prefer to simply avoid displaying the error messages. Figure 85-1 shows an example.

	A	B	C	D	E	F
1	Month	Total Sales	No. Reps	Average		
2	Jan	1,783,983	9	198,220		
3	Feb	2,319,083	12	193,257		
4	Mar	2,654,982	14	189,642		
5	Apr	3,092,002	15	206,133		
6	May			#DIV/0!		
7	Jun			#DIV/0!		
8	Jul			#DIV/0!		
9	Aug			#DIV/0!		
10	Sep			#DIV/0!		
11	Oct			#DIV/0!		
12	Nov			#DIV/0!		
13	Dec			#DIV/0!		
14						
15						

Figure 85-1: The formulas in column D display an error if the data is missing.

Column D contains formulas that calculate the average sales volume. For example, cell D2 contains this formula:

```
=B2/C2
```

Using the ISERROR function

As you can see, the formula displays an error if the cells used in the calculation are empty. If you prefer to hide those error values, you can do so by using an IF function to check for an error.

For this example, change the formula in cell D1 to

```
=IF(ISERROR(B2/C2),"",B2/C2)
```

The ISERROR function returns TRUE if its argument evaluates to an error. In such a case, the IF function returns an empty string. Otherwise, the IF function returns the calculated value. As you see in Figure 85-2, when this formula is copied down the column, the result is a bit more visually pleasing.

	A	B	C	D	E
1	Month	Total Sales	No. Reps	Average	
2	Jan	1,783,983	9	198,220	
3	Feb	2,319,083	12	193,257	
4	Mar	2,654,982	14	189,642	
5	Apr	3,092,002	15	206,133	
6	May				
7	Jun				
8	Jul				
9	Aug				
10	Sep				
11	Oct				
12	Nov				
13	Dec				
14					
15					

Figure 85-2: Using an IF function to hide error values.

You can adapt this technique to any formula. The original formula (without the initial equal sign) serves as the argument for the ISERROR function, and it repeats as the last argument of the IF function:

```
=IF(ISERROR(OriginalFormula),"",OriginalFormula)
```

By the way, you can put anything you like as the second argument for the ISERROR function. (It doesn't have to be an empty string.) For example, you can make it a cell reference.

Using the IFERROR function

If your workbook will be used only by people who have Excel 2007 or later, you might prefer to use the IFERROR function. This function takes two arguments: The first argument is the expression that's checked for an error, and the second is the value to return if the formula evaluates to an error. The formula presented in the preceding section can be rewritten as

```
=IFERROR(B2/C2,"")
```

Using this function has two advantages:

> ➤ Writing error-checking formulas is easier because IFERROR does the work of both the IF function and the ISERROR function.

> ➤ The expression is evaluated only one time, which can result in faster recalculation times.

Keep in mind that because IFERROR was introduced in Excel 2007, it doesn't work with earlier versions of Excel.

Using Goal Seeking

Many Excel worksheets are set up to do what-if analyses. For example, you might have a sales projection worksheet that allows you to answer questions such as "What is the total profit if sales increase by 20 percent?" If you set up your worksheet properly, you can change the value in one cell to see what happens to the profit cell.

Excel offers a useful tool that can best be described as a what-if analysis in reverse. If you know what a formula result *should* be, Excel can tell you the value that you need to enter in an input cell to produce that result. In other words, you can ask a question such as "How much do sales need to increase to produce a profit of $1.2 million?"

Figure 86-1 shows a simple worksheet that calculates mortgage loan information. This worksheet has four input cells (C4:C7) and four formula cells (C10:C13).

	A	B	C	D
1		**Mortgage Loan Worksheet**		
2				
3		**Input Cells**		
4		Purchase Price:	$409,000	
5		Down Payment:	20%	
6		Loan Term (Months):	360	
7		Interest Rate (APR):	6.50%	
8				
9		**Result Cells**		
10		Loan Amount:	$327,200	
11		Monthly Payment:	$2,068	
12		Total Payments:	$744,526	
13		Total Interest:	$417,326	
14				
15				

Figure 86-1: Goal Seeker can tell you the value of an input cell that will result in a desired result.

Assume that you're in the market for a new home and you know that you can afford an $1,800 monthly mortgage payment. You also know that a lender can issue a fixed-rate mortgage loan for 6.50 percent, based on an 80 percent loan-to-value (that is, a 20 percent down payment). The question is "What is the maximum purchase price I can handle?" In other words, which value in cell C4 causes the formula in cell C11 to result in $1,800? One approach is to simply plug a bunch of values into cell C4 until C11 displays $1,800; however, Excel can determine the answer much more efficiently.

To answer this question, follow these steps:

1. Choose Data→Data Tools→What-If Analysis→Goal Seek.

   Excel displays the Goal Seek dialog box.

2. Complete the three fields in the dialog box (shown in Figure 86-2) similar to forming a sentence: You want to set cell C11 to 1800 by changing cell C4.

Enter this information in the dialog box by either typing the cell references or pointing with the mouse.

3. Click OK to begin the goal-seeking process.

Figure 86-2: Enter the information in the Goal Seek dialog box.

In less than a second, Excel displays the Goal Seek Status dialog box, which shows the target value and the value that Excel calculated. In this case, Excel finds an exact value. The worksheet now displays the found value in cell C4 ($284,779). As a result of this value, the monthly payment amount is $1,800. At this point, you have two options:

➤ Click OK to replace the original value with the found value.

➤ Click Cancel to restore your worksheet to the way it was before you chose the Goal Seek command.

This example is very simple. The power of goal seeking is more apparent when you're dealing with a complex model with many interrelated formulas.

Understanding the Secret about Names

Most Excel users have at least a rudimentary understanding of named cells and named ranges. You can use the Formulas→Defined Names→Define Name command to provide a meaningful name to a cell or range. Then you can use those defined names in your formulas.

For example, if you give the name Sales to range A2:A13, you can write a formula such as =SUM(Sales). Just about every Excel user I know refers to this concept as named ranges or named cells (even I did, in the first paragraph of this tip). This terminology isn't quite accurate, however.

Here's the secret to understanding names:

When you create a name, you're creating a named formula. Unlike a normal formula, a named formula doesn't exist in a cell. Rather, it exists in Excel's memory.

Although this revelation isn't exactly earth-shaking, keeping this "secret" in mind helps you understand some advanced naming techniques.

When you work with the New Name dialog box, the Refers To field contains the formula, and the Name field contains the formula's name. You'll find that the contents of the Refers To field always begin with an equal sign, which makes it a formula.

As you can see in Figure 87-1, the workbook contains a name (InterestRate) for cell B4 on Sheet1. The Refers To field lists the following formula:

```
=Sheet1!$B$4
```

Figure 87-1: Technically, the name InterestRate is a named formula, not a named cell.

Whenever you use the name InterestRate, Excel evaluates the formula named InterestRate and returns the result. For example, you might type this formula into a cell:

```
=InterestRate*1.05
```

When Excel evaluates this formula, it first evaluates the formula named InterestRate (which exists only in memory, not in a cell). Excel then multiplies the result of this named formula by 1.05 and displays the result. This cell formula, of course, is equivalent to the following formula, which uses the actual cell reference rather than the name:

```
=Sheet1!$B$4*1.05
```

Using Named Constants

This tip describes a useful technique that can remove some clutter from your worksheets: named constants.

Consider a worksheet that generates an invoice and calculates sales tax for a sales amount. The common approach is to insert the sales tax rate value into a cell and then use this cell reference in your formulas. To make things easier, you probably would name this cell something like SalesTax.

You can store your sales tax rate by using a name (and avoid using a cell). Figure 88-1 demonstrates the following steps:

1. Choose Formulas➜Defined Names➜Define Name to open the New Name dialog box.

2. Enter the name (in this case, SalesTax) into the Name field.

3. Click the Refers To field, delete its contents, and replace it with a simple formula, such as **=7.5%**.

4. Click OK to close the dialog box.

Figure 88-1: Defining a name that refers to a constant.

The preceding steps create a named formula that doesn't use any cell references. To try it out, enter the following formula into any cell:

```
=SalesTax
```

This simple formula returns .075, the result of the formula named SalesTax. Because this named formula always returns the same result, you can think of it as a *named constant.* And, you can use this constant in a more complex formula, such as this one:

```
=A1*SalesTax
```

SalesTax is a workbook-level name, so you can use it in any worksheet in the workbook.

A named constant can also consist of text. For example, you can define a constant for a company's name. You can use the New Name dialog box to create the following formula, named MSFT:

```
="Microsoft Corporation"
```

Then you can use a cell formula, such as this one:

```
="Annual Report: "&MSFT
```

This formula returns the text Annual Report: Microsoft Corporation.

Note

Names that don't refer to ranges don't appear in the Name box or in the Go To dialog box (which appears when you press F5). This situation makes sense because these constants don't reside anywhere tangible. They do, however, appear in the Paste Name dialog box (which appears when you press F3). This _does_ make sense, because you use these names in formulas.

As you might expect, you can change the value of the constant at any time by using the Name Manager dialog box (choose Formulas→Defined Names→Name Manager). Just click the Edit button to display the Edit Name dialog box. Then change the value in the Refers To field. When you close the dialog box, Excel uses the new value to recalculate the formulas that use this name.

Using Functions in Names

Tip 88 describes how to create a named constant. This tip, however, takes the concept one step further and describes how to use worksheet functions in your names.

Figure 89-1 shows an example of a named formula. In this case, the formula is named ThisMonth, and the actual formula is

```
=MONTH(TODAY())
```

Figure 89-1: Defining a named formula that uses worksheet functions.

The named formula uses two worksheet functions. The TODAY function returns the current date, and the MONTH function returns the month number of its date argument. Therefore, you can enter a formula such as the following into a cell and it returns the number of the current month. For example, if the current month is April, the following formula returns 4:

```
=ThisMonth
```

A more useful version of this named formula returns the month name as text. To do so, create a formula named ThisMonthName, defined this way:

```
=TEXT(TODAY(),"mmmm")
```

Now enter the following formula into a cell, and it returns the current month name as text. In the month of April, the formula returns the text April:

```
=ThisMonthName
```

Here's another example of a named formula that uses a function. Create a formula with the name SumA, defined this way:

```
=SUM(Sheet1!$A:A$)
```

As you might expect, this named formula returns the sum of all values in column A.

Note

Note that the name is defined by using absolute references. This is critical. If you use relative references, the formula evaluates differently, depending on the location of the active cell.

Creating a List of Names

The Name Manager dialog box, shown in Figure 90-1, is a handy tool that displays a list of all names defined in the active workbook. Display this dialog box by choosing Formulas➜Defined Names➜Name Manager. Or, just press Ctrl+F3.

Figure 90-1: The Name Manager dialog box displays a sortable list of all names.

Suppose that you want to put a list of those names into a worksheet range, as a way to document your project. Although the Name Manager dialog box doesn't provide a way to paste a list of names, doing so is possible — you just need to know where to look.

The secret Paste List button is in the Paste Name dialog box. To display this dialog box, choose Formulas➜Defined Names➜Use in Formula➜Paste Name. Or, press F3. Then click the Paste List button to create a list of names (and their definitions) starting at the active cell. Figure 90-2 shows the Paste Name dialog box, along with the list it created.

	A	B	C	D	E	F	G	H	I	J
1										
2										
3										
4							April	=Sheet9!$B$4:$J$4		
5							August	=Sheet9!$B$8:$J$8		
6							December	=Sheet9!$B$12:$J$12		
7							February	=Sheet9!$B$2:$J$2		
8							January	=Sheet9!$B$1:$J$1		
9							July	=Sheet9!$B$7:$J$7		
10							June	=Sheet9!$B$6:$J$6		
11							March	=Sheet9!$B$3:$J$3		
12							May	=Sheet9!$B$5:$J$5		
13							November	=Sheet9!$B$11:$J$11		
14							October	=Sheet9!$B$10:$J$10		
15							Region_1	=Sheet6!$D$4:$D$15		
16							Region_2	=Sheet6!$E$4:$E$15		
17							SalesTax	=Sheet3!$E$23		
18							September	=Sheet9!$B$9:$J$9		
19							ThisMonthName	=TEXT(TODAY(),"mmmm")		
20										
21										

Overlaid dialog box (Paste Name):

Paste Name

Paste name

April
August
December
February
January
July
June
March

[Paste List] [OK] [Cancel]

Figure 90-2: Use the Paste List button to create a list of names in your worksheet.

Note

If you display the Paste Name dialog box when you're editing a formula, the dialog box doesn't display the Paste List button.

Using Dynamic Names

This tip describes a useful concept that can save you lots of time: the *dynamic named formula,* which is a named formula that refers to a range that isn't fixed in size. This idea can be difficult to grasp, so I provide a quick example.

Examine the worksheet shown in Figure 91-1. This sheet contains a listing of sales by month, through the month of May.

	A	B	C	D	E
1	January	1,498			
2	February	1,633			
3	March	1,231			
4	April	1,487			
5	May	1,764			
6	June				
7	July				
8	August				
9	September				
10	October				
11	November				
12	December				
13					
14					

Figure 91-1: You can use a dynamic named formula to represent the sales data in column B.

Suppose that you want to create a name (SalesData) for the data in column B and you don't want this name to refer to empty cells. In other words, the reference for the SalesData range changes each month as you add a new sales figure. You can, of course, use the Name Manager dialog box to change the range name definition each month. Or, you can create a dynamic named formula that changes automatically as you enter new data (or delete existing data).

To create a dynamic named formula, start by re-creating the worksheet shown in Figure 91-1. Then follow these steps:

1. Select Formulas➜Defined Names➜Define Name to display the New Name dialog box.

2. Enter **SalesData** in the Name field.

3. Enter the following formula in the Refers To field (see Figure 91-2):

   ```
   =OFFSET(Sheet1!$B$1,0,0,COUNTA(Sheet1!$B:$B),1)
   ```

4. Click OK to close the New Name dialog box.

New Name

Name: SalesData

Scope: Workbook

Comment:

Refers to: =OFFSET(Sheet1!$B$1,0,0,COUNTA(Sheet1!$B:$B),1)

OK   Cancel

Figure 91-2: Creating a dynamic named formula.

The preceding steps create a named formula that uses the Excel OFFSET and COUNTA functions to return a range that changes, based on the number of non-empty cells in column B. To try out this formula, enter the following formula into any cell not in column B:

```
=SUM(SalesData)
```

This formula returns the sum of the values in column B. To verify that the name refers to only the nonblank cells, try this formula:

```
=ROWS(SalesData)
```

The formula returns 5, the number of rows in the range. Add more data or delete data from the end of the column, and you see that the SalesData name adjusts according.

Note that SalesData isn't displayed in the Name box and doesn't appear in the Go To dialog box. You can, however, open the Go To dialog box and type **SalesData** to select the range.

Note

This formula works only for data that doesn't contain gaps. In this example, if cell B3 is empty, the SalesData name doesn't include the last value in the column.

At this point, you might be wondering about the value of this exercise. After all, a simple formula such as the following does the same job, without the need to define a formula:

```
=SUM(B:B)
```

One of the most common uses for a dynamic named formula is for setting up data to be used in a chart. You can use this technique to create a chart with a data series that adjusts automatically as you enter new data:

```
=Sheet1!$E$1:$K$490
```

Beginning with Excel 2007, a chart's data adjusts automatically if the data is in a table (specified by choosing Insert➔Tables➔Table), but creating a dynamic name is useful if you want to chart continually changing data that's not in a table.

Cross-Ref

For more on charts, see the tips in Part VII.

Creating Worksheet-Level Names

Normally, when you name a cell or range, you can use that name in all worksheets in the workbook. For example, if you create a name, RegionTotal, that refers to cell M32 on Sheet1, you can use this name in any formula in any worksheet. This name is a *workbook-level* name (or a *global* name). By default, all cell and range names are workbook-level names.

Suppose that you have several worksheets in a workbook and you want to use the same name (such as RegionTotal) on each sheet. In this case, you should create worksheet-level names (sometimes referred to as *local* names).

To define the worksheet-level name RegionTotal, activate the worksheet in which you want to define the name and choose Formulas➜Defined Names➜Define Name. The New Name dialog box then appears. Enter the name in the Name field, and use the Scope drop-down list to select the sheet in which the name is valid. Figure 92-1 shows a worksheet-level name being created.

Figure 92-1: Creating a worksheet-level name.

You can also create a worksheet-level name by using the Name box (located to the left of the Formula bar). Select the cell or range you want named, click in the Name box, and type the name, preceded by the sheet name and an exclamation point. Press Enter to create the name. Here's an example of a worksheet-level name:

```
Sheet3!RegionTotal
```

If the worksheet name contains at least one space, enclose the worksheet name in apostrophes, like this:

```
'Western Region'!RegionTotal
```

When you write a formula that uses a worksheet-level name on the sheet in which you defined it, you don't need to include the worksheet name in the range name. (The Name box doesn't display the worksheet name, either.) If you use the name in a formula on a *different* worksheet, however, you must use the entire name (sheet name, exclamation point, and name).

The Name Manager dialog box clearly identifies each name by its scope (see Figure 92-2). If the scope of a name isn't Workbook, the dialog box lists the sheet on which the name is defined.

Name	Value	Refers To	Scope	Comment
RegionTotal	12763	=Sheet1!$E$14	Sheet1	
RegionTotal	8772	=Sheet2!$E$14	Sheet2	
RegionTotal	6345	=Sheet3!$E$14	Sheet3	
RegionTotal	9832	=Sheet4!$E$14	Sheet4	

Refers to: =Sheet1!$E$14

Figure 92-2: The Name Manager makes it easy to distinguish between workbook-level names and worksheet-level names.

Note Only the worksheet-level names on the current sheet appear in the Name box. Similarly, only worksheet-level names in the current sheet appear in the list when you open the Paste Name dialog box (by pressing F3).

Working with Pre-1900 Dates

According to Excel, the world began on January 1, 1900. If you work with historical information, you may have noticed that Excel doesn't recognize pre-1900 dates. For example, if you enter July 4, 1776 into a cell, Excel interprets it as text, not as a date.

Unfortunately, the only way to work with pre-1900 dates is to enter the date into a cell as text. The problem, however, is that you can't perform any manipulation on dates recognized as text. For example, you can't change its numeric formatting, you can't determine which day of the week this date occurred on, and you can't calculate the date that occurs seven days later.

To be able to sort by dates that precede 1900, enter the year, month, and day into separate cells. Figure 93-1 shows a simple example.

	A	B	C	D	E
1	**President Birthdays**				
2					
3	**President**	**Year**	**Month**	**Day**	
4	Abraham Lincoln	1809	2	12	
5	Franklin D. Roosevelt	1882	1	30	
6	James A. Garfield	1831	11	19	
7	Warren G. Harding	1865	11	2	
8	William Henry Harrison	1773	2	9	
9	William McKinley	1843	1	29	
10	Zachary Taylor	1784	11	24	
11					
12					

Figure 93-1: To allow sorting by pre-1900 dates, enter the year, month, and day into separate cells.

To sort the presidents by birthday, first do an ascending sort on column D, an ascending sort on column C, and, finally, an ascending sort on column B. The result is shown in Figure 93-2.

Unfortunately, you can't perform other date-related operations for these pre-1900 dates. For example, you cannot perform subtraction to determine ages.

	A	B	C	D	E
1	**President Birthdays**				
2					
3	**President**	**Year**	**Month**	**Day**	
4	William Henry Harrison	1773	2	9	
5	Zachary Taylor	1784	11	24	
6	Abraham Lincoln	1809	2	12	
7	James A. Garfield	1831	11	19	
8	William McKinley	1843	1	29	
9	Warren G. Harding	1865	11	2	
10	Franklin D. Roosevelt	1882	1	30	
11					
12					

Figure 93-2: The presidents sorted by birthday, after performing three sorts.

Note

I created an Excel add-in, XDATE, which contains a number of functions that make it possible to work with pre-1900 dates. You can download a free copy from my Web site: `http://spreadsheetpage.com`.

Working with Negative Time Values

Because Excel stores dates and times as numeric values, you can add or subtract one from the other. Figure 94-1 shows a simple example that tracks the number of hours worked. The total is calculated in cell B8 by using this formula and formatting the cell using the [h]:mm number format (see Tip 59 for details):

```
=SUM(B2:B6)
```

Cell B9 uses the following formula to calculate the amount of time required to make up a 40-hour work week:

```
=(40/24)-B8
```

	A	B	C
1	**Day**	**Hours Worked**	
2	Monday	8:00	
3	Tuesday	8:00	
4	Wednesday	7:30	
5	Thursday	7:00	
6	Friday	8:00	
7			
8	Total	38:30	
9	Hours Remaining:	1:30	
10			
11			

Figure 94-1: Cell B8 displays the time left in a 40-hour workweek.

If the number of hours worked exceeds 40 hours, the formula in cell B9 returns a negative number. But, as you can see in Figure 94-2, Excel can't deal with a negative time value.

	A	B	C
1	**Day**	**Hours Worked**	
2	Monday	8:00	
3	Tuesday	8:00	
4	Wednesday	7:30	
5	Thursday	7:00	
6	Friday	11:00	
7			
8	Total	41:30	
9	Hours Remaining:	################	
10			

Figure 94-2: Excel displays a series of hash marks for negative time values.

By default, Excel uses a date system that begins with January 1, 1900. A negative time value generates a date-time combination that falls before this date, which is invalid.

One solution is to use the optional 1904 date system, which assigns the date serial number 1 to January 2, 1904. Choose File→Options to display the Excel Options dialog box. Click the Advanced tab and select the Use 1904 Date System check box. Your negative times are now displayed correctly, as shown in Figure 94-3.

	A	B	C
1	Day	Hours Worked	
2	Monday	8:00	
3	Tuesday	8:00	
4	Wednesday	7:30	
5	Thursday	7:00	
6	Friday	11:00	
7			
8	Total	41:30	
9	Hours Remaining:	-1:30	
10			
11			

Figure 94-3: Switching to the 1904 date system causes negative times to display properly.

Caution

Be careful if your workbook contains links to other workbooks that don't use the 1904 date system. In such a case, the mismatch of date systems can cause erroneous results.

Useful Formula Examples

In this part, you'll find many formula examples. Some are useful as is. Others can be adapted to your own needs.

Tips and Where to Find Them

Calculating Holidays

Determining the date for a particular holiday can be tricky. Some holidays, such as New Year's Day and Independence Day (U.S.), are no-brainers because they always occur on the same date. For these kinds of holidays, you can simply use the DATE function. For example, to calculate New Year's Day (which always falls on January 1) for a specific year stored in cell A1, you can enter this function:

```
=DATE(A1,1,1)
```

Other holidays are defined in terms of a particular occurrence of a particular weekday in a particular month. For example, Labor Day in the U.S. falls on the first Monday in September.

The formulas that follow all assume that cell A1 contains a year value (for example, 2010). Notice that because New Year's Day, Independence Day, Veterans Day, and Christmas Day all fall on the same days of the year, their dates can be calculated by using the simple DATE function.

New Year's Day

This holiday always falls on January 1:

```
=DATE(A1,1,1)
```

Martin Luther King Jr. Day

This holiday occurs on the third Monday in January. The following formula calculates Martin Luther King Jr. Day for the year in cell A1:

```
=DATE(A1,1,1)+IF(2<WEEKDAY(DATE(A1,1,1)),7-WEEKDAY(DATE(A1,1,1))
+2,2-WEEKDAY(DATE(A1,1,1)))+((3-1)*7)
```

Presidents' Day

Presidents' Day occurs on the third Monday in February. This formula calculates Presidents' Day for the year in cell A1:

```
=DATE(A1,2,1)+IF(2<WEEKDAY(DATE(A1,2,1)),7-WEEKDAY(DATE(A1,2,1))
+2,2-WEEKDAY(DATE(A1,2,1)))+((3-1)*7)
```

Easter

Calculating the date for Easter is difficult because of the complicated manner in which Easter is determined. Easter Day is the first Sunday after the next full moon occurs after the vernal equinox. I found these formulas to calculate Easter on the Web. I have no idea how they work. They don't work if your workbook uses the 1904 date system. (Refer to Tip 94 for more about the 1904 date system.)

```
=DOLLAR(("4/"&A1)/7+MOD(19*MOD(A1,19)-7,30)*14%,)*7-6
```

This one is slightly shorter, but equally obtuse:

```
=FLOOR("5/"&DAY(MINUTE(A1/38)/2+56)&"/"&A1,7)-34
```

Memorial Day

The last Monday in May is Memorial Day. This formula calculates Memorial Day for the year in cell A1:

```
=DATE(A1,6,1)+IF(2<WEEKDAY(DATE(A1,6,1)),7-WEEKDAY(DATE(A1,6,1))
+2,2-WEEKDAY(DATE(A1,6,1)))+((1-1)*7)-7
```

Notice that this formula calculates the first Monday in June and then subtracts 7 from the result, to return the last Monday in May.

Independence Day

The Independence Day holiday always falls on July 4:

```
=DATE(A1,7,4)
```

Labor Day

Labor Day occurs on the first Monday in September. This formula calculates Labor Day for the year in cell A1:

```
=DATE(A1,9,1)+IF(2<WEEKDAY(DATE(A1,9,1)),7-WEEKDAY(DATE(A1,9,1))
+2,2-WEEKDAY(DATE(A1,9,1)))+((1-1)*7)
```

Columbus Day

The Columbus Day holiday occurs on the second Monday in October. The following formula calculates Columbus Day for the year in cell A1:

```
=DATE(A1,10,1)+IF(2<WEEKDAY(DATE(A1,10,1)),7-WEEKDAY(DATE(A1,10,1))
+2,2-WEEKDAY(DATE(A1,10,1)))+((2-1)*7)
```

Veterans Day

The Veterans Day holiday always falls on November 11:

```
=DATE(A1,11,11)
```

Thanksgiving Day

Thanksgiving Day is celebrated on the fourth Thursday in November. This formula calculates Thanksgiving Day for the year in cell A1:

```
=DATE(A1,11,1)+IF(5<WEEKDAY(DATE(A1,11,1)),7-WEEKDAY(DATE(A1,11,1))
+5,5-WEEKDAY(DATE(A1,11,1)))+((4-1)*7)
```

Christmas Day

Christmas Day always falls on December 25:

```
=DATE(A1,12,25)
```

Calculating a Weighted Average

The Excel AVERAGE function returns the average (or mean) of a range of data. Often, users need to calculate a weighted average. You can search all day, and you won't find a function to do the calculation. You can, however, calculate a weighted average by creating a formula that uses the SUMPRODUCT and the SUM function.

Figure 96-1 shows a simple worksheet that contains 30 days of gasoline prices. For example, the price was $2.48 for the first five days. Then it decreased to $2.41 for two days. The price then dipped to $2.39 for three days, and so on.

	A	B	C	D	E
1	Gas Prices For January				
2					
3		Price	No. Days		
4		2.48	5		
5		2.41	2		
6		2.39	3		
7		2.35	1		
8		2.34	1		
9		2.41	2		
10		2.37	2		
11		2.42	4		
12		2.41	3		
13		2.47	8		
14					
15	Average:	2.405			
16	Wt. Avg:	2.429			
17					

Figure 96-1: The formula in cell B16 calculates the weighted average of the gas prices.

Cell B15 contains a formula that uses the AVERAGE function:

```
=AVERAGE(B4:B13)
```

If you think about it, this formula doesn't return an accurate result. Rather, the prices must be weighted by factoring in the number of days that each price was in effect. In other words, a weighted average is the appropriate type of calculation.

The following formula, in cell B16, does the job:

```
=SUMPRODUCT(B4:B13,C4:C13)/SUM(C4:C13)
```

This formula multiplies each price by its corresponding number of days and then adds all those products. The result is then divided by the number of days. You can easily adapt this formula for other types of weighted average calculations.

Calculating a Person's Age

Calculating a person's age is a bit tricky because the calculation depends on not only the current year but also the current day. And then you have to consider the complications resulting from leap years.

In this tip, I present three methods to calculate a person's age. These formulas assume that cell B1 contains the date of birth (for example, 2/16/1952) and that cell B2 contains the current date (calculated with the TODAY function).

Method 1

The following formula subtracts the date of birth from the current date and divides by 365.25. The INT function then eliminates the decimal part of the result:

```
=INT((B2-B1)/365.25)
```

This formula isn't 100 percent accurate because it divides by the average number of days in a year. For example, consider a child who is exactly one year old. This formula returns 0, not 1.

Method 2

A more accurate way to calculate age uses the YEARFRAC function:

```
=INT(YEARFRAC(B2, B1))
```

The YEARFRAC function is normally used in financial calculations, but it works just fine for calculating ages. This function calculates the fraction of the year represented by the number of whole days between two dates. Using the INT function gets rid of the fraction and returns an integer.

Method 3

The third method for calculating age uses the DATEDIF function. This undocumented function isn't described in the Excel Help system:

```
=DATEDIF(B1,B2,"Y")
```

If you're a stickler for accuracy, here's another version:

```
=DATEDIF(B1,B2,"y") & " years, "&DATEDIF(B1,B2,"ym") &
" months, "&DATEDIF(B1,B2,"md") & " days"
```

This function returns a text string, like this:

```
33 years, 8 months, 17 days
```

Cross-Ref

For more information about the elusive DATEDIF function, see Tip 100.

Ranking Values

Often, computing the rank order for the values in a range of data is helpful. For example, if you have a worksheet containing the annual sales figures for your sales staff, you might want to know how each person ranks, from highest to lowest.

If you've used the RANK function, you might have noticed that the ranks produced by this function don't handle ties the way that you might like. For example, if two values are tied for third place, the RANK function gives both of them a rank of 3. You might prefer to assign each an average (or midpoint) of the ranks — in other words, a rank of 3.5 for both values tied for third place.

Excel 2010 includes a new function, RANK.AVG, that corrects this problem.

Figure 98-1 shows a worksheet that uses two methods to rank a column of values. The first method (column C) uses the RANK function, and column D uses the new RANK.AVG function. The range B2:B16 is named Sales.

	A	B	C	D	E
1	Ranking data with an array formula				
2					
3	Salesperson	Sales	Excel's Rank Function	XL 2010 RANK.AVG	
4	Adams	123,000	6	6	
5	Bigelow	98,000	9	10	
6	Fredericks	98,000	9	10	Assigned middle rank
7	Georgio	98,000	9	10	
8	Jensen	25,000	12	12	
9	Juarez	101,000	8	8	
10	Klein	305,000	1	1	
11	Lynch	145,000	3	3.5	
12	Mayne	145,000	3	3.5	Assigned average rank
13	Roberton	121,000	7	7	
14	Slokum	124,000	5	5	
15	Wu	150,000	2	2	
16					

Figure 98-1: Ranking data with the Excel RANK function and with array formulas.

Notice that two people are tied for third place. The RANK function assigns each person a rank of 3, but the RANK.AVG function gives each one a rank of 3.5. Also, three people are tied for tenth place. The RANK function gives each one a rank of 10. The RANK.AVG function, on the other hand, gives these three people a rank of 11, which is the average of 10, 11, and 12.

Formulas that use RANK.AVG function will return an error in previous versions of Excel. If you plan to share your workbook with someone who uses a version prior to Excel 2010, you can use an array formula instead of the RANK.AVG function.

Refer to Figure 98-1 and enter the following array formula in row 4. Then copy it to the cells below it. The result will be exactly the same as using the RANK.AVG function.

```
=SUM(1*(B4<=Sales))-(SUM(1*(B5=Sales))-1)/2
```

Note

An *array* formula is a special type of formula that works with internal arrays of data. When you enter an array formula, you must press Ctrl+Shift+Enter (not just Enter) to indicate that it's an array formula. Excel displays curly braces around the formula to remind you that it's an array formula. If you don't press Ctrl+Shift+Enter, the formula will not work.

Converting Inches to Feet and Inches

If you ever need to convert inches to feet and inches, you'll quickly understand the merits of the metric system. Converting inches to feet and inches is basically a division problem, in which you need to pay attention to the remainder (leftover inches).

The following formula assumes that cell A2 contains a value that represents inches. The formula displays the result in feet and inches (for example, if A2 contains 43, the result is 3'7"):

```
=TEXT(INT(A2/12),"#,##0")&"' "&MOD(A2,12)&""""
```

This formula returns a text string, so you can't perform mathematical operations on the result. If you want to convert a feet-and-inches text string back to inches, this formula does the job (it assumes that cell A1 contains a string such as 9'11"):

```
=(LEFT(B2,FIND("'",B2)-1)+((MID(B2,FIND("'",B2)+1,LEN(B2)-
FIND("'",B2)-1))/12))*12
```

These formulas work with positive inches only.

Note

Figure 99-1 shows these formulas in use.

	A	B	C	D
1	**Inches**	**Feet & Inches**	**Back to Inches**	
2	43	3'7"	43	
3	12	1'0"	12	
4	1	0'1"	1	
5	600	50'0"	600	
6	632	52'8"	632	
7	12.5	1'0.5"	12.5	
8	36.25	3'0.25"	36.25	
9	119	9'11"	119	
10				

Figure 99-1: Converting inches to feet and inches and then back to inches.

Using the DATEDIF Function

In Tip 97, I present a formula that uses the DATEDIF function, which calculates the difference between two dates and expresses the result in terms of months, days, or years.

This useful function, which isn't documented in the Help system, is one of the little Excel mysteries. Although the Excel 2000 Help system has an entry for DATEDIF, it's not documented in earlier or later versions.

The old Lotus 1-2-3 spreadsheet program introduced DATEDIF, and Excel likely included the function for compatibility purposes. But, for some reason, Microsoft doesn't want to acknowledge its existence. Lawyers are probably somehow involved in this mystery.

In any case, this tip describes the DATEDIF function and tells you what Microsoft isn't willing to tell you. The syntax for the DATEDIF function is

```
=DATEDIF(Date1,Date2,Interval)
```

Date1 and Date2 are standard dates (or a reference to a cell that contains a date). Date1 must be earlier than (or equal to) Date2. The third argument, Interval, is a text string that specifies the unit of time that will be returned.

Valid interval codes are described in this list:

- ➤ **m:** The number of complete months between Date1 and Date2.
- ➤ **d:** The number of days between Date1 and Date2.
- ➤ **y:** The number of complete years between Date1 and Date2.
- ➤ **ym:** The number of months between Date1 and Date2. This interval excludes years, so it works as though the two dates are in the same year.
- ➤ **yd:** The number of days between Date1 and Date2. This interval excludes years, so it works as though Date1 and Date2 are in the same year.
- ➤ **md:** The number of days between Date1 and Date2. This interval excludes both month and year, so it works as though Date1 and Date2 are in the same month and the same year.

Figure 100-1 shows a few examples of using the DATEDIF function with each of its possible interval arguments. The formula in D2, which was copied to the cells below, is:

```
=DATEDIF(A2,B2,C2)
```

	A	B	C	D	E
1	Date1	Date2	Interval	Result	Explanation
2	12/2/2008	9/21/2010	m	21	Complete months
3	12/2/2008	9/21/2010	d	658	Total days
4	12/2/2008	9/21/2010	y	1	Complete years
5	12/2/2008	9/21/2010	ym	9	Months (ignoring years)
6	12/2/2008	9/21/2010	yd	293	Days (ignorng years)
7	12/2/2008	9/21/2010	md	19	Days (ignoring years and months)
8					
9					

Figure 100-1: Examples of using the DATEDIF function.

Counting Characters in a Cell

This tip contains formula examples that count characters in a cell.

Counting all characters in a cell

The LEN function returns the number of characters in a cell. For example, if cell A1 contains the text Inventory, the following formula returns 9:

```
=LEN(A1)
```

When you use the LEN function with a value, it returns the number of characters in the number — which might be different from the number of characters displayed as a result of number formatting.

Counting specific characters in a cell

The following formula counts the instances of *B* (uppercase only) in the string in cell A1:

```
=LEN(A1)-LEN(SUBSTITUTE(A1,"B",""))
```

This formula works by using the SUBSTITUTE function to create a new string (in memory) that has all instances of *B* removed. Then the length of this string is subtracted from the length of the original string. The result reveals the number of occurrences of *B* in the original string.

The comparison is case sensitive. So, for example, if cell A1 contains the text Bubble Chart, the formula returns 1.

The following formula is a bit more versatile. It counts the number of Bs (both upper- and lower-case) in the string in cell A1.

```
=LEN(A1)-LEN(SUBSTITUTE(UPPER(A1),"B",""))
```

If cell A1 contains the text Bubble Chart, the formula returns 3.

Counting the occurrences of a substring in a cell

The following formula works with more than one character. It returns the number of occurrences of a particular substring (contained in cell B1) within a string (contained in cell A1). The substring can consist of any number of characters.

```
=(LEN(A1)-LEN(SUBSTITUTE(A1,B1,"")))/LEN(B1)
```

For example, if cell A1 contains the text Blonde On Blonde and B1 contains the text Blonde, the formula returns 2.

The comparison is case sensitive, so if B1 contains the text blonde, the formula returns 0. The following formula is a modified version that performs a case-insensitive comparison:

```
=(LEN(A1)-LEN(SUBSTITUTE(UPPER(A1),UPPER(B1),"")))/LEN(B1)
```

Numbering Weeks

Everyone knows that a year consists of 52 weeks. So, for any given day, you should be able to determine the week number, right? The question seems simple, but in real life, it's a bit more complicated.

To calculate a week number, the WEEKNUM function seems like the ticket. This function accepts a date and returns the week number. It also assumes that the week containing January 1 is the first week of the year. Therefore, the first week of the year can consist of as few as one day (for example, 2011) or as many as seven days (for example, 2006).

The WEEKNUM function doesn't conform to the International Standards Organization (ISO) standard. According to the ISO standard:

> ➤ A week always begins on a Monday and ends on a Sunday.

> ➤ Week 1 is the week that contains the year's first Thursday.

This definition means that, in some years, the first days of the year might have the week number 52 or 53. (They're in a week in the preceding calendar year.)

Note

The Excel WEEKNUM function uses an optional second argument, which lets you specify the weekday that's the first day of the week. If this second argument is 2, weeks are assumed to begin on Monday rather than on Tuesday. However, using this option still doesn't make the WEEKNUM function correspond to the ISO standard.

The following formula, which was created by Laurent Longre, returns the ISO week number for the date in cell A1:

```
=1+INT((A1-DATE(YEAR(A1+4-WEEKDAY(A1+6)),1,5)+
WEEKDAY(DATE(YEAR(A1+4-WEEKDAY(A1+6)),1,3)))/7)
```

Figure 102-1 compares three ways to calculate the week number for the date in column A:

> ➤ Column B: Using the Excel WEEKNUM function (with Sunday as the week start day)

> ➤ Column C: Using the Excel WEEKNUM function (with Monday as the week start day)

> ➤ Column D: Using the previous formulas listed

	Date	Excel WEEKNUM	Excel WEEKNUM2	ISO Week Number	
1	Date	Excel WEEKNUM	Excel WEEKNUM2	ISO Week Number	
2	Saturday, January 01, 2011	1	1	52	
3	Sunday, January 02, 2011	2	1	52	
4	Monday, January 03, 2011	2	2	1	
5	Tuesday, January 04, 2011	2	2	1	
6	Wednesday, January 05, 2011	2	2	1	
7	Thursday, January 06, 2011	2	2	1	
8	Friday, January 07, 2011	2	2	1	
9	Saturday, January 08, 2011	2	2	1	
10	Sunday, January 09, 2011	3	2	1	
11	Monday, January 10, 2011	3	3	2	
12	Tuesday, January 11, 2011	3	3	2	
13	Wednesday, January 12, 2011	3	3	2	
14	Thursday, January 13, 2011	3	3	2	
15	Friday, January 14, 2011	3	3	2	
16	Saturday, January 15, 2011	3	3	2	
17	Sunday, January 16, 2011	4	3	2	
18	Monday, January 17, 2011	4	4	3	
19	Tuesday, January 18, 2011	4	4	3	
20	Wednesday, January 19, 2011	4	4	3	
21	Thursday, January 20, 2011	4	4	3	
22	Friday, January 21, 2011	4	4	3	
23	Saturday, January 22, 2011	4	4	3	
24	Sunday, January 23, 2011	5	4	3	
25					

Figure 102-1: Three ways to calculate a week number.

Using a Pivot Table Instead of Formulas

The Excel pivot table feature is incredibly powerful, and you can often create pivot tables in lieu of creating formulas. This tip describes a simple problem and provides three different solutions.

Figure 103-1 shows a range of data that contains student test scores. The goal is to calculate the average score for all students plus the average score for each gender.

	A	B	C
1	Student	Score	Gender
2	Anne	90	Female
3	Billy	96	Male
4	Chuck	87	Male
5	Darlene	75	Female
6	Ella	84	Female
7	Frank	89	Male
8	George	85	Male
9	Hilda	97	Female
10	Ida	77	Female
11	John	93	Male
12	Keith	89	Male
13	Larry	77	Male
14	Mary	85	Female
15	Nora	100	Female
16	Opie	71	Male
17	Peter	89	Male
18	Quincy	83	Male
19	Rhoda	91	Female
20	Sally	87	Female
21	Tim	97	Male
22	Ubella	83	Female
23	Vince	86	Male
24	Walter	83	Male
25	Xavier	78	Male
26	Yolanda	100	Female
27	Zola	84	Female

Figure 103-1: What's the best way to calculate the average test score for males versus females?

Inserting subtotals

The first solution involves automatically inserting subtotals. To use this method, the data must be sorted by the column that will trigger the subtotaling. In this case, you need to sort by the Gender column. Follow these steps:

1. Select any cell in column C.
2. Right-click and choose Sort➜Sort A To Z from the shortcut menu.
3. Choose Data➜Outline➜Subtotal to display the Subtotal dialog box.

4. In the Subtotal dialog box, specify At Each Change in Gender, Use Function Average, and Add Subtotal to Score.

The result of adding subtotals is shown in Figure 103-2. Notice that Excel also creates an outline, so you can hide the details and view just the summary.

The formulas inserted by Excel use the SUBTOTAL function, with 1 as the first argument (1 represents average). Here are the formulas:

```
=SUBTOTAL(1,B2:B13)
=SUBTOTAL(1,B15:B28)
=SUBTOTAL(1,B2:B28)
```

The formula in cell B30 calculates the Grand Average and uses a range that includes the other two SUBTOTAL formulas in cells B14 and B29. The SUBTOTAL function ignores cells that contain other SUBTOTAL formulas.

	A	B	C	D
1	Student	Score	Gender	
2	Anne	90	Female	
3	Darlene	75	Female	
4	Ella	84	Female	
5	Hilda	97	Female	
6	Ida	77	Female	
7	Mary	85	Female	
8	Nora	100	Female	
9	Rhoda	91	Female	
10	Sally	87	Female	
11	Ubella	83	Female	
12	Yolanda	100	Female	
13	Zola	84	Female	
14		87.75	Female Average	
15	Billy	96	Male	
16	Chuck	87	Male	
17	Frank	89	Male	
18	George	85	Male	
19	John	93	Male	
20	Keith	89	Male	
21	Larry	77	Male	
22	Opie	71	Male	
23	Peter	89	Male	
24	Quincy	83	Male	
25	Tim	97	Male	
26	Vince	86	Male	
27	Walter	83	Male	
28	Xavier	78	Male	
29		85.92857143	Male Average	
30		86.76923077	Grand Average	
31				

Figure 103-2: Excel adds subtotals automatically.

Using formulas

Another method of creating averages is to use formulas. The formula to calculate the average of all students is simple:

```
=AVERAGE(B2:B27)
```

To calculate the average of the genders, you can take advantage of the AVERAGEIF function to create these formulas:

```
=AVERAGEIF(C2:C27,"Female",B2:B27)
=AVERAGEIF(C2:C27,"Male",B2:B27)
```

The AVERAGEIF function was introduced in Excel 2007. If you need your workbook to be compatible with earlier versions, use these formulas:

```
=SUMIF(C2:C27,"Female",B2:B27)/COUNTIF(C2:C27,"Female")
=SUMIF(C2:C27,"Male",B2:B27)/COUNTIF(C2:C27,"Male")
```

Using a pivot table

A third method of averaging the scores is to create a pivot table. Many users avoid creating pivot tables because they consider this feature too complicated. As you can see, it's simple to use:

1. Select any cell in the data range, and choose Insert➜Tables➜PivotTable, to display the Create PivotTable dialog box.

2. In the dialog box, verify that Excel selected the correct data range and specify a cell on the existing worksheet as the location.

   Cell E1 is a good choice.

3. Click OK, and Excel displays the PivotTable Field List.

4. In the PivotTable Field List, drag the Gender item to the Row Labels section, at the bottom.

5. Drag the Score item to the Values section.

   Excel creates the pivot table but displays the SUM function rather than the average.

6. To change the summary function that's used, right-click any of the values in the pivot table and choose Summarize Data By➜Average from the shortcut menu.

Figure 103-3 shows the pivot table.

	E	F	G	H	I	J	K
1	Row Labels ▾	Average of Score					
2	Female	87.75					
3	Male	85.92857143					
4	**Grand Total**	**86.76923077**					
5							
6							
7							
8							
9							
10							
11							
12							
13							
14							
15							
16							
17							
18							
19							
20							
21							
22							
23							
24							
25							

PivotTable Field List

Choose fields to add to report:

- ☐ Student
- ☑ **Score**
- ☑ **Gender**

Drag fields between areas below:

▼ Report Filter   ▦ Column Labels

▦ Row Labels   Σ Values

Gender ▾   Average of Score ▾

☐ Defer Layout Update   Update

Figure 103-3: This pivot table calculates the averages without using formulas.

Note

Unlike a formula-based solution, a pivot table doesn't update itself automatically if the data changes. If the data changes, you must refresh the pivot table. Just right-click any cell in the pivot table and choose Refresh from the shortcut menu.

The pivot table in this example is extremely simple, but it's also very easy to create. Pivot tables can be much more complex, and they can summarize massive amounts of data in just about any way you can think of — without using any formulas.

Expressing a Number as an Ordinal

You might need to express a value as an ordinal number — for example, Today is the 21st day of the month. In this case, the number 21 is converted to an ordinal number by appending the characters *st* to the number. Excel doesn't have a number format to do this, but you can convert a number to an ordinal by using a formula.

The specific characters appended to a number (st, nd, rd, or th) depend on the number. The pattern is a little convoluted, making the construction of a formula tricky. Most numbers use the *th* suffix. Exceptions occur for numbers that end with 1, 2, or 3 — except if the preceding number is a 1 (numbers that end with 11, 12, or 13). These rules might seem fairly complex, but you can translate them into an Excel formula.

The following formula converts the number in cell A1 (assumed to be an integer) to an ordinal number:

```
=A1&IF(OR(VALUE(RIGHT(A1,2))={11,12,13}),"th",IF(OR(VALUE(RIGHT(A1))={1,2,3}),
CHOOSE(RIGHT(A1),"st","nd","rd"),"th"))
```

This formula is rather complicated, so it might help to examine its components. Basically, the formula works this way:

1. If the last two digits of the number consist of 11, 12, or 13, use *th*.

2. If Rule 1 doesn't apply, check the last digit. If the last digit is 1, use *st*. If the last digit is 2, use *nd*. If the last digit is 3, use *rd*.

3. If neither Rule 1 nor Rule 2 applies, use *th*.

Figure 104-1 shows the formula in use.

	A	B	C	D	E
1	Number	Ordinal			
2	1	1st			
3	4	4th			
4	7	7th			
5	10	10th			
6	13	13th			
7	16	16th			
8	19	19th			
9	22	22nd			
10	25	25th			
11	28	28th			
12	31	31st			
13	34	34th			
14	37	37th			
15	40	40th			
16	43	43rd			
17	46	46th			
18	49	49th			
19	52	52nd			
20	55	55th			
21					

Figure 104-1: Using a formula to express a number as an ordinal.

Note

The formula returns a text string, not a number. Therefore, you can't use the result in any numerical calculations.

Extracting Words from a String

The formulas in this tip are useful for extracting words from text contained in a cell. For example, you can use a formula to extract the first word in a sentence.

Extracting the first word of a string

To extract the first word of a string, a formula must locate the position of the first space character and then use this information as an argument for the LEFT function. The following formula does that:

```
=LEFT(A1,FIND(" ",A1)-1)
```

This formula returns all the text before the first space in cell A1. However, the formula has a slight problem: It returns an error if the text in cell A1 contains no space characters, because it consists of a single word. A slightly more complex formula solves the problem by using the new IFERROR function to display the entire cell contents if an error occurs:

```
=IFERROR(LEFT(A1,FIND(" ",A1)-1),A1)
```

If you need the formula to be compatible with earlier versions of Excel, you can't use IFERROR. Therefore, use an IF function and an ISERR function to check for the error:

```
=IF(ISERR(FIND(" ",A1)),A1,LEFT(A1,FIND(" ",A1)-1))
```

Extracting the last word of a string

Extracting the last word of a string is more complicated because the FIND function works only from left to right. Therefore, the problem rests with locating the *last* space character. The following formula, however, solves this problem. The formula returns the last word of a string (all the text following the last space character):

```
=RIGHT(A1,LEN(A1)-FIND("*",SUBSTITUTE(A1," ","*",LEN(A1)-LEN
(SUBSTITUTE(A1," ","")))))
```

This formula, however, has the same problem as the first formula in the preceding section: It fails if the string doesn't contain at least one space character. The solution is to use the IFERROR function and return the entire contents of cell A1 if an error occurs:

```
=IFERROR(RIGHT(A1,LEN(A1)-FIND("*",SUBSTITUTE(A1," ","*",
LEN(A1)-LEN(SUBSTITUTE(A1," ","")))))),A1)
```

The following formula is compatible with all versions of Excel:

```
=IF(ISERR(FIND(" ",A1)),A1,RIGHT(A1,LEN(A1)-FIND("*",SUBSTITUTE
(A1," ","*",LEN(A1)-LEN(SUBSTITUTE(A1," ","")))))))
```

Extracting all except the first word of a string

The following formula returns the contents of cell A1, except for the first word:

```
=RIGHT(A1,LEN(A1)-FIND(" ",A1,1))
```

If cell A1 contains 2008 Operating Budget, the formula returns Operating Budget.

This formula returns an error if the cell contains only one word. The following version uses the IFERROR function to avoid the error; the formula returns an empty string if the cell doesn't contain multiple words:

```
=IFERROR(RIGHT(A1,LEN(A1)-FIND(" ",A1,1)),"")
```

This version is compatible with all versions of Excel:

```
=IF(ISERR(FIND(" ",A1)),"",RIGHT(A1,LEN(A1)-FIND(" ",A1,1)))
```

Parsing Names

Suppose that you have a list of people's names in a single column. You have to separate these names into three columns: one for the first name, one for the middle name or initial, and one for the last name. This task is more complicated than you might initially think, because not every name in the column has a middle name or middle initial. However, you can still do it.

Note

This task becomes a lot more complicated if the list contains names with titles (such as Mrs. or Dr.) or names followed by additional details (such as Jr. or III). In fact, the following formulas don't handle these complex cases. However, they still give you a significant head start if you're willing to do a bit of manual editing to handle the special cases.

The following formulas all assume that the name appears in cell A1.

You can easily construct a formula to return the first name:

```
=LEFT(A1,FIND(" ",A1)-1)
```

This formula returns the last name:

```
=RIGHT(A1,LEN(A1)-FIND("*",SUBSTITUTE(A1," ","*",LEN(A1)-
LEN(SUBSTITUTE(A1," ","")))))
```

The following formula extracts the middle name (if any). It assumes that the first name is in B1 and the last name is in D1:

```
=IF(LEN(B1&D1)+2>=LEN(A1),"",MID(A1,LEN(B1)+2,LEN(A1)-LEN(B1&D1)-2))
```

As you can see in Figure 106-1, the formulas work fairly well. A few problems occurred, however — notably, names that contain either one word or more than three words. But, as I mention earlier in this tip, you can clean these cases up manually.

	A	B	C	D	E
1	**Full Name**	**First**	**Middle**	**Last**	
2	John Q. Public	John	Q.	Public	
3	Lisa Smith	Lisa		Smith	
4	J. R. Robins	J.	R.	Robins	
5	Dr. Lester B. Jones	Dr.	Lester B.	Jones	
6	J. R. R. Tolkien	J.	R. R.	Tolkien	
7	Franklin H. Lee	Franklin	H.	Lee	
8	Melvina Pryce	Melvina		Pryce	
9	Suzette I. Thorson	Suzette	I.	Thorson	
10	J. Frank	J.		Frank	
11	Amanda M. Rowe	Amanda	M.	Rowe	
12	Madonna	#VALUE!	#VALUE!	#VALUE!	
13	Aaron E. Pacheco	Aaron	E.	Pacheco	
14	Dennis Michael Batie	Dennis	Michael	Batie	
15	Lloyd Benedict Arnold	Lloyd	Benedict	Arnold	
16	Agnes K. Saterfiel	Agnes	K.	Saterfiel	
17	Robert M. Simmons	Robert	M.	Simmons	
18	Joseph Q. Glenn	Joseph	Q.	Glenn	

Figure 106-1: This worksheet uses formulas to extract the first name, middle name (or initial), and last name from a list of names in column A.

Note

In many cases, you can avoid formulas and use the Excel Data→Data Tools→Text to Columns command to parse strings into their component parts. Selecting this command displays the Excel Convert Text to Columns Wizard, which consists of a series of dialog boxes that walk you through the steps to convert a single column of data into multiple columns. Generally, you want to select the Delimited option (in Step 1) and use Space as the delimiter (in Step 2).

Removing Titles from Names

If you have a list of names, you might need to remove titles (such as Mr., Ms., or Mrs.) from them. You might want to perform this operation before you parse the name, as described in Tip 106.

You can use the following formula to remove three common titles (Mr., Ms., and Mrs.) from a name; for example, if cell A1 contains Mr. Fred Mertz, the formula returns Fred Mertz:

```
=IF(OR(LEFT(A1,2)="Mr",LEFT(A1,3)="Mrs",LEFT(A1,2)="Ms"),
RIGHT(A1,LEN(A1)-FIND(" ",A1)),A1)
```

This formula tests for three conditions. If you need to test for more, just add arguments to the OR function.

Generating a Series of Dates

If you work with time-based data, you might want to insert a series of dates into a worksheet. For example, in a sales tracking application, you might want to enter a series of dates for a sales quarter — making sure, of course, to skip dates that occur during weekends.

Using AutoFill

The most efficient way to enter a series of dates doesn't require any formulas — just use the AutoFill feature to insert a series of dates. Enter the first date and then drag the cell's fill handle while pressing the right mouse button (right-drag the cell's fill handle). Release the mouse button and choose a command from the shortcut menu (see Figure 108-1).

In some situations, you need to enter two dates before you use the AutoFill. For example, if you want to enter a series of dates that represent consecutive Mondays, you need to enter the first two dates of the series. Then select both dates, right-click, and choose Fill Days from the shortcut menu.

Figure 108-1: Using AutoFill to create a series of dates.

Using formulas

Another way to enter a series of dates is to use formulas. The advantage of using formulas (rather than the AutoFill feature) to create a series of dates is that you can change the first date, and the others are updated automatically. Enter the starting date into a cell and then use formulas (copied down the column) to generate the additional dates.

The following examples assume that you entered the first date of the series into cell A1 and the formula into cell A2. You can then copy this formula down the column as many times as needed.

To generate a series of dates separated by seven days, use this formula:

```
=A1+7
```

To generate a series of dates separated by one month, use this formula:

```
=DATE(YEAR(A1),MONTH(A1)+1,DAY(A1))
```

To generate a series of dates separated by one year, use this formula:

```
=DATE(YEAR(A1)+1,MONTH(A1),DAY(A1))
```

To generate a series of weekdays only (no Saturdays or Sundays), use the following formula. It assumes that the date in cell A1 isn't a weekend day:

```
=IF(WEEKDAY(A1)=6,A1+3,A1+1)
```

This formula returns a date serial number, so you'll need to format the cells to display dates.

Determining Specific Dates

This tip contains a number of useful formulas that return a specific date.

Determining the day of the year

January 1 is the first day of the year, and December 31 is the last day. What about all those days between them? The following formula returns the day of the year for a date stored in cell A1:

```
=A1-DATE(YEAR(A1),1,0)
```

For example, if cell A1 contains the date February 16, 2010, the formula returns 47 because that date is the 47th day of the year.

The following formula returns the number of days remaining in the year from a particular date (assumed to be in cell A1):

```
=DATE(YEAR(A1),12,31)-A1
```

Determining the day of the week

If you need to determine the day of the week for a date, the WEEKDAY function does the job. The WEEKDAY function accepts a date argument and returns an integer between 1 and 7 that corresponds to the day of the week. The following formula, for example, returns 6 because the first day of the year 2010 falls on a Friday:

```
=WEEKDAY(DATE(2010,1,1))
```

The WEEKDAY function uses an optional second argument that specifies the day numbering system for the result. If you specify 2 as the second argument, the function returns 1 for Monday, 2 for Tuesday, and so on. If you specify 3 as the second argument, the function returns 0 for Monday, 1 for Tuesday, and so on.

Note

You can also determine the day of the week for a cell that contains a date by applying a custom number format. A cell that uses the following custom number format displays the day of the week, spelled out:

```
dddd
```

Keep in mind that the cell really contains the full date, not just the day number.

Determining the date of the most recent Sunday

The formula in this section returns the most recent specified day. You can use the following formula to return the date for the previous Sunday. If the current day is Sunday, the formula returns the current date. The result is a date serial number (you need to format the cell to display as a readable date):

```
=TODAY()-MOD(TODAY()-1,7)
```

To modify this formula to find the date of a day other than Sunday, change the 1 to a different number between 2 (for Monday) and 7 (for Saturday).

Determining the first day of the week after a date

The following formula returns the specified day of the week that occurs after a particular date. For example, you can use this formula to determine the date of the first Friday after July 4, 2010.

The formula assumes that cell A1 contains a date and that cell A2 contains a number between 1 and 7 (1 for Sunday, 2 for Monday, and so on):

```
=A1+A2-WEEKDAY(A1)+(A2<WEEKDAY(A1))*7
```

If cell A1 contains July 4, 2010, and cell A2 contains 6 (for Friday), the formula returns July 9, 2010. It's the first Friday after July 4, 2010 (which is a Sunday).

Determining the nth occurrence of a day of the week in a month

You might need a formula to determine the date for a particular occurrence of a weekday. Suppose that your company payday falls on the second Friday of each month and that you need to determine the paydays for each month of the year. The following formula makes this type of calculation:

```
=DATE(A1,A2,1)+A3-WEEKDAY(DATE(A1,A2,1))+(A4-(A3>=WEEKDAY
 (DATE(A1,A2,1))))*7
```

This formula assumes that

> ➤ Cell A1 contains a year.
> ➤ Cell A2 contains a month.

➤ Cell A3 contains a day number (1 for Sunday, 2 for Monday, and so on).

➤ Cell A4 contains the occurrence number (for example, 2 to select the second occurrence of the weekday specified in cell A3).

If you use this formula to determine the date of the second Friday in June 2010, it returns June 11, 2010.

Determining the last day of a month

To determine the date that corresponds to the last day of a month, you can use the DATE function. However, you need to increment the month by 1 and use a day value of 0. In other words, the "0th" day of the next month is the last day of the current month.

The following formula assumes that a date is stored in cell A1. The formula returns the date that corresponds to the last day of the month:

```
=DATE(YEAR(A1),MONTH(A1)+1,0)
```

You can use a variation of this formula to determine how many days comprise a specified month. The following formula returns an integer that corresponds to the number of days in the month for the date in cell A1 (make sure that you format the cell as a number, not as a date):

```
=DAY(DATE(YEAR(A1),MONTH(A1)+1,0))
```

Determining a date's quarter

For financial reports, you might find it useful to present information in terms of quarters. The following formula returns an integer between 1 and 4 that corresponds to the calendar quarter for the date in cell A1:

```
=ROUNDUP(MONTH(A1)/3,0)
```

This formula divides the month number by 3 and then rounds up the result.

Displaying a Calendar in a Range

This tip describes how to create a "live" calendar in a range of cells. Figure 110-1 shows an example. If you change the date that's displayed at the top of the calendar, the calendar recalculates to display the dates for the month and year.

Figure 110-1: This calendar was created with a complex array formula.

To create this calendar in the range B2:H9, follow these steps:

1. Select B2:H2 and then merge the cells by choosing Home→Alignment→Merge & Center.

2. Enter a date into the merged range.

   The day of the month isn't important, so change the format of the cell to a custom format that doesn't display the day: mmmm, yyyy.

3. Enter the abbreviated day names in the range B3:H3.

4. Select B4:H9 and then enter the following array formula without the line breaks.

   Remember: To enter an array formula, press Ctrl+Shift+Enter (not just Enter):

   ```
   =IF(MONTH(DATE(YEAR(B2),MONTH(B2),1))
   <>MONTH(DATE(YEAR(B2),MONTH(B2),1)-
   (WEEKDAY(DATE(YEAR(B2),MONTH(B2),1))-1)
   +{0;1;2;3;4;5}*7+{1,2,3,4,5,6,7}-1),"",
   DATE(YEAR(B2),MONTH(B2),1)-
   (WEEKDAY(DATE(YEAR(B2),MONTH(B2),1))-1)
   +{0;1;2;3;4;5}*7+{1,2,3,4,5,6,7}-1)
   ```

5. Format the range B4:H9 to use this custom number format, which displays only the day: d.

6. Adjust the column widths, and format the cells the way you like.

Change the date and year, and the calendar updates automatically. After creating this calendar, you can copy the range to any other worksheet or workbook.

Various Methods of Rounding Numbers

Rounding numbers is a common task, and Excel provides quite a few functions that round values in various ways.

You must understand the difference between *rounding* a value and *formatting* a value. When you *format* a number to display a specific number of decimal places, formulas that refer to that number use the actual value, which might differ from the displayed value. When you *round* a number, formulas that refer to that value use the rounded number.

Table 111-1 summarizes the Excel rounding functions.

Table 111-1: Excel Rounding Functions

Function	What It Does
CEILING	Rounds a number up (away from zero) to the nearest specified multiple
DOLLARDE	Converts a dollar price, expressed as a fraction, into a decimal number
DOLLARFR	Converts a dollar price, expressed as a decimal, into a fractional number
EVEN	Rounds up (away from zero) positive numbers to the nearest even integer; rounds down (away from zero) negative numbers to the nearest even integer
FLOOR	Rounds down (toward zero) a number to the nearest specified multiple
INT	Rounds down a number to make it an integer
MROUND	Rounds a number to a specified multiple
ODD	Rounds up (away from zero) numbers to the nearest odd integer; rounds down (away from zero) negative numbers to the nearest odd integer
ROUND	Rounds a number to a specified number of digits
ROUNDDOWN	Rounds down (toward zero) a number to a specified number of digits
ROUNDUP	Rounds up (away from zero) a number to a specified number of digits
TRUNC	Truncates a number to a specified number of significant digits

The following sections provide examples of formulas that use various types of rounding.

Rounding to the nearest multiple

The MROUND function is useful for rounding values to the nearest multiple. For example, you can use this function to round a number to the nearest 5. The following formula returns 135:

```
=MROUND(133,5)
```

Rounding currency values

Often, you need to round currency values. For example, a calculated price might be a number like $45.78923. In such a case, you want to round the calculated price to the nearest penny. This process might sound simple, but you can round this type of value in one of three ways:

> ➤ Round it up to the nearest penny.
> ➤ Round it down to the nearest penny.
> ➤ Round it to the nearest penny (the rounding can be up or down).

The following formula assumes that a dollar-and-cents value is in cell A1. The formula rounds the value to the nearest penny. For example, if cell A1 contains $12.421, the formula returns $12.42.

```
=ROUND(A1,2)
```

If you need to round up the value to the nearest penny, use the CEILING function. The following formula rounds up the value in cell A1 to the nearest penny (if, for example, cell A1 contains $12.421, the formula returns $12.43):

```
=CEILING(A1,0.01)
```

To round down a dollar value, use the FLOOR function. The following formula, for example, rounds down the dollar value in cell A1 to the nearest penny (if cell A1 contains $12.421, the formula returns $12.42):

```
=FLOOR(A1,0.01)
```

To round up a dollar value to the nearest nickel, use this formula:

```
=CEILING(A1,0.05)
```

Using the INT and TRUNC functions

On the surface, the INT and TRUNC functions seem similar. Both convert a value to an integer. The TRUNC function simply removes the fractional part of a number. The INT function rounds down a number to the nearest integer, based on the value of the fractional part of the number.

In practice, INT and TRUNC return different results only when using negative numbers. For example, the following formula returns –14.0:

```
=TRUNC(-14.2)
```

The next formula returns –15.0 because –14.2 is rounded down to the next lower integer:

```
=INT(-14.2)
```

The TRUNC function takes an additional (optional) argument that's useful for truncating decimal values. For example, the following formula returns 54.33 (the value truncated to two decimal places):

```
=TRUNC(54.3333333,2)
```

Rounding to n significant digits

In some situations, you might need to round a value to a particular number of significant digits. For example, you might want to express the value 1,432,187 in terms of two significant digits (that is, as 1,400,000). The value 84,356 expressed in terms of three significant digits is 84,300.

If the value is a positive number with no decimal places, the following formula does the job. This formula rounds the number in cell A1 to two significant digits. To round to a different number of significant digits, replace the 2 in this formula with a different number:

```
=ROUNDDOWN(A1,2-LEN(A1))
```

For nonintegers and negative numbers, the solution is a bit trickier. The following formula provides a more general solution that rounds the value in cell A1 to the number of significant digits specified in cell A2. This formula works for positive and negative integers and nonintegers:

```
=ROUND(A1,A2-1-INT(LOG10(ABS(A1))))
```

For example, if cell A1 contains 1.27845 and cell A2 contains 3, the formula returns 1.28000 (the value, rounded to three significant digits).

Rounding Time Values

You might need to create a formula that rounds a time to a particular number of minutes. For example, you might need to enter your company's time records rounded to the nearest 15 minutes. This tip presents examples of various ways to round a time value.

The following formula rounds the time in cell A1 to the nearest minute:

```
=ROUND(A1*1440,0)/1440
```

This formula works by multiplying the time by 1440 (to get the total number of minutes). This value is passed to the ROUND function, and the result is divided by 1440. For example, if cell A1 contains 11:52:34, the formula returns 11:53:00.

The following formula is similar, except that it rounds the time in cell A1 to the nearest hour:

```
=ROUND(A1*24,0)/24
```

If cell A1 contains 5:21:31, the formula returns 5:00:00.

The following formula rounds the time in cell A1 to the nearest 15 minutes (quarter of an hour):

```
=ROUND(A1*24/0.25,0)*(0.25/24)
```

In this formula, 0.25 represents the fractional hour. To round a time to the nearest 30 minutes, change 0.25 to 0.5, as in the following formula:

```
=ROUND(A1*24/0.5,0)*(0.5/24)
```

Using the New AGGREGATE Function

One of the new worksheet functions introduced in Excel 2010 is AGGREGATE. You can use this multipurpose function to sum values, calculate an average, count entries, and more. What makes this function useful is that it can (optionally) ignore hidden cells and error values.

The first argument for the AGGREGATE function is a value between 1 and 19 that determines the calculation type. The calculation type, in essence, is one of Excel's other functions. Table 113-1 contains a list of these values, with the function it mimics.

Table 113-1: Values for the First Argument of the AGGREGATE Function

Function_num	Function
1	AVERAGE
2	COUNT
3	COUNTA
4	MAX
5	MIN
6	PRODUCT
7	STDEV.S
8	STDEV.P
9	SUM
10	VAR.S
11	VAR.P
12	MEDIAN
13	MODE.SNGL
14	LARGE
15	SMALL
16	PERCENTILE.INC
17	QUARTILE.INC
18	PERCENTILE.EXC
19	QUARTILE.EXC

The second argument for the AGGREGATE function is an integer between 0 and 7 that specifies how hidden cells and errors are handled. Table 113-2 summarizes these options.

Table 113-2: Values for the Second Argument of the AGGREGATE Function

Option	Behavior
0 or omitted	Ignore nested SUBTOTAL and AGGREGATE functions
1	Ignore hidden rows, nested SUBTOTAL and AGGREGATE functions
2	Ignore error values, nested SUBTOTAL and AGGREGATE functions
3	Ignore hidden rows, error values, nested SUBTOTAL and AGGREGATE functions
4	Ignore nothing
5	Ignore hidden rows
6	Ignore error values
7	Ignore hidden rows and error values

The third argument of the AGGREGATE function is a range reference for the data to be aggregated.

Note

The SUBTOTAL function always ignores data that is hidden, but only if the hiding is a result of autofiltering or contracting an outline. The AGGREGATE function works similarly, but also ignores data in rows that have been hidden manually. Note that this function does *not* ignore data in hidden columns. In other words, the AGGREGATE function was designed to work only with vertical ranges.

Figure 113-1 shows an example of how the AGGREGATE function can be useful. The worksheet contains pre-test and post-scores for eight students. Note that Diane did not take the post-test, so cell C8 contains the NA/# error value (to indicate not available).

Cell D11 contains a formula that uses the AVERAGE function to calculate the average change. This formula returns an error:

```
=AVERAGE(D2:D8)
```

The formula in cell D12 uses the AGGREGGATE function, with the option to ignore error values:

```
=AGGREGATE(1,6,D2:D8)
```

	A	B	C	D	E
1	Student	Pre-Test	Post-Test	Change	
2	Arnold	67	76	9	
3	Betty	75	78	3	
4	Charles	81	80	-1	
5	Diane	90	#N/A	#N/A	
6	Elvin	84	83	-1	
7	Francis	79	86	7	
8	Georgy	81	81	0	
9					
10					
11	Average Change (AVERAGE):			#N/A	
12	Average Change (AGGREGATE):			2.833333333	
13					
14					

Figure 113-1: Using the AGGREGATE function to calculate an average when the range contains an error value.

Remember that AGGREGATE works only with Excel 2010. If a workbook that uses this function is opened in a previous version of Excel, the formula will display an error.

Returning the Last Nonblank Cell in a Column or Row

Suppose that you update a worksheet frequently by adding new data to its columns. You might need a way to reference the last value in a particular column (the value most recently entered).

Figure 114-1 shows an example. The worksheet tracks the value of three funds in columns B:D. Notice that the information does not arrive at the same time. The goal is to get the sum of the most recent data for each fund. These values are calculated in the range G4:G6.

▲	A	B	C	D	E	F	G	H
1	Month	Fund A	Fund B	Fund C				
2	January	189.74	98.32	212.92				
3	February	175.34	84.55	210.54		Latest Values		
4	March	159.54	81.41	215.85		Fund -A	174.54	
5	April	162.44	80.03			Fund-B	81.18	
6	May	174.54	77.43			Fund-C	215.85	
7	June		81.18					
8	July					Total:	471.57	
9	August							
10	September							
11	October							
12	November							
13	December							
14								

Figure 114-1: Use a formula to return the last nonempty cell in columns B:D.

The formulas in G4, G5, and G6 are as follows:

```
=INDEX(B:B,COUNTA(B:B))
=INDEX(C:C,COUNTA(C:C))
=INDEX(D:D,COUNTA(D:D))
```

These formulas use the COUNTA function to count the number of nonempty cells in column C. This value is used as the second argument for the INDEX function. For example, in column B the last value is in row 6, COUNTA returns 6, and the INDEX function returns the 6th value in the column.

The preceding formulas work in most, but not all, situations. If the column has one or more empty cells interspersed, determining the last nonblank cell is a bit more challenging because the COUNTA function doesn't count the empty cells.

The following array formula returns the contents of the last nonempty cell in the first 500 rows of column C, even if column C contains blank cells:

```
=INDEX(C1:C500,MAX(ROW(C1:C500)*(C1:C500<>"")))
```

Note   **Press Ctrl+Shift+Enter (not just Enter) to enter an array formula.**

You can, of course, modify the formula to work with a column other than column C. To use a different column, change the four column references from C to whatever column you need. If the last nonempty cell occurs in a row beyond row 500, you need to change the two instances of 500 to a larger number. The fewer rows referenced in the formula, the faster the calculation speed.

The following array formula is similar to the previous formula, but it returns the last nonempty cell in a row (in this case, row 1):

```
=INDEX(1:1,MAX(COLUMN(1:1)*(1:1<>"")))
```

To use this formula for a different row, change the three 1:1 row references to correspond to the correct row number.

Using the COUNTIF Function

The Excel COUNT and COUNTA functions are useful for basic counting, but sometimes you need more flexibility. This tip contains many examples of the powerful Excel COUNTIF function, useful for counting cells based on various types of criteria.

These formulas all work with a range named Data, so you need to adjust the formulas to refer to your own range. As you can see in Table 115-1, the criteria argument proves quite flexible. You can use constants, expressions, functions, cell references, and even wildcard characters (* and ?).

Table 115-1: COUNTIF Formulas

Formula	Number of Cells or Values It Returns
=COUNTIF(Data,12)	Cells containing the value 12
=COUNTIF(Data,"<0")	Cells containing a negative value
=COUNTIF(Data,"<>0")	Cells not equal to 0
=COUNTIF(Data,">5")	Cells greater than 5
=COUNTIF(Data,A1)	Cells equal to the contents of cell A1
=COUNTIF(Data,">"&A1)	Cells greater than the value in cell A1
=COUNTIF(Data,"*")	Cells containing text
=COUNTIF(Data,"???")	Text cells containing exactly three characters
=COUNTIF(Data,"budget")	Cells containing the single word budget and nothing else (not case sensitive)
=COUNTIF(Data,"*budget*")	Cells containing the text budget anywhere within the text (not case sensitive)
=COUNTIF(Data,"A*")	Cells containing text that begins with the letter A (not case sensitive)
=COUNTIF(Data,TODAY())	Cells containing the current date
=COUNTIF(Data,">"&AVERAGE(Data))	Cells with a value greater than the average
=COUNTIF(Data,">"&AVERAGE(Data)+ STDEV(Data)*3)	Values exceeding three standard deviations above the mean
=COUNTIF(Data,3)+COUNTIF(Data,-3)	Cells containing the value 3 or –3
=COUNTIF(Data,TRUE)	Cells containing logical TRUE
=COUNTIF(Data,TRUE)+COUNTIF(Data, FALSE)	Cells containing a logical value (TRUE or FALSE)
=COUNTIF(Data,"#N/A")	Cells containing the #N/A error value

Counting Cells That Meet Multiple Criteria

Tip 116 presents examples of formulas that use the COUNTIF function. Those formulas are useful for counting cells that match a single criterion. The formula examples in this tip are useful when you need to count cells only if two or more criteria are met. These criteria can be based on the cells that are being counted or based on a range of corresponding cells.

New Feature

Some of these formulas use the COUNTIFS function, which was introduced in Excel 2007. For compatibility purposes, I also present an alternative formula that works with previous versions of Excel.

Using "And" criteria

The And criterion counts cells if all specified conditions are met. A common example is a formula that counts the number of values that fall within a numerical range. For example, you might want to count cells that contain a value greater than 0 *and* less than or equal to 12. Any cell that has a positive value less than or equal to 12 is included in the count.

The following formula, which works only in Excel 2007 and later, counts the cells in a range named Data that fall between 0 and 12:

```
=COUNTIFS(Data,">=0",Data,"<=12")
```

Arguments for the COUNTIFS function always come in pairs. This formula has two sets of paired arguments: The first argument in each pair is the range of interest, and the second argument is the criterion. Values are counted if they meet *all* criteria specified by each argument pair.

For compatibility with previous versions of Excel, use this formula:

```
=COUNTIF(Data,">0")-COUNTIF(Data,">12")
```

This formula counts the number of values that are greater than 0 and then subtracts the number of values that are greater than 12. The result is the number of cells that contain a value greater than 0 and less than or equal to 12.

Creating this type of formula can be confusing because the formula refers to the condition `">12"` even though the goal is to count values that are less than or equal to 12. An alternative technique is to use an array formula, such as the following one (you might find creating this type of formula easier):

```
=SUM((Data>0)*(Data<=12))
```

Note

When you enter an array formula, press Ctrl+Shift+Enter, not just Enter.

Figure 116-1 shows a worksheet that I use for some of the examples that follow. This sheet shows sales amount categorized by Month, SalesRep, and Type. The worksheet contains named ranges that correspond to the labels in Row 1.

Sometimes, the counting criteria are based on cells other than the cells being counted. You might, for example, want to count the number of sales that meet the following criteria:

➤ Month is January, *and*

➤ SalesRep is Brooks, *and*

➤ Amount is greater than 1000

	A	B	C	D
1	**Month**	**SalesRep**	**Type**	**Amount**
2	January	Albert	New	85
3	January	Albert	New	675
4	January	Brooks	New	130
5	January	Cook	New	1350
6	January	Cook	Existing	685
7	January	Brooks	New	1350
8	January	Cook	New	475
9	January	Brooks	New	1205
10	February	Brooks	Existing	450
11	February	Albert	New	495
12	February	Cook	New	210
13	February	Cook	Existing	1050
14	February	Albert	New	140
15	February	Brooks	New	900
16	February	Brooks	New	900
17	February	Cook	New	95
18	February	Cook	New	780
19	March	Brooks	New	900
20	March	Albert	Existing	875
21	March	Brooks	New	50
22	March	Brooks	New	875
23	March	Cook	Existing	225
24	March	Cook	New	175
25	March	Brooks	Existing	400
26	March	Albert	New	840
27	March	Cook	New	132
28				

Figure 116-1: This worksheet demonstrates various counting techniques that use multiple criteria.

The following formula (for Excel 2007 and later only) uses three sets of paired arguments to return the count:

```
=COUNTIFS(Month,"January",SalesRep,"Brooks",Amount,">1000")
```

For compatibility with previous versions of Excel, use the following formula to count the number of items that meet all three criteria:

```
=SUMPRODUCT((Month="January")*(SalesRep="Brooks")*(Amount>1000))
```

Note

If your data is in a table (created by choosing Insert➔Tables➔Table), you can use filtering to display only the rows that meet multiple And criteria. Figure 116-2 shows the data filtered to show only the January sales for Brooks that exceed 1000. I also added a Total Row to this table, which displays the count. However, filtering cannot be used for Or criteria, which is discussed next.

	A	B	C	D	E
1	Month	SalesRep	Type	Amount	
7	January	Brooks	New	1350	
9	January	Brooks	New	1205	
28					
29					
30					
31					

Figure 116-2: Using table filtering to count rows that meet multiple And criteria.

Using "Or" criteria

To count cells by using an Or criterion, you can sometimes use multiple COUNTIF functions. The following formula, for example, counts the number of instances of 1, 3, and 5 in the range named Data:

```
=COUNTIF(Data,1)+COUNTIF(Data,3)+COUNTIF(Data,5)
```

You can also use the COUNTIF function in an array formula. The following array formula, for example, returns the same result as the previous formula:

```
=SUM(COUNTIF(Data,{1,3,5}))
```

Note

Enter an array formula by using Ctrl+Shift+Enter.

If you base your Or criteria on cells other than the cells being counted, the COUNTIF function doesn't work. Refer to Figure 116-1. Suppose that you want to count the number of sales that meet one of the following criteria:

> ➤ Month is January, *or*
> ➤ SalesRep is Brooks, *or*
> ➤ Amount is greater than 1000

The following array formula returns the correct count:

```
=SUM(IF((Month="January")+(SalesRep="Brooks")+(Amount>1000),1))
```

Combining "And" and "Or" criteria

You can combine And and Or criteria when counting. Perhaps you want to count sales that meet the following criteria:

> ➤ Month is January, *and*
> ➤ SalesRep is Brooks, *or*
> ➤ SalesRep is Cook

This array formula returns the number of sales that meet the criteria:

```
=SUM((Month="January")*IF((SalesRep="Brooks")+(SalesRep="Cook"),1))
```

Counting Nonduplicated Entries in a Range

In some situations, you might need to count the number of nonduplicated entries in a range. Figure 117-1 shows an example. Column A has a list of animals, and the goal is to count the number of different animals in the list. The formula in cell B2 returns 8, which is the number of nonduplicated animals. This formula (an array formula, by the way) is

```
=SUM(1/COUNTIF(A1:A10,A1:A10))
```

Note

When you enter an array formula, press Ctrl+Shift+Enter (not just Enter). Excel surrounds the formula with braces to remind you that it's an array formula.

	A	B	C	D	E	F
1	dog					
2	cat		8	different animals		
3	monkey					
4	cow					
5	pig					
6	donkey					
7	horse					
8	chicken					
9	cat					
10	cow					
11						

Figure 117-1: Use an array formula to count the number of nonduplicated entries in a range.

This formula is one of those "Internet classics" that is passed around on various Web sites and newsgroups. Credit goes to David Hager, who first came up with the formula.

The preceding array formula works fine unless the range contains one or more empty cells. The following modified version of this array formula uses the new IFERROR function to overcome this problem:

```
=SUM(IFERROR(1/COUNTIF(A1:A10,A1:A10),0))
```

The preceding formulas work with both values and text. If the range contains only numeric values or blank cells (but no text), you can use the following formula (which isn't an array formula) to count the number of nonduplicated values:

```
=SUM(N(FREQUENCY(A1:A10,A1:A10)>0))
```

Calculating Single-Criterion Conditional Sums

The SUM function is easily the most commonly used function. But sometimes you need more flexibility than the SUM function provides. The SUMIF function is useful when you need to compute conditional sums. For example, you might need to calculate the sum of just the negative values in a range of cells.

The examples in this tip demonstrate how to use the SUMIF function for conditional sums by using a single criterion.

These formulas are based on the worksheet shown in Figure 118-1, which is set up to track invoices. Column F contains a formula that subtracts the date in column E from the date in column D. A negative number in column F indicates that the payment is past due. The worksheet uses named ranges that correspond to the labels in row 1.

	A	B	C	D	E	F
1	InvoiceNum	Office	Amount	DateDue	Today	Difference
2	AG-0145	Oregon	$5,000.00	4/1/2010	5/5/2010	-34
3	AG-0189	California	$450.00	4/19/2010	5/5/2010	-16
4	AG-0220	Washington	$3,211.56	4/28/2010	5/5/2010	-7
5	AG-0310	Oregon	$250.00	4/30/2010	5/5/2010	-5
6	AG-0355	Washington	$125.50	5/4/2010	5/5/2010	-1
7	AG-0409	Washington	$3,000.00	5/10/2010	5/5/2010	5
8	AG-0581	Oregon	$2,100.00	5/24/2010	5/5/2010	19
9	AG-0600	Oregon	$335.39	5/24/2010	5/5/2010	19
10	AG-0602	Washington	$65.00	5/28/2010	5/5/2010	23
11	AG-0633	California	$250.00	5/31/2010	5/5/2010	26
12	TOTAL		$14,787.45			29
13						
14						

Figure 118-1: A negative value in column F indicates a past-due payment.

Summing only negative values

The following formula returns the sum of the negative values in column F. In other words, it returns the total number of past-due days for all invoices (for this worksheet, the formula returns –63):

```
=SUMIF(Difference,"<0")
```

The SUMIF function can use three arguments. Because you omit the third argument, the second argument ("<0") applies to the values in the Difference range.

Summing values based on a different range

The following formula returns the sum of the past-due invoice amounts (in column C):

```
=SUMIF(Difference,"<0",Amount)
```

This formula uses the values in the Difference range to determine whether the corresponding values in the Amount range contribute to the sum.

Summing values based on a text comparison

The following formula returns the total invoice amounts for the Oregon office:

```
=SUMIF(Office,"=Oregon",Amount)
```

Using the equal sign is optional. The following formula has the same result:

```
=SUMIF(Office,"Oregon",Amount)
```

To sum the invoice amounts for all offices except Oregon, use this formula:

```
=SUMIF(Office,"<>Oregon",Amount)
```

Summing values based on a date comparison

The following formula returns the total invoice amounts that have a due date of May 10, 2010, or later:

```
=SUMIF(DateDue,">="&DATE(2010,5,10),Amount)
```

Notice that the second argument for the SUMIF function is an expression. The expression uses the DATE function, which returns a date. Also, the comparison operator, enclosed in quotation marks, is concatenated (using the & operator) with the result of the DATE function.

The following formula returns the total invoice amounts that have a future due date (including today):

```
=SUMIF(DateDue,">="&TODAY(),Amount)
```

Calculating Multiple-Criterion Conditional Sums

Tip 118 contains summing examples that use a single comparison criterion. The examples in this tip involve summing cells based on multiple criteria. Because the SUMIF function doesn't work with multiple criteria, you need to use an array formula.

Figure 119-1 shows the sample worksheet again, for your reference. The formulas in this tip, of course, can be adapted to your own worksheets.

	A	B	C	D	E	F
1	**InvoiceNum**	**Office**	**Amount**	**DateDue**	**Today**	**Difference**
2	AG-0145	Oregon	$5,000.00	4/1/2010	5/5/2010	-34
3	AG-0189	California	$450.00	4/19/2010	5/5/2010	-16
4	AG-0220	Washington	$3,211.56	4/28/2010	5/5/2010	-7
5	AG-0310	Oregon	$250.00	4/30/2010	5/5/2010	-5
6	AG-0355	Washington	$125.50	5/4/2010	5/5/2010	-1
7	AG-0409	Washington	$3,000.00	5/10/2010	5/5/2010	5
8	AG-0581	Oregon	$2,100.00	5/24/2010	5/5/2010	19
9	AG-0600	Oregon	$335.39	5/24/2010	5/5/2010	19
10	AG-0602	Washington	$65.00	5/28/2010	5/5/2010	23
11	AG-0633	California	$250.00	5/31/2010	5/5/2010	26
12	TOTAL		$14,787.45			29
13						
14						

Figure 119-1: This worksheet demonstrates summing based on multiple criteria.

Using "And" criteria

Suppose that you want to get a sum of the invoice amounts that are past due *and* associated with the Oregon office. In other words, the value in the Amount range is summed only if both of these criteria are met:

➤ The corresponding value in the Difference range is negative.

➤ The corresponding text in the Office range is "Oregon".

The following formula, which uses the new SUMIFS function, does the job:

```
=SUMIFS(Amount,Difference,"<0",Office,"Oregon")
```

The first argument of the SUMIFS function is the range to be summed. Subsequent arguments come in pairs: the range on which the criterion is based, followed by the actual criterion.

If you plan to share your work with someone who uses an earlier version of Excel, you can't use the SUMIFS function. The following formula returns the same result:

```
=SUMPRODUCT(1*(Difference<0),1*(Office="Oregon"),Amount)
```

Using "Or" criteria

Suppose that you want to get a sum of past-due invoice amounts *or* ones associated with the Oregon office (regardless of their past-due status). In other words, the value in the Amount range is summed if either of the following criteria is met:

> ➤ The corresponding value in the Difference range is negative.

> ➤ The corresponding text in the Office range is "Oregon".

This type of sum requires an array formula:

```
=SUM(IF((Office="Oregon")+(Difference<0),1,0)*Amount)
```

A plus sign (+) joins the conditions, and you can include more than two conditions.

Note

When you enter an array formula, remember to press Ctrl+Shift+Enter.

Using "And" and "Or" criteria

Things get a bit tricky when your criteria consists of both And and Or operations. For example, you might want to sum the values in the Amount range when both of the following conditions are met:

> ➤ The corresponding value in the Difference range is negative.

> ➤ The corresponding text in the Office range is "Oregon" or "California".

Notice that the second condition consists of *two* conditions, joined with Or. The following array formula does the trick:

```
=SUM((Difference<0)*IF((Office="Oregon")+(Office="California"),1)*Amount)
```

Looking Up an Exact Value

The VLOOKUP and HLOOKUP functions are useful if you need to return a value from a table (in a range) by looking up another value.

The classic example of a lookup formula involves an income tax rate schedule (see Figure 120-1). The tax rate schedule shows the income tax rates for various income levels. The following formula (in cell B3) returns the tax rate for the income value in cell B2:

```
=VLOOKUP(B2,D2:F7,3)
```

◢	A	B	C	D	E	F	G
1				Income is Greater Than or Equal To...	But Less Than or Equal To...	Tax Rate	
2	Enter Income:	$45,500		$0	$2,650	15.00%	
3	The Tax Rate is:	31.00%		$2,651	$27,300	28.00%	
4				$27,301	$58,500	31.00%	
5				$58,501	$131,800	36.00%	
6				$131,801	$284,700	39.60%	
7				$284,701		45.25%	
8							
9							

Figure 120-1: Using VLOOKUP to look up a tax rate.

The tax table example demonstrates that VLOOKUP and HLOOKUP don't require an exact match between the value to be looked up and the values in the lookup table. In some cases, though, you might require a perfect match. For example, when looking up an employee number, close doesn't count. You require a perfect match for the number.

To look up only an exact value, use the VLOOKUP (or HLOOKUP) function with the optional fourth argument set to FALSE.

Figure 120-2 shows a worksheet with a lookup table that contains employee numbers (column D) and employee names (column E). The formula in cell B2, which follows, looks up the employee number entered in cell B1 and returns the corresponding employee name:

```
=VLOOKUP(B1,D1:E11,2,FALSE)
```

Because the last argument for the VLOOKUP function is FALSE, the function returns a value only if an exact match is found. If the value isn't found, the formula returns #N/A. This is exactly what you want to happen, of course, because returning an approximate match for an employee number makes no sense. Also, notice that the employee numbers in column D aren't in ascending order. If the last argument for VLOOKUP is FALSE, the values don't need to be in ascending order.

⊿	A	B	C	D	E
1	Employee No.:	983		Employee Number	Employee Name
2	Employee Name:	Peter Yates		873	Charles K. Barkley
3				1109	Francis Jenikins
4				1549	James Brackman
5				1334	Linda Harper
6				1643	Louise Victor
7				1101	Melinda Hindquest
8				1873	Michael Orenthal
9				983	Peter Yates
10				972	Sally Rice
11				1398	Walter Franklin
12					
13					

Figure 120-2: This lookup table requires an exact match.

If you prefer to see something other than #N/A when the employee number isn't found, you can use the IFERROR function to test for the #N/A result (using the ISNA function) and substitute a different string. The following formula displays the text "Not Found" rather than #N/A:

```
=IFERROR(VLOOKUP(B2,D1:E11,2,FALSE),"Not Found")
```

The IFERROR function was introduced in Excel 2007, so if your workbook must be compatible with earlier versions, use this formula:

```
=IF(ISERROR(VLOOKUP(B2,D1:E11,2,FALSE)),"Not Found",
VLOOKUP(B2,D1:E11,2,FALSE))
```

Performing a Two-Way Lookup

A two-way lookup identifies the value at the intersection of a column and a row. This tip describes two methods to perform a two-way lookup.

Using a formula

Figure 121-1 shows a worksheet with a range that displays product sales by month. To retrieve sales for a particular month and product, the user enters a month in cell B1 and a product name in cell B2.

	A	B	C	D	E	F	G	H
1	Month:	July			Widgets	Sprockets	Snapholytes	Combined
2	Product:	Sprockets		January	2,892	1,771	4,718	9,381
3				February	3,380	4,711	2,615	10,706
4	Month Offset:	8		March	3,744	3,223	5,312	12,279
5	Product Offset:	3		April	3,221	2,438	1,108	6,767
6	Sales:	3,337		May	4,839	1,999	1,994	8,832
7				June	3,767	5,140	3,830	12,737
8				July	5,467	3,337	3,232	12,036
9				August	3,154	4,895	1,607	9,656
10				September	1,718	2,040	1,563	5,321
11				October	1,548	1,061	2,590	5,199
12				November	5,083	3,558	3,960	12,601
13				December	5,753	2,839	3,013	11,605
14				Total	44,566	37,012	35,542	117,120
15								
16								

Figure 121-1: This table demonstrates a two-way lookup.

To simplify the process, the worksheet uses the following named ranges:

Name	Refers To
Month	B1
Product	B2
Table	D1:H14
MonthList	D1:D14
ProductList	D1:H1

The following formula (in cell B4) uses the MATCH function to return the position of the Month within the MonthList range. For example, if the month is January, the formula returns 2 because January is the second item in the MonthList range (the first item is a blank cell, D1):

```
=MATCH(Month,MonthList,0)
```

The formula in cell B5 works similarly but uses the ProductList range:

```
=MATCH(Product,ProductList,0)
```

The final formula, in cell B6, returns the corresponding sales amount. It uses the INDEX function with the results from cells B4 and B5:

```
=INDEX(Table,B4,B5)
```

You can combine these formulas into a single formula, as shown here:

```
=INDEX(Table,MATCH(Month,MonthList,0),MATCH(Product,ProductList,0))
```

Using implicit intersection

The second method to accomplish a two-way lookup is quite a bit simpler, but it requires that you create a name for each row and column in the table.

A quick way to name each row and column is to select the table and choose Formulas➜Defined Names➜Create From Selection. In the Create Names From Selection dialog box, specify that the names are in the top row and left column. Click OK, and Excel creates the names. After creating the names, you can use a simple formula to perform the two-way lookup, such as

```
=Sprockets July
```

This formula, which uses the range intersection operator (a space), returns July sales data for Sprockets.

Performing a Two-Column Lookup

Some situations might require a lookup based on the values in two columns. Figure 122-1 shows an example.

⊿	A	B	C	D	E	F	G
1	Make:	Jeep		**Make**	**Model**	**Code**	
2	Model:	Grand Cherokee		Chevy	Blazer	C-094	
3	Code:	J-701		Chevy	Tahoe	C-823	
4				Ford	Explorer	F-772	
5				Ford	Expedition	F-229	
6				Isuzu	Rodeo	I-897	
7				Isuzu	Trooper	I-900	
8				Jeep	Cherokee	J-983	
9				Jeep	Grand Cherokee	J-701	
10				Nissan	Pathfinder	N-231	
11				Toyota	4Runner	T-871	
12				Toyota	Land Cruiser	T-981	
13							

Figure 122-1: This workbook performs a lookup by using information in two columns (D and E).

The lookup table contains automobile makes and models and a corresponding code for each one. The technique described here allows you to look up the value based on the car's make and model.

The worksheet uses named ranges, as shown in this table:

Range	Name
F2:F12	Code
B1	Make
B2	Model
D2:D12	Range1
E2:E12	Range2

The following array formula displays the corresponding code for an automobile make and model:

```
=INDEX(Code,MATCH(Make&Model,Range1&Range2,0))
```

When you enter an array formula, press Ctrl+Shift+Enter (not just Enter).

Note

This formula works by concatenating the contents of Make and Model and then searching for this text in an array consisting of the corresponding concatenated text in Range1 and Range2.

An alternative approach is to create a new two-column lookup table, as shown in Figure 122-2. This table contains the same information as the original table, but column H contains the data from columns D and E, concatenated.

	A	B	C	D	E	F	G	H	I
1	Make:	Jeep		Make	Model	Code		MakeModel	Code
2	Model:	Grand Cherokee		Chevy	Blazer	C-094		ChevyBlazer	C-094
3	Code:	J-701		Chevy	Tahoe	C-823		ChevyTahoe	C-823
4				Ford	Explorer	F-772		FordExplorer	F-772
5				Ford	Expedition	F-229		FordExpedition	F-229
6				Isuzu	Rodeo	I-897		IsuzuRodeo	I-897
7				Isuzu	Trooper	I-900		IsuzuTrooper	I-900
8				Jeep	Cherokee	J-983		JeepCherokee	J-983
9				Jeep	Grand Cherokee	J-701		JeepGrand Cherokee	J-701
10				Nissan	Pathfinder	N-231		NissanPathfinder	N-231
11				Toyota	4Runner	T-871		Toyota4Runner	T-871
12				Toyota	Land Cruiser	T-981		ToyotaLand Cruiser	T-981
13									

Figure 122-2: Avoid a two-column lookup by combing two columns into one.

After you create this new table, you can use a simpler formula to perform the lookup:

```
=VLOOKUP(Make&Model,H1:I12,2)
```

Performing a Lookup by Using an Array

If your lookup table is small, you might be able to avoid using a table altogether and store the lookup information in an array. This tip describes a typical lookup problem that uses a standard lookup table — and an alternative method that uses an array.

Using a lookup table

Figure 123-1 shows a worksheet with student test scores. The range E2:F6 (named GradeList) displays a lookup table used to assign a letter grade to a test score.

	A	B	C	D	E	F
1	**Student**	**Score**	**Grade**		**Score**	**Grade**
2	Adams	36	F		0	F
3	Baker	68	D		40	D
4	Camden	50	D		70	C
5	Dailey	77	C		80	B
6	Gomez	92	A		90	A
7	Hernandez	100	A			
8	Jackson	74	C			
9	Maplethorpe	45	D			
10	Paulson	60	D			
11	Ramirez	89	B			
12	Sosa	99	A			
13	Thompson	91	A			
14	Wilson	59	D			
15						
16						

Figure 123-1: Looking up letter grades for test scores.

Column C contains formulas that use the VLOOKUP function and the lookup table to assign a grade based on the score in column B. The formula in C2, for example, is

```
=VLOOKUP(B2,GradeList,2)
```

Using an array

When the lookup table is small (as in this example), you can use a literal array in place of the lookup table. Using an array in lieu of a table can remove a bit of clutter on your worksheet. The following formula, for example, returns a letter grade without using a lookup table. Rather, the information in the lookup table is hard-coded into an array constant. Note the use of curly braces to indicate the array and note the use of semicolons to separate rows:

```
=VLOOKUP(B2,{0,"F";40,"D";70,"C";80,"B";90,"A"},2)
```

Another approach, which uses a more legible formula, is to use the LOOKUP function with two array arguments:

```
=LOOKUP(B2,{0,40,70,80,90},{"F","D","C","B","A"})
```

Note

The preceding formulas use arrays as arguments, but they're not array formulas. Therefore, you don't need to use Ctrl+Shift+Enter when you enter these formulas.

Using the INDIRECT Function

To make a formula more flexible, you can use the Excel INDIRECT function to create a range reference. This rarely used function accepts a text argument that resembles a range reference and then converts the argument to an actual range reference. When you understand how this function works, you can use it to create more powerful interactive spreadsheets.

Specifying rows indirectly

Figure 124-1 shows an example that uses the INDIRECT function. The formula in cell E5 is

```
=SUM(INDIRECT("B"&E2&":B"&E3))
```

	A	B	C	D	E	F
1	Month	Sales				
2	January	55,045		First Row:	2	
3	February	53,391		Last Row:	4	
4	March	48,545				
5	April	50,841		SUM:	156,981	
6	May	48,488				
7	June	51,460				
8	July	49,678				
9	August	54,624				
10	September	48,078				
11	October	53,907				
12	November	51,653				
13	December	50,724				
14						

Figure 124-1: Using the INDIRECT function to sum user-supplied rows.

Notice that the argument for the INDIRECT function uses the concatenation operator to build a range reference by using the values in cells E2 and E3. So, if E2 contains 2 and E3 contains 4, the range reference evaluates to this string:

```
"B2:B4"
```

The INDIRECT function converts that string to an actual range reference, which is then passed to the SUM function. In effect, the formula returns

```
=SUM(B2:B4)
```

When you change the values in E2 or E3, the formula is updated to display the sum of the specified rows.

Specifying worksheet names indirectly

Figure 124-2 shows another example, this time using a worksheet reference.

Column A, on the Summary worksheet, contains text that corresponds to other worksheets in the workbook. Column B contains formulas that reference these text items. For example, the formula in cell B2 is

```
=SUM(INDIRECT(A2&"!F1:F10"))
```

Figure 124-2: Using the INDIRECT function to create references.

This formula concatenates the text in A2 with a range reference. The INDIRECT function evaluates the result and converts it to an actual range reference. The result is equivalent to this formula:

```
=SUM(North!F1:F10)
```

That formula is copied down the column. Each formula returns the sum of range F1:F10 on the corresponding worksheet.

Making a cell reference unchangeable

Another use for the INDIRECT function is to create a reference to a cell that never changes. For example, consider this formula, which sums the values in the first 12 rows of column A:

```
=SUM(A1:A12)
```

If you insert a new row 1, Excel changes the formula to

```
=SUM(A2:A13)
```

In other words, the formula adjusts so that it continues to refer to the original data (and it no longer sums the first 12 rows of column A). To prevent Excel from changing the cell references, use the INDIRECT function:

```
=SUM(INDIRECT("A1:A12"))
```

This formula *always* returns the sum of the first 12 rows in column A.

Creating Megaformulas

This tip describes a method of combining several intermediate formulas to create a single long formula (a *megaformula*). If you've used Excel for a while, you might have seen some lengthy formulas that were virtually incomprehensible. Here, you learn how they were created.

The goal is to create a single formula that removes the middle name (for example, Billy Joe Shaver becomes Billy Shaver). Figure 125-1 shows a worksheet with some names, plus six columns of intermediate formulas that accomplish the goal. Notice that the formulas aren't perfect; they can't handle a single-word name.

	A	B	C	D	E	F	G	H	I	J
1	Name	Formula-1	Formula-2	Formula-3	Formula-4	Formula-5	Formula-6	Result		Megaformula
2	Bob Smith	Bob Smith	4	#VALUE!	4	Bob	Smith	Bob Smith		Bob Smith
3	Mike A. Jones	Mike A. Jones	5	8	8	Mike	Jones	Mike Jones		Mike Jones
4	Cher	Cher	#VALUE!	#VALUE!	#VALUE!	#VALUE!	#VALUE!	#VALUE!		#VALUE!
5	Tom Alvin Jacobs	Tom Alvin Jacobs	4	10	10	Tom	Jacobs	Tom Jacobs		Tom Jacobs
6	John Q. Public	John Q. Public	5	8	8	John	Public	John Public		John Public
7	R.J Smith	R.J Smith	4	#VALUE!	4	R.J	Smith	R.J Smith		R.J Smith
8	R. Jay Smith	R. Jay Smith	3	7	7	R.	Smith	R. Smith		R. Smith
9	Tim Jones	Tim Jones	4	#VALUE!	4	Tim	Jones	Tim Jones		Tim Jones
10										

Figure 125-1: Removing the middle names and initials requires six intermediate formulas — or one megaformula.

The formulas in row 2 are listed in Table 125-1.

Table 125-1: Intermediate Formulas

Cell	Intermediate Formula	What It Does
B2	=TRIM(A2)	Removes excess spaces
C2	=FIND(" ",B2,1)	Locates the first space
D2	=FIND(" ",B2,C2+1)	Locates the second space, if any
E2	=IFERROR(D2,C2)	Uses the first space if no second space exists
F2	=LEFT(B2,C2)	Extracts the first name
G2	=RIGHT(B2,LEN(B2)-E2)	Extracts the last name
H2	=F2&G2	Concatenates the two names

With a bit of work, you can eliminate all of the intermediate formulas and replace them with a single megaformula. You do so by creating all the intermediate formulas and then editing the final result formula (in this case, the formula in column H) by replacing each cell reference with a copy of the formula in the cell that's referred to. Fortunately, you can use the Clipboard to copy and paste the formulas rather than type them over again. Keep repeating this process until cell H1 contains nothing other than references to cell A1. You end up with the following megaformula in one cell:

```
=LEFT(TRIM(A2),FIND(" ",TRIM(A2),1))&
RIGHT(TRIM(A2),LEN(TRIM(A2))-
IFERROR(FIND(" ",TRIM(A2),FIND(" ",TRIM(A2),1)+1),
FIND(" ",TRIM(A2),1)))
```

When you're satisfied that the megaformula works, you can delete the columns that hold the intermediate formulas because they're no longer used.

If you're still not clear about this process, take a look at the step-by-step procedure:

1. Examine the formula in H2.

    This formula contains two cell references (F2 and G2):

    ```
    =F2&G2
    ```

2. Activate cell G2 and copy the contents of the formula (without the equal sign) to the Clipboard.

3. Activate cell H2 and replace the reference to cell G2 with the Clipboard contents.

    Now cell H2 contains the following formula:

    ```
    =F2&RIGHT(B2,LEN(B2)-E2)
    ```

4. Activate cell F2 and copy the contents of the formula (without the equal sign) to the Clipboard.

5. Activate cell H2 and replace the reference to cell F2 with the Clipboard contents.

    Now the formula in cell H2 is

    ```
    =LEFT(B2,C2)&RIGHT(B2,LEN(B2)-E2)
    ```

6. Now cell H2 contains references to three cells (B2, C2, and E2).

    The formulas in those cells replace each of the references to those cells.

7. Replace the reference to cell E2 with the formula in E2.

    The result is

    ```
    =LEFT(B2,C2)&RIGHT(B2,LEN(B2)-IFERROR(D2,C2))
    ```

8. Copy the formula from D2 and replace the references to cell D2.

   The formula now looks like this:

   ```
   =LEFT(B2,C2)&RIGHT(B2,LEN(B2)-IFERROR(FIND(" ",B2,C2+1},C2))
   ```

   The formula has three references to cell C2.

9. Replace each of those references with the formula contained in cell C2.

   The formula in cell H2 is

   ```
   =LEFT(B2,FIND(" ",B2,1))&RIGHT(B2,LEN(B2)-IFERROR(FIND(" ",B2,FIND
   (" ",B2,1)+1),FIND(" ",B2,1)))
   ```

10. Finally, replace the seven references to cell B2 with the formula in cell B2.

    The result is

    ```
    =LEFT(TRIM(A2),FIND(" ",TRIM(A2),1))&
    RIGHT(TRIM(A2),LEN(TRIM(A2))-
    IFERROR(FIND(" ",TRIM(A2),FIND(" ",TRIM(A2),1)+1),
    FIND(" ",TRIM(A2),1)))
    ```

Notice that the formula in cell H2 now contains references only to cell A2. The megaformula is complete, and it performs exactly same tasks as all the intermediate formulas (which you can now delete).

You can, of course, adapt this technique to your own needs. A nice byproduct is that a single megaformula often calculates faster than a series of formulas does.

Note

While you're replacing the cell references with formula text, make sure that the formula continues to display the correct result after each replacement. In some situations, you might need to enclose the copied formula in parentheses.

Conversions and Mathematical Calculations

This part provides you with a variety of handy measurement conversion tables and several calculations that you might find useful as you work away in Excel 2010.

Tips and Where to Find Them

Converting Between Measurement Systems

You know the distance from New York to London in miles, but your European office needs the numbers in kilometers. What's the conversion factor?

The Excel CONVERT function can convert between a variety of measurements in these categories:

➤ Weight and mass

➤ Distance

➤ Time

➤ Pressure

➤ Force

➤ Energy

➤ Power

➤ Magnetism

➤ Temperature

➤ Liquid measures

New Feature

In versions prior to Excel 2007, the CONVERT function required the Analysis ToolPak add-in. This useful function is now built in, and an add-in is not required.

The CONVERT function requires three arguments: the value to be converted, the from-unit, and the to-unit. For example, if cell A1 contains a distance expressed in miles, use this formula to convert miles to kilometers:

```
=CONVERT(A1,"mi","km")
```

The second and third arguments are unit abbreviations, which are listed in the Help system. Some abbreviations are commonly used, but others aren't. And, of course, you must use the *exact* abbreviation. Furthermore, the unit abbreviations are case sensitive, so the following formula returns an error:

```
=CONVERT(A1,"Mi","km")
```

The CONVERT function is even more versatile than it seems. When using metric units, you can apply a multiplier. In fact, the first example I presented uses a multiplier. The unit abbreviation for the third argument is *m,* for meters. I added the kilo-multiplier — *k* — to express the result in kilometers.

In some situations, the CONVERT function requires some creativity. For example, what if you need to convert ten square yards to square feet? Neither of these units is available, but the following formula does the job:

```
=CONVERT(CONVERT(10,"yd","ft"),"yd","ft")
```

The nested instance of CONVERT converts ten yards into feet, and this result (30) is used as the first argument of the outer instance of the function. Similarly, to convert ten cubic yards into unit cubic feet, use this formula:

```
=CONVERT(CONVERT(CONVERT(10,"yd","ft"),"yd","ft"),"yd","ft")
```

Converting Temperatures

This tip presents formulas for conversion among three units of temperature: Fahrenheit, Celsius, and Kelvin.

The formulas in Table 127-1 assume that the temperature for conversion is in a cell named temp.

Table 127-1: Temperature Conversion Formulas

Type of Conversion	Formula
Fahrenheit to Celsius	=(temp-32)*(5/9)
Fahrenheit to Kelvin	=(temp-32)*(5/9)+273
Celsius to Fahrenheit	=(temp*1.8)+32
Celsius to Kelvin	=temp+273
Kelvin to Celsius	=temp-273
Kelvin to Fahrenheit	=((temp-273)*1.8)+32

Solving Simultaneous Equations

This tip describes how to use formulas to solve simultaneous linear equations. The following example shows a set of simultaneous linear equations:

```
3x + 4y = 8
4x + 8y = 1
```

Solving a set of simultaneous equations involves finding the values for *x* and *y* that satisfy both equations. This set of equations has one solution:

```
x = 7.5
y = -3.625
```

The number of variables in the set of equations must be equal to the number of equations. The preceding example uses two equations with two variables. Three equations are required in order to solve for three variables (*x, y,* and *z*).

The general steps for solving a set of simultaneous equations follow. See Figure 128-1, which uses the equations presented in the first paragraph of this tip.

Figure 128-1: Using formulas to solve a set of two simultaneous equations.

1. Express the equations in standard form.

    If necessary, use basic algebra to rewrite the equations so that all variables appear on the left side of the equal sign. The following two equations are identical, but the second one is in standard form:

```
3x -8 = -4y
3x + 4y = 8
```

2. Place the coefficients in an *n*-by-*n* range of cells, where *n* represents the number of equations.

   In Figure 128-1, the coefficients are in the range I2:J3.

3. Place the constants (the numbers on the right side of the equal sign) in a vertical range of cells.

   In Figure 128-1, the constants are in the range L2:L3.

4. Use an array formula to calculate the inverse of the coefficient matrix.

   In Figure 128-1, the following array formula is entered into the range I6:J7. (Remember to press Ctrl+Shift+Enter to enter an array formula.)

   ```
   =MINVERSE(I2:J3)
   ```

5. Use an array formula to multiply the inverse of the coefficient matrix by the constant matrix.

   In Figure 128-1, the following array formula is entered into the range J10:J11. This range holds the solution (x = 7.5, and y = –3.625).

   ```
   =MMULT(I6:J7,L2:L3)
   ```

Figure 128-2 shows a worksheet set up to solve a set of three simultaneous equations.

Figure 128-2: Using formulas to solve a set of three simultaneous equations.

Solving Recursive Equations

A *recursive* equation is an equation in which a variable appears on both sides of the equal sign. The following equations are examples of recursive equations:

```
x = 1/(x+1)
x = COS(x)
x = SQRT(X+5)
x = 2^(1/x)
x = 5 + (1/x)
```

You can solve a recursive equation by using an intentional circular reference.

Note

This technique uses iterative calculations. By default, Excel doesn't perform iterative calculations, so you need to change a setting, by selecting the Enable Iterative Calculation check box on the Formulas tab of the Excel Options dialog box (see Figure 129-1).

Figure 129-1: To solve a recursive equation, you must specify the Enable Iterative Calculation option.

The first step is to convert the recursive equation into a self-referencing formula. To solve the first equation, enter the following formula into cell A1:

```
=1/(A1+1)
```

The formula converges at 0.618033989, which is the value of *x* that satisfies the equation.

Note

Excel uses an iterative process to calculate the solution. The maximum number of iterations performed for each calculation is specified in Formulas tab of the Excel Options dialog box. You might need to press F9 several times before the solution stops changing.

Sometimes, this technique doesn't work. For example, the formula allows the possibility of a division-by-zero error. The solution is to check for an error. If the formula displays an error, modify the iterated value slightly. For example, the preceding formula can be rewritten using the IFERROR function:

```
=IFERROR(1/(A1+1),A1+0.01)
```

IFERROR works only with Excel 2007 and later. The following version of the formula is compatible with previous versions of Excel:

```
=IF(ISERR(1/(A1+1)),A1+0.01,1/(A1+1))
```

Figure 129-2 shows a worksheet that calculates several recursive equations in column B. The formulas in column D provide a check of the results. For example, the formula in column D2 is

```
=1/(B2+1)
```

Formulas in column E display the difference between the values in column B and column D. If the solution is correct, column E displays a zero (or a value very close to zero).

	A	B	C	D	E
1	Equation	Circular Ref Formula		Check	Difference
2	x = 1/(x+1)	0.618033989		0.6180340	0.000000000
3	x = COS(x)	0.739085133		0.7390851	0.000000000
4	x = SQRT(X+5)	2.791287847		2.7912878	0.000000000
5	x = 2^(1/x)	1.559610469		1.5596105	0.000000000
6	x = 5+(1/x)	5.192582404		5.1925824	0.000000000
7					
8					

Figure 129-2: This workbook uses circular references to calculate several recursive equations.

Generating Random Numbers

Random numbers are often useful in spreadsheet applications. For example, you can fill a range with random numbers in order to test formulas. Or, you can generate random numbers to simulate various processes.

Excel provides several ways to generate random numbers.

Using the RAND function

The Excel RAND function generates a uniform random number between 0 and 1. In other words, every number between 0 and 1 has an equal probability of being returned by the function.

If you need larger random numbers, just use a simple multiplication formula. The following formula, for example, generates a uniform random number between 0 and 1000:

```
=RAND()*1000
```

To limit the random number to whole numbers, use the ROUND function:

```
=ROUND((RAND()*1000),0)
```

Using the RANDBETWEEN function

To generate uniform random integers between any two numbers, you can use the RANDBETWEEN function. The following formula, for example, generates a random number between 100 and 200:

```
=RANDBETWEEN(100,200)
```

In versions prior to Excel 2007, the RANDBETWEEN function is available only when the Analysis Toolpak add-in is installed. For compatibility with previous versions (and to avoid using the add-in), use a formula like the following, where a represents the lower limit and b represents the upper limit:

```
=RAND()*(b-a)+a
```

To generate a random number between 40 and 50, use this formula:

```
=RAND()*(50-40)+40
```

Using the Analysis Toolpak add-in

Another way of getting random numbers into a worksheet is to use the Analysis Toolpak add-in (an add-in that's included with Excel). This tool can generate non-uniform random numbers. These numbers aren't generated by formulas, so if you want a new set of random numbers, you need to rerun the procedure.

Access the Analysis Toolpak add-in by choosing Data➜Analysis➜Data Analysis. If this command isn't available, install the Analysis Toolpak by using the Add-Ins dialog box. The easiest way to display this dialog box is to press Atl+TI.

In the Data Analysis dialog box, select the Random Number Generation option and click OK. The dialog box shown in Figure 130-1 appears.

Figure 130-1: The Random Number Generation dialog box.

Choose a distribution from the Distribution drop-down list and then specify additional parameters (the parameters vary, depending on the distribution). Don't forget to specify the Output Range, which stores the random numbers.

Calculating Roots

If you need to calculate the square root of a value, use the SQRT function. The following formula, for example, calculates the square root of the value in cell A1:

```
=SQRT(A1)
```

What about other roots? You won't find a CUBEROOT function, and there certainly isn't a FOURTHROOT function. The trick is to raise the number to the (1/root) power. For example, to calculate the cube root of the value in cell A1, use this formula:

```
=A1^(1/3)
```

To calculate the fourth root, use this formula:

```
=A1^(1/4)
```

Calculating a Remainder

When you divide two numbers, if the result isn't a whole number, you end up with a remainder. When Excel performs division, the result is a decimal value. How can you determine the remainder (if any) that results from a division?

The solution is to use the MOD function, which takes two arguments: the number and the divisor. The MOD function returns the remainder.

For example, if you have 187 books to be divided equally among 5 offices, how many will be left over? Use this formula to determine the number of books per office (which is 37):

```
=INT(187/5)
```

Use this formula to calculate how many books will be left over (which is 2):

```
=MOD(187,5)
```

PART VII

Charts and Graphics

A well-conceived chart can make a range of incomprehensible numbers make sense. The tips in this part deal with various aspects of chart making.

Tips and Where to Find Them

Creating a Text Chart Directly in a Range

Tip 54 presents an example of the Data Bars Conditional Formatting option, which enables you to create a simple bar chart directly in a range of cells. The Data Bars feature is quick and easy, but if you share your workbook with others who use a version prior to Excel 2007, they will not see the Data Bars.

This tip describes another way to create a bar chart directly in a range. Figure 133-1 shows an example of a chart created by using formulas.

	A	B	C	D
1				
2		Month	Employees	Graphic
3		January	60	******************************
4		February	64	********************************
5		March	62	*******************************
6		April	67	**********************************
7		May	71	***********************************
8		June	72	************************************
9		July	77	***************************************
10		August	79	**
11		September	79	**
12		October	80	**
13		November	81	***
14		December	89	**
15				

Figure 133-1: A histogram created directly in a range of cells.

Column D contains formulas that feature the rarely used REPT function, which repeats a text string a specified number of times. For example, the following formula displays five asterisks:

```
=REPT("*",5)
```

In the example shown in Figure 133-1, cell D3 contains this formula, which was copied down the column:

```
=REPT("*",C3/2)
```

Notice that the formula divides the value in column C by 2. This is a way to scale the chart. Instead of displaying 60 asterisks, the cell displays 30 asterisks. For improved accuracy, you can use the ROUND function:

```
=REPT("*",ROUND(C3/2,0))
```

Without the ROUND function, the formula *truncates* the result of the division (disregards the decimal part of the argument). For example, the value 67 in column C displays 33 characters in column D. Using ROUND rounds up the result to 34 characters.

You can use this type of graphical display in place of a column chart. As long as you don't require strict accuracy (because of rounding errors), this type of nonchart might fit the bill.

Figure 133-2 shows some other examples that use different characters and fonts. The chart that displays the solid bars (beginning in row 39) uses the pipe character of the Script font. On most keyboards, the pipe character is generated when you press Shift+Backslash. The formula in cell D39 is

```
=REPT("|",C39/2000)
```

Figure 133-2: Examples of in-cell charting using the REPT function.

The example in Figure 133-3 uses formulas in columns F and H to graphically depict monthly budget variances by displaying a series of characters. You can then easily see which budget items are under or over budget. This pseudo bar chart uses the character *n*, which appears as a small square in the Wingdings font.

The key formulas are

```
F3:  =IF(D3<0,REPT("n",-ROUND(D3*100,0)),"")
G3:  =A3
H3:  =IF(D3>0,REPT("n",-ROUND(D3*-100,0)),"")
```

	A	B	C	D	E	F	G	H
1								
2	Month	Budget	Actual	Pct. Diff		Under Budget		Exceeded Budget
3	Jan	300	311	3.7%			Jan	■■■■
4	Feb	300	343	14.3%			Feb	■■■■■■■■■■■■■■
5	Mar	300	305	1.7%			Mar	■■
6	Apr	350	351	0.3%			Apr	
7	May	350	402	14.9%			May	■■■■■■■■■■■■■■■
8	Jun	350	409	16.9%			Jun	■■■■■■■■■■■■■■■■
9	Jul	500	421	-15.8%		■■■■■■■■■■■■■■■■	Jul	
10	Aug	500	454	-9.2%		■■■■■■■■■	Aug	
11	Sep	500	474	-5.2%		■■■■■	Sep	
12	Oct	500	521	4.2%			Oct	■■■■
13	Nov	500	476	-4.8%		■■■■■	Nov	
14	Dec	500	487	-2.6%		■■■	Dec	
15								

Figure 133-3: Displaying monthly budget variances by using the REPT function.

For this example, follow these steps to set up the bar chart after entering the preceding formulas:

1. Assign the Wingdings font to cells F3 and H3.
2. Copy the formulas down columns F, G, and H to accommodate all the data.
3. Right-align the text in column E and adjust any other formatting.

Depending on the numerical range of your data, you might need to change the scaling. Experiment by replacing the 100 value in the formulas. You can substitute any character you like for the *n* in the formulas to produce a different character in the chart.

Selecting Elements in a Chart

An Excel chart consists of a number of different elements. For example, all charts contain a plot area and at least one data series. A chart can also contain elements such as a chart title, axes, data labels, and so on. To work with a particular chart element, you need to select it — something that is often easier said than done.

Excel provides three ways to select a particular chart element:

> ➤ Use the mouse.

> ➤ Use the keyboard.

> ➤ Use the Chart Elements control.

Selecting with the mouse

To select a chart element with your mouse, just click it. The chart element appears with small circles at the corners.

To ensure that you selected the chart element you intended to select, view the Chart Element control, located in the Chart Tools➜Format➜Current Selection group on the Ribbon. Also, notice that when you move the mouse over a chart, a small chart tip displays the name of the chart element under the mouse pointer. Figure 134-1 shows the Chart Elements control and the tooltip when a chart's vertical axis is selected.

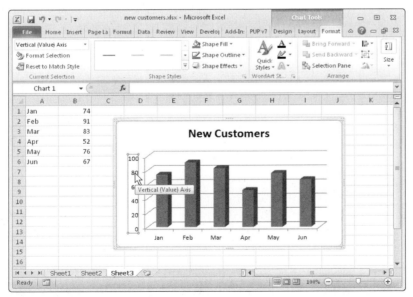

Figure 134-1: The Chart Element control displays the name of the selected chart element, and a tooltip also describes the selection. In this example, Vertical (Value) Axis is selected.

Note

If these chart tips annoy you, you can turn them off. Choose File➜Options and click the Advanced tab in the Excel Options dialog box. Locate the Chart section and deselect either or both of the check boxes labeled Show Chart Element Names On Hover or Show Data Point Values On Hover.

Some chart elements (such as a series, legend, or data label) consist of multiple items. For example, a chart series element is made up of individual data points. To select a particular data point, click twice: First click the series to select it; then click the specific element within the series (such as a column or a line chart marker). Selecting the element enables you to apply formatting to only a particular data point in a series.

You might find that some chart elements are difficult to select with the mouse. If you rely on the mouse for selecting a chart element, you might have to click it several times before the element you want is selected. Fortunately, Excel provides other ways to select a chart element, and it's worth your while to be familiar with them.

Selecting with the keyboard

When a chart is active, you can use the up-arrow and down-arrow keys on your keyboard to cycle among the chart's elements. Again, keep your eye on the Chart Elements control, to ensure that the selected chart element is what you think it is.

When a chart series is selected, use the left-arrow and right-arrow keys to select an individual item within the series. Similarly, when a set of data labels is selected, you can select a specific data label by pressing the left-arrow or right-arrow key. And, when a legend is selected, you can select individual elements within the legend by using the left-arrow or right-arrow key.

Selecting with the Chart Element control

The Chart Element control is so useful, that it's available in three locations:

> In the Chart Tools➜Layout➜Current Selection group of the Ribbon

> In the Chart Tools➜Format➜Current Selection group of the Ribbon

> In the Mini Toolbar that appears when you right-click a chart element

This control displays the name of the selected chart element. Because it's a drop-down control, you can also use it to select a particular element in the active chart. Figure 134-2 shows the Chart Element control in the Mini Toolbar.

This control lists only the top-level elements in the chart. To select an individual data point within a series, for example, you need to select the series and then use the left and right arrow keys (or your mouse) to select the data point.

Figure 134-2: Using the Chart Element drop-down control to select a chart element.

Note

When a single data point is selected, the Chart Element control *will* display the name of the selected element, even though it's not available for selection in the drop-down list.

If you do a lot of work with charts, you might want to add the Chart Element to yet another location: your Quick Access toolbar. That way, it's always visible regardless of which Ribbon tab is selected. To add the control to your Quick Access toolbar, right-click the down-arrow in the control, and choose Add to Quick Access Toolbar.

Creating a Self-Expanding Chart

This tip describes how to create a chart that expands automatically when you add new data to a worksheet. Figure 135-1 illustrates the problem: The chart displays all data in the sheet. But when new data is entered, the chart series must be manually expanded to include the new data. It would be nice if Excel could do this automatically.

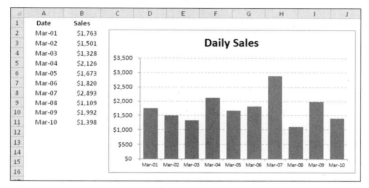

Figure 135-1: If this chart were self-expanding, it would update automatically when additional data is entered.

Excel can do it, and it's very easy. The trick is to make sure that the data the chart uses is in a table. If your chart is using data that's not in a table, select the data and choose Insert➡ Tables➡Tables to convert the range to a table.

That's all there is to it. Excel recognizes the data as a table, and data added to the table is shown in the chart. And if you delete rows from the top or bottom of the table, the chart also adjusts accordingly.

Creating Combination Charts

Typically, a chart uses a single style: a column chart, a line chart, or a pie chart, for example. If your chart has more than one data series, you might want to display multiple styles within the same chart — a combination chart. Figure 136-1 shows a chart that's a good candidate for a combination chart. The chart shows average temperature and precipitation, by month. But there's a problem. The two ranges of data vary in magnitude, so the precipitation columns are barely visible in the chart.

Figure 136-1: This chart would be more effective as a combination chart.

Figure 136-2 shows the chart after I converted it to a combination chart. In this chart, the precipitation values are depicted with a line, and it uses a second vertical axis on the right. Most would agree that this chart is a vast improvement over the original.

Figure 136-2: This combination chart displays two data series that vary in magnitude.

You can search the Excel Ribbon all day, and you won't find a command to create a combination chart. If you already created your chart (that has at least two data series), you can easily convert it to a combination chart. Follow these steps:

1. Click the series that you want to change.

2. Choose Chart Tools→Design→Type→Change Chart Type.

3. In the Change Chart Type dialog box, choose the icon that represents the chart type for the selected series.

4. If you'd like to use a second vertical axis for the converted series, select the series and press Ctrl+1 to display the Format Data Series dialog box; click the Series Options tab and select Secondary Axis.

The chart in Figure 136-1 started out as a standard column chart with two series. A few mouse clicks later, one of the series (named Precipitation, in this case) is converted from columns to a line. I also added a secondary axis and labeled the axes to make it perfectly clear which scale is used for which series. To add axis titles, use Chart Tools→Layout→Axis Titles.

Figure 136-3 shows another combination chart. This chart combines a column chart and a line chart, and both series use the same vertical axis. In this case, depicting the monthly sales goal as a line chart makes it easier to identify the months in which the goal was met.

Figure 136-3: A combination chart that uses a single vertical axis.

Figure 136-4 shows how far you can go with a combination chart. This chart combines five different chart types: Pie, Area, Column, Line, and XY. I can't think of any situation that would warrant such a chart, but it's an interesting demo.

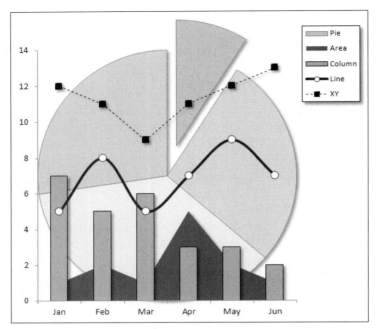

Figure 136-4: A five-way combination chart.

In some cases, you can't combine chart types. For example, you can't create a combination chart that involves a bubble chart or a 3-D chart. If you choose an incompatible chart type for the series, Excel lets you know.

Creating a Gantt Chart

A *Gantt chart* is a horizontal bar chart that's often used in project management applications. Although Excel doesn't support Gantt charts per se, creating a simple Gantt chart is fairly easy. The key is setting up your data properly.

Figure 137-1 shows a Gantt chart created from the data in the range A2:C13. In the chart, the horizontal axis represents the total time span of the project, and each bar represents a project task. The viewer can quickly see the duration for each task and identify overlapping tasks.

Figure 137-1: You can create a simple Gantt chart from a stacked bar chart.

Column A contains the task name, column B contains the corresponding start date, and column C contains the duration of the task, in days. Note that cell A1 does *not* have a descriptive label. Leaving that cell empty ensures that Excel does not use columns A and B as the category axis.

Follow these steps to create this chart:

1. Select the range A1:C13, choose Insert➜Charts➜Bar, and select the Stacked Bar Chart option.

2. Delete the legend.

3. Select the category (vertical) axis, and press Ctrl+1 to display the Format Axis dialog box.

4. In the Format Axis dialog box, click the Axis Options tab and specify Categories in Reverse Order to display the tasks in order, starting at the top; choose Horizontal Axis Crosses at Maximum Category to display the dates at the bottom.

5. Select the Start Date data series and display the Format Data Series dialog box.

6. In the Format Data Series dialog box, click the Fill tab and specify No Fill; click the Border Color tab and specify No Line.

   These steps effectively hide the data series.

7. Select the value (horizontal) axis and display the Format Axis dialog box.

8. In the Format Axis dialog box, adjust the Minimum and Maximum settings to accommodate the dates that you want to display on the axis.

   In this example, the minimum is 5/3/2010, and the maximum is 7/21/2010.

9. Specify **7** for the Major Unit option, to display one-week intervals, and use the Number tab to specify a date format for the axis labels.

10. Apply other formatting as desired.

Creating a Gauge Chart

In some cases, you might want to depict, graphically, progress towards a goal. One way to do that is by using a gauge chart, as shown in Figure 138-1. There's only one problem: Excel doesn't have a gauge chart! But Excel does have a pie chart. In this tip, I describe how to use a pie chart to display a single value that ranges between 0 and 100 percent.

Figure 138-1: This chart resembles a speedometer gauge and displays a value between 0 and 100 percent.

The chart depicts the value in cell F1, which contains this formula:

```
=SUM(B4:B18)/500
```

The pie chart actually uses three data points (in H2:H4).

One slice of the pie — the slice at the bottom, represented by cell H4 — always consists of 50 percent. I rotated the pie so that the 50 percent slice was at the bottom. Then I hid that slice, by specifying No Fill and No Border for the data point.

The other two slices are apportioned based on the value in cell F11. The formula in cell H2 is

```
=MIN(F1,100%)/2
```

This formula uses the MIN function to display the smaller of two values: either the value in cell F1 or 100 percent. It then divides this value by 2 because only the top half of the pie is relevant. Using the MIN function prevents the chart from displaying more than 100 percent.

The formula in cell H3 calculates the remaining part of the pie — the part to the right of the gauge's "needle":

```
=50%-H2
```

Following are the steps I took to create this gauge chart:

1. Select range H2:H4, choose Insert→Charts→Pie, and then choose the standard pie chart icon.

2. Delete the chart's legend.

3. Click the pie and press Ctrl+F1 to display the Format Data Series dialog box.

4. In the Format Data Series dialog box, click the Series Options tab and specify a rotation value of 270.

    This puts the 50 percent slice at the bottom of the pie.

5. Click the bottom slice of the pie, to select only that slice.

6. In the Format Data Point dialog box, click the Fill tab and choose No Fill.

    This step hides the 50 percent slice. At this point, two slices are visible.

7. Select the slice on the right, click the Border Color tab in the Format Data Point dialog box, and choose Solid Line.

8. With the same data point selected, click the Fill tab in the Format Data Point dialog box and choose No Fill.

9. Choose Chart→Layout→Chart Title to add a title to the chart; move the title below the visible pie slices.

10. Select the chart title, type an equal sign, and then click in cell F2.

    A linked title displays the percent complete.

11. Use Insert→Text→Text Box to add other text boxes to display the 0%, 100%, and Percent Complete labels.

12. Apply other cosmetic adjustments, as desired.

Using Pictures in Charts

Excel makes it easy to incorporate a pattern, texture, or graphical file for elements in your chart. Figure 139-1 shows a chart that uses a photo as the background for a chart's Chart Area element.

Figure 139-1: The Chart Area contains a photo.

To display an image in a chart element, use the Fill tab in the element's Format dialog box. (Press Ctrl+1 to display this dialog box.) Select the Picture or Text Fill option and then click the button that corresponds to the image source (File, Clipboard, or Clip Art). If you use the Clipboard button, make sure that you copied your image first. The other two options prompt you to supply the image.

Figure 139-2 shows two more examples: a pie chart that uses Office clip art as the fill in the Plot Area, and a column chart that uses a shape, which was inserted on a worksheet and then copied to the Clipboard.

Using images in a chart offers unlimited potential for creativity. The key, of course, is to resist the temptation to go overboard. A chart's primary goal is to convey information, not to impress the viewer with your artistic skills. Also, remember that using images, especially photos, in charts can dramatically increase the size of your workbooks.

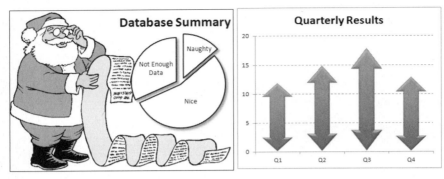

Figure 139-2: The left chart uses clip art, and the right chart uses a shape that was copied to the Clipboard.

Plotting Mathematical Functions

An Excel chart is a good way to display a mathematical or trigonometric function plot. This tip describes two function-plotting techniques:

> ➤ Plot a single-variable function by using a scatter chart.
> ➤ Plot a two-variable function by using a 3-D surface chart.

Plotting single-variable mathematical functions

A *scatter chart* (known as an XY chart in previous versions of Excel) displays a marker for each set of paired values. For example, Figure 140-1 shows a plot of the SIN function. The chart plots the calculated y value for values of x (expressed in radians) from −5 to +5 in increments of 0.5. Each pair of x and y values appears as a data point in the chart, and the points are connected by a line.

Figure 140-1: This chart plots the SIN(x).

The function is expressed as

```
y = SIN(x)
```

The corresponding formula in cell B2 (which is copied to the cells below) is

```
=SIN(A2)
```

To create this chart, follow these steps:

1. Select A1:B22.

2. Choose Insert→Charts→Scatter→Scatter with Straight Lines and Markers.

3. Choose a chart layout that gives you the look you like and then fine-tune it.

Change the values in column A to plot the function for different values of x. And, of course, you can use any single-variable formula you like in column B. Here are a few examples that make interesting plots:

```
=SIN(PI()*A2)*(PI()*A2)
=SIN(A2)/A2
=SIN(A2^3)*COS(A2^2)
=NORMDIST(A2,0,1,FALSE)
```

For more accurate charts, increase the number of plotted values and make the increments in column A smaller.

Plotting two-variable mathematical functions

You also can plot functions that use two variables. For example, the following function calculates a value of z for various values of two variables (x and y):

```
z = SIN(x)*COS(y)
```

Figure 140-2 shows a surface chart that plots the value of z for 21 x values ranging from –3 to 0 and for 21 y values ranging from 2 to 5. Both x and y use an increment of 0.15.

The x values are in A2:A22, and the y values are in B1:V1. The formula in cell B2, which is copied to the other cells in the table, is

```
= SIN($A2)*COS(B$1)
```

To create this chart, follow these steps:

1. Select A1:V22.

2. Choose Insert→Charts→Other Charts→3-D Surface.

3. Choose a chart layout that gives you the look you like, and then fine-tune it.

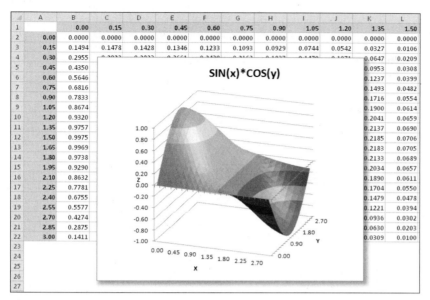

	A	B	C	D	E	F	G	H	I	J	K	L
1		0.00	0.15	0.30	0.45	0.60	0.75	0.90	1.05	1.20	1.35	1.50
2	0.00	0.0000	0.0000	0.0000	0.0000	0.0000	0.0000	0.0000	0.0000	0.0000	0.0000	0.0000
3	0.15	0.1494	0.1478	0.1428	0.1346	0.1233	0.1093	0.0929	0.0744	0.0542	0.0327	0.0106
4	0.30	0.2955									0.0647	0.0209
5	0.45	0.4350									0.0953	0.0308
6	0.60	0.5646									0.1237	0.0399
7	0.75	0.6816									0.1493	0.0482
8	0.90	0.7833									0.1716	0.0554
9	1.05	0.8674									0.1900	0.0614
10	1.20	0.9320									0.2041	0.0659
11	1.35	0.9757									0.2137	0.0690
12	1.50	0.9975									0.2185	0.0706
13	1.65	0.9969									0.2183	0.0705
14	1.80	0.9738									0.2133	0.0689
15	1.95	0.9290									0.2034	0.0657
16	2.10	0.8632									0.1890	0.0611
17	2.25	0.7781									0.1704	0.0550
18	2.40	0.6755									0.1479	0.0478
19	2.55	0.5577									0.1221	0.0394
20	2.70	0.4274									0.0936	0.0302
21	2.85	0.2875									0.0630	0.0203
22	3.00	0.1411									0.0309	0.0100
23												
24												
25												
26												
27												

Figure 140-2: Using a 3-D surface chart to plot a function with two variables.

As long as the x and y values have equal increments, you can specify any two-variable formula you like. You might need to adjust the starting values and increment values for the x and y variables. For a smoother plot, use more x and y values with a smaller increment.

Here are some other formulas you can try:

```
=SIN(SQRT($A2^2 + B$1^2))
=SIN($A2)*COS($A2* B$1)
=COS($A2* B$1)
```

Using High-Low Lines in a Chart

Excel supports a number of stock market charts, used to display stock market data. For example, you can create a chart that shows a stock's high, low, and closing prices. That particular chart requires three data series.

But stock market charts aren't just for stock prices. Figure 141-1 shows a chart that depicts daily temperatures for a month. The vertical lines (called *high-low lines*) show the temperature range for the day.

This chart was created with a single command. I selected the range A3:D34, chose Insert→ Charts→Other Charts, and selected the High-Low-Close option. You can, of course, format the high-low lines any way you like. And you may prefer to have the average temperatures connected with a line.

Figure 141-1: Using a stock market chart to plot temperature data.

When creating stock market charts, the order of the data for the chart series is critical. Because I chose the High-Low-Close chart type, the series must be arranged in that order.

Linking Chart Text to Cells

When you create a chart, you might like to have some of the chart's text elements linked to cells. That way, when you change the text in the cell, the corresponding chart element is updated. You can even link chart text elements to cells that contain a formula. For example, you might link the chart title to a cell that contains a formula that returns the current date.

You can create a link to a cell for the chart title, the axis titles, and the data labels.

1. Select the chart element that will contain the cell link.

2. Click the Formula bar.

3. Type an equal sign (=).

4. Click the cell that will be linked to the chart element.

In addition, you can add a linked text box to a chart:

1. Select the chart.

2. Choose Insert➜Text➜Text Box.

3. Click inside the chart to add an empty text box.

4. Click the Formula bar.

5. Type an equal sign (=).

6. Click the cell that will be linked to the text box.

Creating a Chart Template

If you find that you're continually making the same types of customizations to your charts, you can probably save some time by creating a template. Many users avoid this feature because they think that it's too complicated. Creating a chart template is actually very simple.

To create a chart template, follow these steps:

1. Create a chart to serve as the basis for your template.

   The data you use for this chart isn't critical, but for best results, it should be typical of the data that you will eventually plot with your custom chart type.

2. Apply any formatting and customizations that you like.

   This step determines the appearance of the charts created from the template.

3. Activate the chart and choose Chart Tools➜Design➜Type➜Save As Template.

   Excel displays its Save Chart Template dialog box.

4. Provide a name for the template and click Save.

To create a chart based on a template, follow these steps:

1. Select the data to be used in the chart.

2. Choose Insert➜Charts➜Other Charts➜All Chart Types.

   Excel displays its Insert Chart dialog box.

3. On the left side of the Insert Chart dialog box, select Templates.

   Excel displays an icon for each custom template that has been created.

4. Click the icon that represents the template you want to use and click OK.

   Excel creates the chart based on the template you selected.

You can also apply a template to an existing chart. Select the chart and choose Chart Tools➜Design➜Change Chart Type.

Saving a Chart as a Graphics File

Oddly, Excel doesn't provide a direct way to convert a chart into a stand-alone graphics file, such as a GIF or PNG file. In this tip, I present three methods for saving an Excel chart as a graphics file (one method uses a VBA macro).

Method 1: Paste the chart into a graphics program

This method requires other software — namely, a graphics program. Select your chart and choose Home➜Clipboard➜Copy (or press Ctrl+C). Then access a document in your graphics program and choose Edit➜Paste (or its equivalent command). Then you can save the file by using whichever graphics file format you like.

You might need to experiment to get optimal results. For example, you might need to copy the chart as a picture. To do so, select the chart and then choose Home➜Clipboard➜Copy➜Copy As Picture.

If you don't have a graphics program, try IrfanView, available free at `http://irfanview.com`.

Method 2: Save as an HTML file

To convert all charts in a workbook to PNG files, save your workbook in HTML format and then locate the PNG files that are created. Follow these steps:

1. Save your workbook.

2. Choose File➜Save As.

3. In the Save As dialog box, choose Web Page (*.htm, *.html) from the Save As Type drop-down list.

4. Choose the Entire Workbook option.

5. Select a location for the file.

   Your desktop is a good choice because it's easy to find.

6. Provide a name for the file and click Save.

7. Close the workbook.

8. Open an Explorer window and locate the folder where you saved the file.

9. In addition to the HTML file, you'll find a subdirectory with a name that corresponds to the filename with _files appended; open that folder to see a PNG file that corresponds to each chart in your workbook.

Caution

Save your workbook in a normal Excel file format first. The HTML version of your workbook should be considered a *temporary* version of your workbook. Although you can open the HTML file in Excel, this file format doesn't preserve key information — such as formulas.

Method 3: Use a VBA macro

This method uses a simple VBA macro that saves each chart on the active sheet as a GIF file.

To create the macro, first save your workbook. Then press Alt+F11 to activate the Visual Basic Editor. Select your workbook in the Projects window and choose Insert➜Module to insert a new VBA module. Then type the following procedure into the module:

```
Sub SaveChartsAsGIF()
    Dim ChtObj As ChartObject
    Dim Fname As String
    For Each ChtObj In ActiveSheet.ChartObjects
        Fname = ThisWorkbook.Path & "\" & ChtObj.Name & ".gif"
        ChtObj.Chart.Export Filename:=Fname, FilterName:="gif"
    Next ChtObj
End Sub
```

After the macro is entered, press Alt+F11 to reactivate Excel. Then activate the worksheet that contains your charts. Press Alt+F8 to display the Macro dialog box. Select the SaveChartsAsGIF macro and click Run.

The procedure saves each chart in the active worksheet as a GIF file. (The chart's name is used as the filename.) The files are stored in the same folder as the workbook.

Saving a Range as a Graphic Image

If you need to save a range as a graphic image, the best approach is to use one of several screen capture programs that are available. This type of software makes it easy to capture complete windows, or just a portion of a window. After you capture the screen, click a button to save it as a graphics image in the format you choose (GIF, PNT, TIF, and so on).

If you don't' have a screen capture program, you probably have some other type of graphics software. When you copy a range of cells, that range is stored on the Windows Clipboard in several different formats. One of those formats is a graphic image. Therefore, you can copy a range, activate your graphics software, and press Ctrl+V to paste the range as a graphic. Then, save the graphics file in your desired format.

Figure 145-1 shows a range after it was copied and pasted into IrfanView.

Figure 145-1: A range of data, ready to be saved as a graphic image.

Copying is a what-you-see-is-what-you-get thing. For example, if the selected range contains a chart, the chart will also appear in the image.

You may have noticed that Excel 2010 includes a new Screenshot command. (It's in the Insert➜ Illustrations group on the Ribbon.) This command sounds more useful than it is. Ideally, it would allow you to capture a portion of the screen and save it as a graphics image. But it doesn't. It lets you capture the window of another application and then paste it into your worksheet.

Making Charts the Same Size

If you have several embedded charts on a worksheet, you might want to make them all exactly the same size. Figure 146-1 shows a worksheet with four charts that would look better if they were all the same size and aligned.

Figure 146-1: These charts would look better if they were all the same size.

To make all the charts the same size, first identify the chart that is already the size you want. In this case, you want to make all the charts the same size as the line chart in the upper left area.

1. Click the chart to select it.

2. Choose Chart Tools→Format.

   You see the Height and Width settings in the Size group.

3. Make a note of the Height and Width settings.

4. Press Ctrl while you click the other three charts (so that all four are selected).

5. Choose Drawing Tools→Format, enter the Height and Width settings that you noted in Step 3, and then click OK.

   The charts are now exactly the same size.

You can align the charts manually, or you can use the Chart Tools→ Format→Arrange→Align commands. Figure 146-2 shows the result.

Note that if you Ctrl+click a chart, you select it as a graphic object so that you can use the arrow keys to move the chart (which allows more control than dragging it without your mouse).

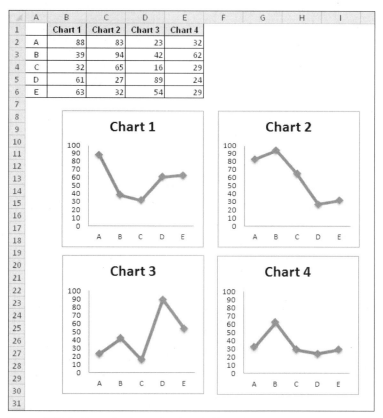

Figure 146-2: Four charts, resized and aligned.

Resetting All Chart Formatting

Excel provides you with many chart formatting options. You can select individual chart elements and apply all sorts of formatting: shadows, glows, bevels, fills, and outline styles, for example. Sometimes, it's easy to go overboard.

If you go overboard in formatting a chart element, you can undo your previous actions, although it's much easier to reset the chart element to its original state. Just select the element and choose Chart Tools→Format→Current Selection→Reset to Match Style. Or, right-click the chart element and choose Reset to Match Style from the shortcut menu.

To reset all formatting changes in the entire chart, select the Chart Area before you choose the Reset to Match Style command.

Figure 147-1 shows a chart with way too much formatting. But, as you can see in Figure 147-2, even the gaudiest chart can be salvaged.

Figure 147-1: Formatting overload.

Figure 147-2: That's much better.

Freezing a Chart

Normally, an Excel chart uses data stored in a range. Change the data, and the chart is updated automatically. Usually, that's a good thing. But sometimes you want to "unlink" the chart from its data range to produce a *static* chart — a snapshot of a chart that never changes. For example, if you plot data generated by various what-if scenarios, you might want to save a chart that represents a baseline so that you can compare it with other scenarios. You can freeze a chart in two ways:

> ➤ Convert the chart to a picture.
> ➤ Convert the range references to arrays.

Converting a chart into a picture

To convert a chart to a static picture, follow these steps:

1. Create the chart as usual and format it the way you want.
2. Click the chart to activate it.
3. Choose Home➜Clipboard➜Copy➜Copy As Picture.
4. In the Copy Picture dialog box, accept the default settings and click OK.
5. Click any cell to deselect the chart.
6. Press Ctrl+V to paste the picture at the cell you selected in Step 5.

The result is a picture of the original chart. This chart can be edited as a picture, but not as a chart. In other words, you can no longer modify properties such as chart type and data labels. It's a dead chart — just what you wanted.

Converting range references into arrays

The other way to unlink a chart from its data is to convert the SERIES formula range references to arrays. Follow these steps:

1. Activate your chart.
2. Click the chart series.

    The Formula bar displays the SERIES formula for the selected data series.
3. Click the Formula bar.
4. Press F9 and then press Enter.

Repeat these steps for each series in the chart.

Figure 148-1 shows a pie chart that has been unlinked from its data range. Notice that the Formula bar displays arrays, not range references. The original data SERIES formula was

```
=SERIES(,Sheet3!$A$1:$A$6,Sheet3!$B$1:$B$6,1)
```

The converted SERIES formula is

```
=SERIES(,{"Work","Sleep","Drive","Eat","Play Banjo","Ot
   her"},{8,7,2,1,3,3},1)
```

Note

Excel places a limit on the length of a SERIES formula. Therefore, this method may not work if the series consists of a large number of data points.

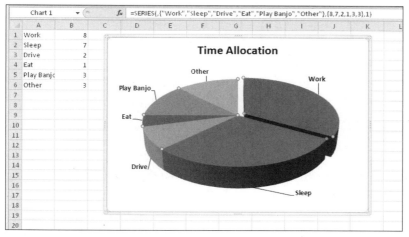

Figure 148-1: This chart isn't linked to a data range.

Creating Picture Effects with a Chart

When you copy a chart as a picture, it opens the door to some creative effects that are possible with pictures, but not with charts.

To create a picture from a chart, select the chart and choose Home➜Clipboard➜Copy➜Copy As Picture. Then click a cell and press Ctrl+V (see Tip 148 for additional information).

When you select the picture, Excel displays its Picture Tools contextual menu. You can use all of the tools in Picture Tools➜Format, plus those available in the Format Picture dialog box (displayed when you press Ctrl+1).

Figure 149-1 shows a few examples of picture styles applied to a chart that was copied as a picture.

Figure 149-1: Applying picture styles to a chart that was copied as a picture.

Creating Sparkline Graphics

One of the new features in Excel 2010 is Sparklines graphics. A Sparkline is a small chart displayed in a single cell. A Sparkline lets you quickly spot time-based trends or variations in data. Because they are so compact, Sparklines are often used in a group.

Although Sparklines look like miniature charts (and can sometimes take the place of a chart), this feature is completely separate from Excel's charting feature. For example, charts are placed on a worksheet's draw layer, and a single chart can display several series of data. A Sparkline is displayed inside of a cell, and it displays only one series of data.

Figure 150-1 shows examples of each of the three types of Sparkline graphics, displayed in column H. Each Sparkline depicts the six data points to the left.

	A	B	C	D	E	F	G	H
1	Line Sparklines							
2								
3	Fund Number	Jan	Feb	Mar	Apr	May	Jun	Sparklines
4	A-13	103.98	98.92	88.12	86.34	75.58	71.2	
5	C-09	212.74	218.7	202.18	198.56	190.12	181.74	
6	K-88	75.74	73.68	69.86	60.34	64.92	59.46	
7	W-91	91.78	95.44	98.1	99.46	98.68	105.86	
8	M-03	324.48	309.14	313.1	287.82	276.24	260.9	
9								
10	Column Sparklines							
11								
12	Fund Number	Jan	Feb	Mar	Apr	May	Jun	Sparklines
13	A-13	103.98	98.92	88.12	86.34	75.58	71.2	
14	C-09	212.74	218.7	202.18	198.56	190.12	181.74	
15	K-88	75.74	73.68	69.86	60.34	64.92	59.46	
16	W-91	91.78	95.44	98.1	99.46	98.68	105.86	
17	M-03	324.48	309.14	313.1	287.82	276.24	260.9	
18								
19	Win/Loss Sparklines							
20								
21	Fund Number	Jan	Feb	Mar	Apr	May	Jun	Sparklines
22	A-13	#N/A	-5.06	-10.8	-1.78	-10.76	-4.38	
23	C-09	#N/A	5.96	-16.52	-3.62	-8.44	-8.38	
24	K-88	#N/A	-2.06	-3.82	-9.52	4.58	-5.46	
25	W-91	#N/A	3.66	2.66	1.36	-0.78	7.18	
26	M-03	#N/A	-15.34	3.96	-25.28	-11.58	-15.34	

Figure 150-1: Examples of Sparkline graphics.

The three types of Sparklines available in Excel 2010 are

> ➤ **Line:** Similar to a line chart. As an option, the line can display with a marker for each data point. The first group shows line Sparklines, with markers. A quick glance reveals that with the exception of Fund Number W-91, the funds have been losing value over the six-month period.

> ➤ **Column:** Similar to a column chart. The second group shows the same data displayed with column Sparklines.

➤ **Win/Loss:** A binary-type chart that displays each data point as a high block or a low block. The third group shows win/loss Sparklines. Notice that the data is different. Each cell displays the *change* from the previous month. In the Sparkline, each data point is depicted as a high block (win) or a low block (loss). In this example, a positive change from the previous month is a win, and a negative change from the previous month is a loss.

To create Sparkline graphics, select the data that will be depicted. Then choose Insert➔Sparklines and click one of the three Sparkline types: Line, Column, or Win/Loss. Excel displays the Create Sparklines dialog box, where you specify the location for the Sparklines.

Typically, you'll put the Sparklines next to the data, but that's not a requirement. Most of the time, you'll use an empty range to hold the Sparklines. However, Excel does not prevent you from inserting Sparklines into cells that already contain data. The Sparkline location that you specify must match the source data in terms of number of rows or number of columns.

After you create some Sparklines, you have a fair amount of control over their appearance. Use the tools in the Sparkline Tools Design tab (which appears when you select a cell that contains a Sparkline).

Figure 150-2 shows a group of Sparklines in the range H3:H12, plus a line chart that uses the same data. The line chart is a bit jumbled, but it's a better choice if you want to compare the cities. The Sparklines, on the other hand, are useful for showing trends for a single city.

Figure 150-2: A group of Sparklines, and a line chart that shows the same data.

Selecting Objects on a Worksheet

Excel lets you place quite a few different types of objects on a worksheet: charts, shapes, clip art, and SmartArt, for example. To work with an object, you must select it. The easiest way to select a single object is to click it. What if you want to select multiple objects? For example, you might want to move several objects, delete them, or apply formatting.

Excel provides several ways to select multiple objects.

Ctrl+click

Pressing the Ctrl key while you click objects is one way to select multiple objects.

The Selection and Visibility pane

The Selection and Visibility pane, shown in Figure 151-1, provides a quick way to select (and hide) objects. To display the Selection and Visibility pane, choose Home➔Editing➔Find & Select➔ Selection Pane.

The pane contains the name of each object on the active worksheet. Click an object name, and the object is selected. Press Ctrl to select multiple objects. You can also use this task pane to hide objects (click the little eyeball icon) and rearrange the stack order of objects (use the two Reorder buttons).

Figure 151-1: You can use the Selection and Visibility pane to easily select objects (if you know their names).

The Go to Special dialog box

To select all objects on a worksheet, choose Home➔Editing➔Find & Select➔Go to Special. Then choose the Objects option in the Go to Special dialog box and click OK.

The Select Object tool

Another way to select multiple objects is to use the Select Object tool (choose Home→Editing→ Find & Select→Select Objects). When you choose this command, Excel goes into a special mode and the mouse pointer changes to an arrow. Click and drag to select all objects in a rectangular area.

To get back to normal mode, press Escape.

Making a Greeting Card

It's your boss's birthday, and you forgot to buy a birthday card! No problem. Follow these steps to create a do-it-yourself greeting card in a worksheet.

1. Start with an empty worksheet.

2. Select columns A and B, choose Home➜Format➜Cells➜Column Width, and then specify 45 as the column width.

3. Select rows 1 and 2, choose Home➜Format➜Cells➜Row Height, and then specify 350 as the row height.

4. Choose View➜Workbook Views➜Page Layout, to enter Page Layout view. You might want to use the Zoom control on the right side of the status bar to reduce the size of the worksheet so you can see the four cells in the range A1:B2.

5. Choose Insert➜Illustrations➜Clip Art to display the Clip Art task pane.

6. Search for an appropriate word (for example, birthday) and locate a suitable clip art image.

7. Add the clip art image to the worksheet and drag it to cell A1.

8. Click the green handle in the clip art image and rotate it so that the image is upside-down.

9. Type some text into cell B2 and format it any way you like.

   Centering vertically and horizontally is a good choice.

Your worksheet should look something like the one shown in Figure 152-1. You may need to tweak the row heights and column widths so range A1:B2 fills exactly one page.

Print the worksheet and fold it once vertically and once horizontally. Voilà! Instant (and cheap) greeting card.

Remember, it's the *thought* that counts.

Figure 152-1: Using Excel to create a greeting card.

Enhancing Text Formatting in Shapes

When you add text to a shape (including a text box), Excel provides you with formatting capabilities that aren't normally available. To try them out, use Insert→ Illustrations→Shapes and add a shape to your worksheet (any shape, except those in the Line group). Then, just start typing to add some text.

You can select individual words or characters by dragging with your mouse or by using the arrow keys while you press Shift. Select some characters, right-click, and choose one of these commands from the shortcut menu:

> ➤ Font
>
> ➤ Paragraph
>
> ➤ Bullets

These commands each display a dialog box that isn't available for normal text formatting in a cell. Unfortunately, you can't preview your formatting; the changes don't appear until you click OK. Figure 153-1 shows some text formatting accomplished using the Font dialog box.

Figure 153-1: Special text formatting, available only in a shape.

For more options, right-click and choose Format Shape (to display the Format Shape dialog box) and click the Text Box tab. Here, you can set margins and even specify snaking columns.

Figure 153-2 shows a shape that uses two columns of text, and four bullets.

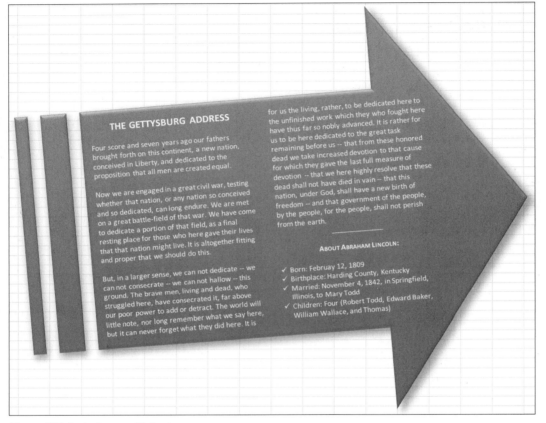

Figure 153-2: A shape with text.

Using Images as Line Chart Markers

When you create a Line chart (or a scatter chart), you can choose from a few different marker styles. For added pizzazz, you might want to use a shape or a simple clip art image for your markers. This technique works best when the chart has a small number of data points.

Figure 154-1 shows an example. This line chart uses a shape for its markers.

Figure 154-1: This line chart uses a shape in place of standard line markers.

The procedure is simple:

1. Create a line chart, with markers.
2. Choose Insert➜Illustrations➜Shapes to add a shape to your worksheet.
3. Format the shape any way you like and size it so that it's suitable for the chart.
4. Select the shape and press Ctrl+C.
5. Activate the chart, select the line series, and press Ctrl+V.

You can even use different shapes for each data point. The trick is to click the series once to select the entire series and then click a single data point marker. When you press Ctrl+V, only the selected marker is changed. Figure 154-2 shows a chart that uses two different shapes.

Figure 154-2: A line chart with two shapes for the line markers.

You can also use clip art for the line markers. For best results, use a relatively simple image. Figure 154-3 shows an example of a chart that uses a clip art image for line markers. I applied a shadow to the image before I pasted it, and the shadow transfers when the image is pasted to the chart series.

Figure 154-3: A line chart with a clip art image for the line markers.

Changing the Shape of a Cell Comment

Cell comments are useful for a variety of purposes. But sometimes you just get tired of looking at the same old yellow rectangle. If you want your comment to get noticed, try changing the shape.

Figure 155-1 shows a normal cell comment, and the same comment after it gets spiffed up a bit.

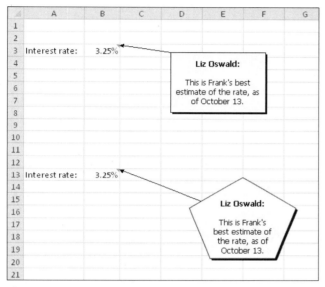

Figure 155-1: A typical cell comment, and a comment with a nonstandard shape.

To change the shape of a cell comment, you need to use a command that's not normally available when a comment is selected. You can add the command to your Quick Access toolbar:

1. Right-click the QAT and choose Customize Quick Access Toolbar.

    The Customization section of the Excel Options dialog box appears.

2. From the Choose Commands From drop-down list, choose Drawing Tools→Format Tab.

3. In the list on the left, select Change Shape and then click the Add button.

4. Click OK to close the Excel Options dialog box.

After you complete these steps, your Quick Access toolbar has a new Change Shape icon.

To change the shape of a comment, make sure that it's visible. If the comment isn't visible, right-click the cell and choose Show/Hide Comments. Then click the comment's border to select it as a shape (or, Ctrl+click the comment to select it as a shape). Click the Change Shape button on the Quick Access toolbar and choose a new shape for the comment from the Shape gallery.

Adding an Image to a Cell Comment

Most users don't realize it, but a cell comment can display an image. The image must reside in a file. In other words, you can't use shapes or clip art images that are copied to the Clipboard.

To add an image to a comment, follow these steps:

1. Make sure that the comment is visible.

    (Right-click the cell and choose Show/Hide Comments.)

2. Click the comment's border to select it as a shape (or, Ctrl+click the comment to select it as a shape).

3. Right-click the comment's border and choose Format Comment from the shortcut menu.

4. In the Format Comment dialog box, click the Colors and Lines tab.

5. In the Fill section of the Format Comment dialog box, click the Color drop-down list and select Fill Effects.

6. In the Fill Effects dialog box, click the Picture tab and then click the Select Picture button to specify a graphics file.

7. Click OK to close the Format Comment dialog box.

Figure 156-1 shows a comment that contains a picture of an ostrich head. Using an image in a comment increases the size of your workbook, so you should use this feature sparingly.

Figure 156-1: Displaying an image in a cell comment.

Enhancing Images

A new set of features in Office 2010 that you might overlook is image enhancement. These tools allow you to modify and enhance images that you insert on a worksheet. This doesn't mean you can uninstall your favorite image editing software, but you might be surprised at the type of enhancements you can perform without even leaving Excel.

To embed an image on a worksheet, choose Insert➡Illustrations➡Picture and then locate the file that contains the image. Or, you can copy an image to the Windows Clipboard and press Ctrl+V to paste it on a worksheet.

When you select an embedded image, use the tools in the Picture Tools➡Format➡Adjust group to work it. The tools include the following:

> **Remove Background:** Makes it very easy to remove extraneous background from a photo.

> **Corrections:** Sharpen or soften the image or adjust the brightness and contrast.

> **Color:** Adjust the color saturation and color tone or convert the image to use just a few colors.

> **Artistic Effects:** Apply some Photoshop-like filters to the image.

In most cases, you get a live preview of the effect when you move your mouse pointer over the icon. Just click to apply it. For more control over the enhancements, right-click the image and choose Format Picture. Then use the Picture Corrections, Picture Color, and Artistic Effects tabs to adjust the parameters.

Figure 157-1 shows a photo before and after I removed the background. The parts of the image that are removed become transparent. This feature works surprisingly well.

Figure 157-1: The result of using the Remove Background command.

Figure 157-2 shows a photo before and after I applied the Pencil Grayscale effect.

Figure 157-2: Applying an artistic effect to a photo.

Even if you have no need to adjust images, you might enjoy playing around with these features when you need a break from number crunching.

Data Analysis and Lists

Much of the data contained in your worksheets is in the form of a list. In this part, you'll find tips that deal with lists and data analysis.

Tips and Where to Find Them

Using the Table Feature

One significant new feature introduced in Excel 2007 is tables. A *table* is a rectangular range of data that has a row of text headings to describe the contents of each column. Excel has always supported tables, of course, but the new implementation makes common tasks much easier to do — and makes the results a lot better looking. More important, the new table features can help eliminate some common errors. Many users overlook this new feature, but it's really worth knowing about.

Understanding what a table is

A *table* is simply a rectangular range of structured data. Each row in the table corresponds to a single entity. For example, a row can contain information about a customer, a bank transaction, an employee, or a product. Each column contains a specific piece of information. For example, if each row contains information about an employee, the columns can contain data, such as name, employee number, hire date, salary, or department. Tables have a header row at the top that describes the information contained in each column.

So far, I've said nothing new. Every previous version of Excel can work with this type of table. The magic happens when you tell Excel to convert a range of data into an "official" table. You do this by selecting any cell within the range and then choosing Insert➔Tables➔Table.

When you explicitly identify a range as a table, Excel can respond more intelligently to the actions you perform with that range. For example, if you create a chart from a table, the chart expands automatically as you add new rows to the table. If you create a pivot table from a table, refreshing the pivot table will include any new data that you added to the table.

Range versus table

What's the difference between a standard range and a table?

> ➤ Activating any cell in the table gives you access to a new Table Tools contextual tab on the Ribbon (see Figure 158-1).

> ➤ You can quickly apply background color and text color formatting by choosing from a gallery. This type of formatting is optional.

> ➤ Each column header contains a drop-down list, which you can use to sort the data or filter the table to hide specific rows.

> ➤ If you scroll down the sheet so that the header row disappears, the table headers replace the column letters in the worksheet header. In other words, you don't need to freeze the top row to keep the column labels visible.

➤ Tables support calculated columns. A single formula in a column is automatically propagated to all cells in the column.

➤ Tables support structured references. Rather than use cell references, formulas can use table names and column headers. (See Tip 160.)

➤ When you move your mouse pointer to the lower right corner of the lower right cell, you can click and drag to extend the table's size, either horizontally (add more columns) or vertically (add more rows).

➤ Selecting rows and columns within the table is simplified.

Figure 158-1: When a table is selected, Excel displays a contextual tab named Table Tools.

Using a table has a few limitations:

➤ For some reason, when a workbook contains at least one table, Excel doesn't allow you to use the custom views feature (choose View➜Workbook Views➜Custom Views).

➤ You can't insert automatic subtotals within a table (by choosing Data➜Outline➜ Subtotal).

Creating a table

Most of the time, you create a table from an existing range of data. Excel also allows you to create a table from an empty range so that you can fill in the details later. The following instructions assume that you already have a range of data that's suitable for a table:

1. Make sure that the range contains no completely blank rows or columns.

2. Activate any cell within the range.

3. Choose Insert➔Tables➔Table (or press Ctrl+T).

   Excel responds with its Create Table dialog box, shown in Figure 158-2. Excel tries to guess the range and whether the table has a header row. Most of the time, it guesses correctly.

4. If Excel does not guess correctly, make your corrections before you click OK.

	A	B	C	D	E	F	G	H
1								
2		Month	Projected	Actual				
3		Jan	4,000	3,255				
4		Feb	4,000	4,102				
5		Mar	4,000	3,982				
6		Apr	5,000	4,598				
7		May	5,000	5,873				
8		Jun	5,000	4,783				
9		Jul	5,000	5,109				
10		Aug	6,000	5,982				
11		Sep	6,000	6,201				
12		Oct	7,000	6,833				
13		Nov	8,000	7,983				
14		Dec	9,000	9,821				
15								
16								

Create Table

Where is the data for your table?

=$B$2:$D$14

☑ My table has headers

OK   Cancel

Figure 158-2: Use the Create Table dialog box to verify that Excel guessed the table dimensions correctly.

The range is converted to a table (it uses the default table style), and the Table Tools contextual tab appears.

Note

Excel might guess the table's dimensions incorrectly if the table isn't separated from other information by at least one empty row or column. If Excel guesses incorrectly, just specify the exact range for the table in the Create Table dialog box. Or, click Cancel and rearrange your worksheet so that the table is separated from your other data by at least one blank row or column.

Working with Tables

Tip 158 presents a brief overview of Excel's table feature. This tip provides a few pointers on working with tables.

Navigating in a table

Selecting cells in a table works just like selecting cells in a normal range. One difference is apparent when you use the Tab key. Pressing Tab moves the cursor to the cell to the right, but when you reach the last column, pressing Tab moves the cursor to the first cell in the next row.

Selecting parts of a table

When you move your mouse around in a table, you might notice that the pointer changes its shape. The pointer shapes help you select various parts of the table:

➤ **Select an entire column:** When you move the mouse to the top of a cell in the header row, the mouse pointer changes to a downward-pointing arrow. Click to select the data in the column. Click a second time to select the entire table column (including the header and total row). You can also press Ctrl+spacebar (once or twice) to select a column.

➤ **Select an entire row:** When you move the mouse pointer to the left of a cell in the first column, the mouse pointer changes to a right-pointing arrow. Click to select the entire table row. You can also press Shift+spacebar to select a table row.

➤ **Select the entire table:** Move the mouse to the upper left part of the upper left cell. When the mouse pointer turns into a diagonal arrow, click to select the data area of the table. Click a second time to select the entire table (including the header row and the total row). You can also press Ctrl+A (once or twice) to select the entire table.

Note

Right-clicking a cell in a table displays several selection options on the shortcut menu.

Adding new rows or columns

To add a new column to the right of a table, activate a cell in the column to the right of the table and start entering the data. Excel automatically extends the table horizontally. Similarly, if you enter data in the row below a table, Excel extends the table vertically to include the new row.

An exception to automatically extending tables vertically is when the table is displaying a total row. If you enter data below the totals row, the table isn't extended.

To add rows or columns within the table, right-click and choose Insert from the shortcut menu. The Insert shortcut menu command displays additional menu items.

Note

When the cell pointer is in the lower right cell of a table, pressing Tab inserts a new row at the bottom.

Another way to extend a table is to drag its resize handle, which appears in the lower right corner of the table (but only when the entire table is selected). When you move the mouse pointer to the resize handle, the mouse pointer turns into a diagonal line with two arrow heads. Click and drag down to add more rows to the table. Click and drag to the right to add more columns.

When you insert a new column, the header row displays a generic description, such as Column 1 or Column 2. Normally, you want to change these names to more descriptive labels.

Deleting rows or columns

To delete a row (or column) in a table, select any cell in the row (or column) to be deleted. If you want to delete multiple rows or columns, select them all. Then right-click and choose Delete➜ Table Rows (or Delete➜Table Columns).

Moving a table

To move a table to a new location in the same worksheet, move the mouse pointer to any of its borders. When the mouse pointer turns into a cross with four arrows, click and drag the table to its new location.

To move a table to a different worksheet (in the same workbook or in a different workbook):

1. Press Alt+A *twice* to select the entire table.
2. Press Ctrl+X to cut the selected cells.
3. Activate the new worksheet and select the upper left cell for the table.
4. Press Ctrl+V to paste the table.

Sorting and filtering a table

The header row of a table contains a drop-down arrow that, when clicked, displays sorting and filtering options (see Figure 159-1). When you filter a table, rows that don't meet the filter criteria are temporarily hidden and are not included in summary formulas in the total row.

Figure 159-1: Each column in a table contains sorting and filtering options.

Using Formulas with a Table

This tip describes some ways to use formulas with a table. The example uses a simple sales summary table with three columns: Month, Projected, and Actual, as shown in Figure 160-1. I entered the data and then converted the range to a table by using the Insert➜Tables➜Table command. Note that I didn't define any names, but the data area of the table is named Table1 by default.

Figure 160-1: A simple table with three columns.

Working with the total row

If you want to calculate the total projected and total actual sales, you don't even need to write a formula. Just click a button to add a row of summary formulas to the table:

1. Activate any cell in the table.

2. Select the Table Tools➜Design➜Table Style Options➜Total Row check box.

3. Activate a cell in the total row and select a summary formula from the drop-down list (see Figure 160-2).

   For example, to calculate the sum of the Actual column, select SUM from the drop-down list in cell D15. Excel creates this formula:

   ```
   =SUBTOTAL(109,[Actual])
   ```

For the SUBTOTAL function, 109 is an enumerated argument that represents SUM. The second argument for the SUBTOTAL function is the column name, in square brackets. Using the column name within brackets is a way to create structured references within a table.

Tip 160: Using Formulas with a Table

	A	B	C	D	E	F
1						
2		Month ▾	Projected ▾	Actual ▾		
3		Jan	4,000	3,255		
4		Feb	4,000	4,102		
5		Mar	4,000	3,982		
6		Apr	5,000	4,598		
7		May	5,000	5,873		
8		Jun	5,000	4,783		
9		Jul	5,000	5,109		
10		Aug	6,000	5,982		
11		Sep	6,000	6,201		
12		Oct	7,000	6,833		
13		Nov	8,000	7,983		
14		Dec	9,000	9,821		
15		Total		68,522 ▾		
16				None		
17				Average		
18				Count		
				Count Numbers		
19				Max		
20				Min		
21				Sum		
22				StdDev		
23				Var		
				More Functions...		

Figure 160-2: A drop-down list enables you to select a summary formula for a table column.

Note

You can toggle the total row display on and off by choosing Table Tools➜Design➜ Table Style Options➜Total Row. If you turn it off, the summary options you selected are remembered when you turn it back on.

Using formulas within a table

In many cases, you want to use formulas within a table. For example, in the table shown in Figure 160-1, you might want a column that shows the difference between the actual and projected amounts for each month. As you'll see, Excel makes this process very easy:

1. Activate cell E2 and type **Difference** for the column header.

    Excel automatically expands the table for you.

2. Move to cell E3 and type an equal sign to signal the beginning of a formula.

3. Press the left-arrow key to point to the corresponding value in the Actual column.

4. Type a minus sign and then press the left-arrow key twice to point to the corresponding value in the Projected column.

5. Press Enter to end the formula.

The formula is entered into the other cells in the column, and the Formula bar displays this formula:

```
=[@Actual]-[@Projected]
```

Figure 160-3 shows the table with the new column.

	A	B	C	D	E	F
1						
2		Month ▼	Projected ▼	Actual ▼	Difference ▼	
3		Jan	4,000	3,255	-745	
4		Feb	4,000	4,102	102	
5		Mar	4,000	3,982	-18	
6		Apr	5,000	4,598	-402	
7		May	5,000	5,873	873	
8		Jun	5,000	4,783	-217	
9		Jul	5,000	5,109	109	
10		Aug	6,000	5,982	-18	
11		Sep	6,000	6,201	201	
12		Oct	7,000	6,833	-167	
13		Nov	8,000	7,983	-17	
14		Dec	9,000	9,821	821	
15		Total	68,000	68,522		
16						

Figure 160-3: The Difference column contains a formula.

Although the formula was entered into the first row of the table, that's not necessary. Anytime a formula is entered into an empty table column, it propagates to the other cells in the column. If you need to edit the formula, edit any formula in the column, and the change is applied to the other cells in the column.

Note

Propagating a formula to other cells in a table column is actually one of Excel's AutoCorrect options. To turn off this feature, click the icon that appears when you enter a formula and choose Stop Automatically Creating Calculated Columns.

The preceding set of steps used the column names to create the formula. Alternatively, you can enter the formula by using standard cell references. For example, you can enter the following formula in cell E3:

```
=D3-C3
```

If you type the cell references, Excel still automatically copies the formula to other cells in the column.

Referencing data in a table

Formulas that are outside of a table can refer to data within a table by using the table name and column headers. You don't need to create names for these items. The table itself has a name (for example, Table1), and you can refer to data within the table by using column headers.

You can, of course, use standard cell references to refer to data in a table, but using table references has a distinct advantage: The names adjust automatically if the table size changes by adding or deleting rows.

Refer to the table shown earlier, in Figure 160-1. This table was given the name Table1 when it was created. To calculate the sum of all data in the table, use this formula:

```
=SUM(Table1)
```

This formula always returns the sum of all the data, even if rows or columns are added or deleted. And, if you change the name of Table1, Excel automatically adjusts formulas that refer to that table. For example, if you rename Table1 as AnnualData (by using the Name Manager), the preceding formula changes to

```
=SUM(AnnualData)
```

Most of the time, you want to refer to a specific column in the table. The following formula returns the sum of the data in the Actual column (but ignores the total row):

```
=SUM(Table1[Actual])
```

Notice that the column name is enclosed in square brackets. Again, the formula adjusts automatically if you change the text in the column heading.

Even better, Excel provides some helpful assistance when you create a formula that refers to data within a table. Figure 160-4 shows the Formula AutoComplete feature helping to create a formula by showing a list of the elements in the table.

Figure 160-4: The Formula AutoComplete feature is useful when creating a formula that refers to data in a table.

Numbering Rows in a Table

If you have a table (created by choosing Insert➔Tables➔Table), you might want to number the rows in the table. Excel doesn't provide a direct way to number table rows, but this tip describes how to accomplish it with a formula.

Figure 161-1 shows a table with an empty column labeled Number. The goal is to create a formula that displays the row number — and that remains correct even if table rows are added or deleted or if the table is filtered or sorted.

	A	B	C	D	E
1					
2					
3					
4		Number	Name	Score	
5			Abe	81	
6			Benjamin	82	
7			Cathy	88	
8			David	76	
9			Elmer	85	
10			Francis	96	
11			Georgia	89	
12			Herbert	91	
13			Isabelle	91	
14			James	86	
15			Kenneth	80	
16			Lulu	84	
17					
18					

Figure 161-1: This table needs a row number in the first column.

The following formula, entered in column B5, does the job:

```
=SUBTOTAL(3,C$4:C4)
```

This formula (which Excel copies to other cells in column B) uses the SUBTOTAL function with an argument of 3 (COUNTA). The formula returns the count of all cells in column C, starting with the header row and ending with the row that's one cell above the cell with the formula. Notice that the formula is in column B but references column C, to avoid a circular reference.

Figure 161-2 shows the table after entering the formula.

This formula continues to show consecutive row numbers if the table is sorted or filtered or if new rows are added or deleted.

Figure 161-3 shows the table after sorting and filtering to show only rows in which the score is greater than 90. Notice that the Number column continues to show consecutive numbers.

⬜	A	B	C	D	E
1					
2					
3					
4		Number ▼	Name ▼	Score ▼	
5		1	Abe	81	
6		2	Benjamin	82	
7		3	Cathy	88	
8		4	David	76	
9		5	Elmer	85	
10		6	Francis	96	
11		7	Georgia	89	
12		8	Herbert	91	
13		9	Isabelle	91	
14		10	James	86	
15		11	Kenneth	80	
16		12	Lulu	84	
17					
18					

Figure 161-2: The table now has row numbers.

table formulas.xlsx

⬜	A	B	C	D	E
1					
2					
3					
4		Number ▼	Name ▼	Score ▼	
7		1	Francis	96	
9		2	Herbert	91	
10		3	Isabelle	91	
16					
17					
18					
19					

Sheet1   Sheet2

Figure 161-3: When rows are filtered, the first column still shows consecutive numbers.

Using Custom Views with Filtering

The Excel Filter feature is handy for hiding specific items in a list. For example, if you have a mailing list, you can choose to display only the rows in which the State column contains Montana. You can filter a list by using as many columns as you need, and the Custom option provides even more flexibility.

This tip describes how to save various filter configurations by using custom views.

Caution

For reasons known only to Microsoft, the View➜Workbook Views➜Custom Views command isn't available if your workbook contains a table (created by choosing Insert➜Tables➜Table). Therefore, this tip applies only to filtering done using a normal range of data. If your data is in a table, convert it to a normal range by using Table Tools➜Design➜Convert to Range.

To enable filtering of a range, select a cell in the range and choose Data➜Sort & Filter➜Filter. Excel displays drop-down arrows in the header row of the range. Use these drop-down arrows to filter the data.

Note

In a range that has filtering enabled, the column headers make it look like a table, but it's not a table. For example you can't add a Total row to such a range.

Excel doesn't allow you to give a name to a particular set of filters. Therefore, if you tend to use several different filtering criteria for a particular list, you can waste a lot of time specifying and re-specifying the filters manually.

The solution: The rarely used View➜Workbook Views➜Custom Views command. Here's how to do it:

1. Apply filtering to your range and specify the filters to your liking.
2. Choose View➜Workbook Views➜Custom Views to display the Custom Views dialog box.
3. Click the Add button to display the Add View dialog box, shown in Figure 162-1.
4. Provide a name for the view and make sure that the Hidden Rows, Columns and Filter Settings check box is selected.
5. Click OK to close the Add View dialog box.

Repeat these steps for as many different filter settings as you like. You might also want to create an unfiltered view, to display the list with no filtering applied.

Then, to apply a set of filter settings, choose View➜Workbook Views➜Custom Views and select the named view from the list displayed in the Custom Views dialog box.

If you prefer, you can customize your Quick Access toolbar by adding the Custom Views control (it's in the Commands Not in the Ribbon category). This control is a drop-down list that shows all named views. Just select a view from the list, and your data is filtered.

	A	B	C	D	E	F	G
1	County	State Name	Region	Census 2000	Census 1990	Land Area	WaterArea
60	Worcester	Massachusetts	Region I	750,963	709,705	1,513	66
322	Penobscot	Maine	Region I	144,919	146,601	3,396	160
526	Aroostook	Maine	Region I	73,938	86,936	6,672	157
602	Grafton	New Hampshire	Region I	81,743	74,929	1,713	37
807	Oxford	Maine	Region I	54,755	52,602	2,078	97
845	Somerset	Maine	Region I	50,888	49,767	3,926	169
892	Hancock	Maine			46,948	1,588	763
1121	Washington	Maine			35,308	2,568	686
1138	Coos	New Hampshire			34,828	1,800	31
1330	Franklin	Maine			29,008	1,698	46
1757	Piscataquis	Maine			18,653	3,966	411
3146							
3147							
3148							
3149							
3150							
3151							

Add View

Name: Region 1, Land Area > 1,000

Include in view
☑ Print settings
☑ Hidden rows, columns and filter settings

OK   Cancel

Figure 162-1: Adding a custom view after applying a filter to a range

Putting Advanced Filter Results on a Different Sheet

If you use Excel's Advanced Filter feature, you may have discovered that Excel is rather picky about where you choose to put the results.

Figure 163-1 shows an Advanced Filter operation in progress. Notice that the list range and the criteria range are on the active sheet (Sheet1), but the user has specified a cell on Sheet2 as the Copy To range. Clicking the OK button results in an error message: *You can only copy filtered data to the active sheet.*

Figure 163-1: Specifying a different sheet as the Copy To range causes an error.

Fortunately, you have a simple way around this meaningless limitation:

1. Start out on the sheet that will contain the results; if the list range and criteria range are on Sheet1 and you want the results on Sheet2, just activate Sheet2 when you choose the Data➜Sort & Filter➜Advanced Filter command.

2. To specify the List Range and Criteria Range settings, click the sheet tab for Sheet1 and select the ranges.

3. Enter a range on the active sheet (Sheet2) for the Copy To range.

Comparing Two Ranges by Using Conditional Formatting

A common task is comparing two lists of items. Doing it manually is far too tedious and error-prone, but Excel can make it easy. This tip describes a method that uses conditional formatting.

Figure 164-1 shows an example of two multicolumn lists of names. Applying conditional formatting can make the differences in the lists become immediately apparent. These list examples contain text, but this technique also works with numeric data.

	A	B	C	D	E
1	Old List			New List	
2	Arnold Goodwin	Pauline Farmer		Bridget Garza	Mary White
3	Kristin Baxter	Helen Griffin		Nancy Williams	Mary Nelson
4	Howard Lee	Mike Carter		Carol Smith	Mike Carter
5	Emily Brooks	Lee Scott		Lisa Thomas	Robyn Fox
6	Gretchen Smith	Amy Jordan		Lynda R. Rice	Cheyenne Sullivan
7	Janette Reeves	Ruth Gonzalez		Sonia Washington	Jane Winters
8	Amy Walker	Susan Williams		Eddie Brown	Michael Dodson
9	Johnnie D. Anderson	Charles Torres		Calvin O. Flores	Sharon Parker
10	Christopher Collins	Robyn Fox		Helen Griffin	Ruth Gonzalez
11	Krystle Ferrell	Burt Morrow		Janette Reeves	Gretchen Smith
12	Mary Nelson	Darryl Marsh		Richard Lee	Charles Roberts
13	Timothy Moore	Leigh Johnson		Chris Stevenson	Terrell Jones
14	David White	Dennis Nichols		Robert Jones	Timothy Moore
15	James Smith	Michael Dodson		David White	John Bryant
16	Nancy Anderson	Chris Stevenson		Nancy Anderson	Jolie A. Cooper
17	Alta Watkins	Clinton Ramirez		Patrick Gutierrez	Sylvia O. Cummings
18	Jane Winters	Charles Roberts		Darlene Roman	Darryl Marsh
19	Susan Reynolds	Kimberly Smith		Arnold Goodwin	Kristin Baxter
20	Janet Cooper	Samantha Davis		Jeffrey Garrett	Krystle Ferrell
21	Kimberly Wolfe	Terrell Jones		Lee Scott	Samantha Davis
22	Robert Jones	Patricia Hart		Dennis Nichols	Susan Williams
23	Ida Davis	Chester Robinson		Brian Thomas	Ida Davis
24	Sharon Parker	Patrick Gutierrez		Emily Brooks	Burt Morrow
25	Jeffrey Garrett	Mildred Thompson		Jeffrey Carter	Amy Jordan
26	Curtis N. Hill	Janet Adams		James Smith	Janet Adams
27	Masako Jones	Richard Lee		Mildred Thompson	Curtis N. Hill
28	Jeffrey Carter	Cheyenne Sullivan		Pauline Farmer	Chester Robinson
29	John Bryant	Kim Roman		Kimberly Smith	Mark Tiller
30	Reinaldo Collins	Brian Thomas		Christopher Collins	Howard Jackson
31	Mary White	Sylvia O. Cummings		Alta Watkins	Frank Peachpit
32					

Figure 164-1: You can use conditional formatting to highlight the differences in these two ranges.

The first list is in A2:B31, and this range is named OldList. The second list is in D2:E31, and the range is named NewList. The ranges were named by using the Formulas➜Defined Names➜Define Name command. Naming the ranges isn't necessary, but it makes them easier to work with.

Start by adding conditional formatting to the old list:

1. Select the cells in the OldList range.
2. Choose Home➜Conditional Formatting➜New Rule to display the New Formatting Rule dialog box.

3. In the New Formatting Rule dialog box, click the option labeled Use a Formula to Determine Which Cells to Format.

4. Enter this formula in the dialog box (see Figure 164-2):

```
=COUNTIF(NewList,A2)=0
```

5. Click the Format button and specify the formatting to apply when the condition is true. A different fill color is a good choice.

6. Click OK.

Figure 164-2: Applying conditional formatting.

The cells in the NewList range use a similar conditional formatting formula.

1. Select the cells in the NewList range.

2. Choose Home➜Conditional Formatting➜New Rule to display the New Formatting Rule dialog box.

3. In the New Formatting Rule dialog box, click the option labeled Use a Formula to Determine Which Cells to Format.

4. Enter this formula in the dialog box:

```
=COUNTIF(OldList,D2)=0
```

5. Click the Format button and specify the formatting to apply when the condition is true (a different fill color).

6. Click OK.

Figure 164-3 shows the result. Names that are in the old list but not in the new list are highlighted. In addition, Names in the new list that aren't in the old list are highlighted in a different color. Names that are not highlighted appear in both lists.

	A	B	C	D	E
1	Old List			New List	
2	Arnold Goodwin	Pauline Farmer		Bridget Garza	Mary White
3	Kristin Baxter	Helen Griffin		Nancy Williams	Mary Nelson
4	Howard Lee	Mike Carter		Carol Smith	Mike Carter
5	Emily Brooks	Lee Scott		Lisa Thomas	Robyn Fox
6	Gretchen Smith	Amy Jordan		Lynda R. Rice	Cheyenne Sullivan
7	Janette Reeves	Ruth Gonzalez		Sonia Washington	Jane Winters
8	Amy Walker	Susan Williams		Eddie Brown	Michael Dodson
9	Johnnie D. Anderson	Charles Torres		Calvin O. Flores	Sharon Parker
10	Christopher Collins	Robyn Fox		Helen Griffin	Ruth Gonzalez
11	Krystle Ferrell	Burt Morrow		Janette Reeves	Gretchen Smith
12	Mary Nelson	Darryl Marsh		Richard Lee	Charles Roberts
13	Timothy Moore	Leigh Johnson		Chris Stevenson	Terrell Jones
14	David White	Dennis Nichols		Robert Jones	Timothy Moore
15	James Smith	Michael Dodson		David White	John Bryant
16	Nancy Anderson	Chris Stevenson		Nancy Anderson	Jolie A. Cooper
17	Alta Watkins	Clinton Ramirez		Patrick Gutierrez	Sylvia O. Cummings
18	Jane Winters	Charles Roberts		Darlene Roman	Darryl Marsh
19	Susan Reynolds	Kimberly Smith		Arnold Goodwin	Kristin Baxter
20	Janet Cooper	Samantha Davis		Jeffrey Garrett	Krystle Ferrell
21	Kimberly Wolfe	Terrell Jones		Lee Scott	Samantha Davis
22	Robert Jones	Patricia Hart		Dennis Nichols	Susan Williams
23	Ida Davis	Chester Robinson		Brian Thomas	Ida Davis
24	Sharon Parker	Patrick Gutierrez		Emily Brooks	Burt Morrow
25	Jeffrey Garrett	Mildred Thompson		Jeffrey Carter	Amy Jordan
26	Curtis N. Hill	Janet Adams		James Smith	Janet Adams
27	Masako Jones	Richard Lee		Mildred Thompson	Curtis N. Hill
28	Jeffrey Carter	Cheyenne Sullivan		Pauline Farmer	Chester Robinson
29	John Bryant	Kim Roman		Kimberly Smith	Mark Tiller
30	Reinaldo Collins	Brian Thomas		Christopher Collins	Howard Jackson
31	Mary White	Sylvia O. Cummings		Alta Watkins	Frank Peachpit
32					

Figure 164-3: Conditional formatting causes differences in the two lists to be highlighted.

Both of these conditional formatting formulas use the COUNTIF function. This function counts the number of times a particular value appears in a range. If the formula returns 0, it means that the item doesn't appear in the range. Therefore, the conditional formatting kicks in and the cell's background color is changed.

Note

The cell reference in the COUNTIF function should always be the upper left cell of the selected range.

Randomizing a List

This tip describes a quick method to randomize a list. It's like shuffling a deck of cards, where each row is a card.

Figure 165-1 shows a two-column list, arranged alphabetically by column A. The goal is to arrange the rows in random order.

	A	B	C	D
1	**Artist**	**DVD**		
2	Alanis Morissette	Jagged Little Pill, Live		
3	Alberta Hunter	My Castle's Rocking		
4	Animusic	Special Edition		
5	B.B. King	The Jazz Channel Presents B.B. King		
6	Blue Man Group	Audio		
7	Brian Setzer Orchestra	Live In Japan		
8	Cheryl Crow	Rockin' The Globe Live		
9	Dayna Kurtz	Postcards From Amsterdam		
10	Diana Krall	Live At The Montreal Jazz Festival		
11	Diana Krall	Live In Paris		
12	Eagles	Hell Freezes Over		
13	Eric Clapton	Live On Tour 2001		
14	Gillian Welch	The Revelator Collection		
15	J.J. Cale & Leon Russell	Sessions At The Paradise Studios		
16	James Taylor	Live At The Beacon Theatre		
17	John Prine	Live From Sessions At West 54th		
18	Joni Mitchell	Painting With Words And Music		
19	Joni Mitchell	Woman Of Heart And Mind		
20	Joni Mitchell	Refuge Of The Roads		
21	Joni Mitchell	Shadows And Light		
22	Keb' Mo'	Sessions At West 54th		
23	Keola Beamer	Ki Ho Alu		
24	King Crimson	Deja Vrooom		
25	Norah Jones	Live In 2004		
26	Norah Jones	Live In New Orleans		
27	Peter Frampton	Live In Detroit		
28	Randy Travis	Live: It Was Just A Matter Of Time		
29	Richard Thompson Band	Live In Providence		
30	Robert Earl Keen	Live From Austin TX		
31	Roger Waters	In The Flesh - Live		
32	Roy Orbison	Black & White Night		

Figure 165-1: This alphabetized list will be randomly arranged.

1. In cell C1, enter the column heading **Random**.
2. In cell C2, enter this formula:

   ```
   =RAND()
   ```

3. Copy C2 down the column to accommodate the number of rows in the list.

4. Activate any cell in column C and choose Home➔Editing➔Sort & Filter➔Sort Smallest to Largest (or, right-click and choose the Sort command on the shortcut menu).

To get a different random configuration, press F9 to generate new random numbers and then sort again. Figure 165-2 shows the randomized list.

	A	B	C	D
1	**Artist**	**DVD**	**Random**	
2	Various	Naxos Musical Journey: Bach	0.727696122	
3	Roy Orbison	Black & White Night	0.23645386	
4	Joni Mitchell	Woman Of Heart And Mind	0.854081681	
5	John Prine	Live From Sessions At West 54th	0.452289551	
6	Peter Frampton	Live In Detroit	0.743273235	
7	Steve Goodman	Live From Austin City Limits And More	0.604145335	
8	Willie Nelson	Live At Billy Bob's Texas	0.160866256	
9	Alanis Morissette	Jagged Little Pill, Live	0.560102474	
10	Norah Jones	Live In New Orleans	0.589155875	
11	Diana Krall	Live At The Montreal Jazz Festival	0.780332698	
12	Various	Concert For George	0.369355352	
13	Brian Setzer Orchestra	Live In Japan	0.253116702	
14	Gillian Welch	The Revelator Collection	0.762298361	
15	Stevie Ray Vaughan	Live At The El Cmocambo	0.380492741	
16	Alberta Hunter	My Castle's Rocking	0.087620274	
17	Various	Bridge To Havana	0.369439874	
18	Sade	Sade Live	0.224480311	
19	Randy Travis	Live: It Was Just A Matter Of Time	0.032259712	
20	Richard Thompson Band	Live In Providence	0.071292885	
21	Various	Naxos Musical Journey: Vivaldi	0.276575568	
22	Animusic	Special Edition	0.31224982	
23	Blue Man Group	Audio	0.679099382	
24	Various	The Velvet Lounge	0.631762511	
25	J.J. Cale & Leon Russell	Sessions At The Paradise Studios	0.794216171	
26	Diana Krall	Live In Paris	0.31195065	
27	Keola Beamer	Ki Ho Alu	0.976692635	
28	Dayna Kurtz	Postcards From Amsterdam	0.763674862	
29	Townes Van Zandt	Houston 1988	0.658888077	
30	Sarah McLachlan	Mirrorball	0.842676908	
31	Eric Clapton	Live On Tour 2001	0.676792541	
32	King Crimson	Deja Vrooom	0.439000833	
33	Norah Jones	Live In 2004	0.106839179	
34	Cheryl Crow	Rockin' The Globe Live	0.676415975	

Figure 165-2: The list after being randomized.

Filling the Gaps in a Report

When you import data, you can end up with a worksheet that looks something like the one shown in Figure 166-1. This type of report formatting is common. As you can see, an entry in column A applies to several rows of data. If you sort this type of list, the missing data messes things up, and you can no longer tell who sold what when.

	A	B	C	D	E
1					
2	Sales Rep	Month	Units Sold	Amount	
3	Dorothy Harrison	Jan	182	$15,101	
4		Feb	3350	$34,230	
5		Mar	114	$9,033	
6	Andrew Stephens	Jan	135	$8,054	
7		Feb	401	$9,322	
8		Mar	357	$32,143	
9	Colleen Allen	Jan	509	$29,239	
10		Feb	414	$38,993	
11		Mar	53	$309	
12	Lowell Marshall	Jan	323	$9,092	
13		Feb	283	$12,332	
14		Mar	401	$32,933	
15					

Figure 166-1: This report contains gaps in the Sales Rep column.

If your list is small, you can enter the missing cell values manually or by using a series of Home➜Editing➜Fill➜Down commands (or its Ctrl+D shortcut). But if you have a large list that's in this format, you need a better way of filling in those cell values. Here's how:

1. Select the range that has the gaps (A3:A14, in this example).
2. Choose Home➜Editing➜Find & Select➜Go to Special to display the Go To Special dialog box.
3. In the Go To Special dialog box, select the Blanks option and click OK.

   This action selects the blank cells in the original selection.
4. On the Formula bar, type an equal sign (**=**) followed by the address of the first cell with an entry in the column (**=A3,** in this example) and press Ctrl+Enter.
5. Reselect the original range and press Ctrl+C to copy the selection.
6. Choose Home➜Clipboard➜Paste➜Paste Values to convert the formulas to values.

After you complete these steps, the gaps are filled in with the correct information, and your worksheet looks similar to the one shown in Figure 166-2. Now it's a more traditional list, and you can do whatever you like with it — including sorting.

	A	B	C	D	E
1					
2	**Sales Rep**	**Month**	**Units Sold**	**Amount**	
3	Dorothy Harrison	Jan	182	$15,101	
4	Dorothy Harrison	Feb	3350	$34,230	
5	Dorothy Harrison	Mar	114	$9,033	
6	Andrew Stephens	Jan	135	$8,054	
7	Andrew Stephens	Feb	401	$9,322	
8	Andrew Stephens	Mar	357	$32,143	
9	Colleen Allen	Jan	509	$29,239	
10	Colleen Allen	Feb	414	$38,993	
11	Colleen Allen	Mar	53	$309	
12	Lowell Marshall	Jan	323	$9,092	
13	Lowell Marshall	Feb	283	$12,332	
14	Lowell Marshall	Mar	401	$32,933	
15					

Figure 166-2: The gaps are gone, and this list can now be sorted.

Creating a List from a Summary Table

You might be familiar with Excel's PivotTable feature, which creates a summary table from a list. But what if you want to perform the opposite operation? This tip describes how to create a list from a simple two-variable summary table.

The worksheet shown in Figure 167-1 shows the type of transformation I'm talking about. Range A1:E13 contains the original summary table: 48 data points. Columns G:I show part of a 48-row table derived from the summary table. In other words, every value in the original summary table is converted to a row, which also contains the value's corresponding product name and month. This type of list is useful because it can be sorted and manipulated in other ways.

	A	B	C	D	E	F	G	H	I	J
1		North	South	East	West		Month	Region	Sales	
2	Jan	132	233	314	441		Jan	North	132	
3	Feb	143	251	314	447		Jan	South	233	
4	Mar	172	252	345	450		Jan	East	314	
5	Apr	184	290	365	452		Jan	West	441	
6	May	212	299	401	453		Feb	North	143	
7	Jun	239	317	413	457		Feb	South	251	
8	Jul	249	350	427	460		Feb	East	314	
9	Aug	263	354	448	468		Feb	West	447	
10	Sep	291	373	367	472		Mar	North	172	
11	Oct	294	401	392	479		Mar	South	252	
12	Nov	302	437	495	484		Mar	East	345	
13	Dec	305	466	504	490		Mar	West	450	
14							Apr	North	184	
15							Apr	South	290	
16							Apr	East	365	
17							Apr	West	452	
18							May	North	212	
19							May	South	299	
20							May	East	401	
21							May	West	453	
22							Jun	North	239	
23							Jun	South	317	
24							Jun	East	413	
25							Jun	West	457	
26							Jul	North	249	
27							Jul	South	350	
28							Jul	East	427	

Figure 167-1: Converting a summary table to a list.

The trick to creating this reverse pivot table is to use a pivot table. But before you can make use of this technique, you must add the PivotTable Wizard command to your Quick Access toolbar. Excel 2007 and Excel 2010 still support the PivotTable Wizard, but it's not available on the Ribbon. To gain access to the PivotTable Wizard, follow these steps:

1. Right-click the Quick Access toolbar and choose Customize Quick Access Toolbar from the shortcut menu.

2. On the Quick Access Toolbar tab of the Excel Options dialog box, choose Commands Not in the Ribbon from the drop-down list on the left.

3. Scroll down the list and select PivotTable and PivotChart Wizard from the list.

4. Click Add.

5. Click OK to close the Excel Options dialog box.

After you perform these steps, your Quick Access toolbar displays a new icon.

Now it's time to convert the summary table to a list. Keep in mind that, although the following steps are specific to the sample data shown here, you can easily modify the steps to work with your data. First, create the pivot table:

1. Activate any cell in your summary table.

2. Click the PivotTable and PivotChart Wizard icon, which you added to your Quick Access toolbar.

3. In the PivotTable and PivotChart Wizard dialog box, select the Multiple Consolidation Ranges option and click Next.

4. In Step 2a of the PivotTable and PivotChart Wizard dialog box, choose the I Will Create the Page Fields option and click Next.

5. In Step 2b, specify a summary table range in the Range field (A1:E13 for the sample data) and click Add; click Next to move on to Step 3.

6. In Step 3, select a location for the pivot table and click the Finish button.

Excel creates a pivot table from the data and displays the PivotTable Field list.

7. In the PivotTable Field List, deselect the check boxes from the fields named Row and Column.

This leaves the pivot table with only a data field: Sum of Value.

At this point, a small pivot table shows only the sum of all values (see Figure 167-2).

	A	B	C	D	E	F	G	H	I
1		North	South	East	West		Sum of Value		
2	Jan	132	233	314	441		17147		
3	Feb	143	251	314	447				
4	Mar	172	252	345	450				
5	Apr	184	290	365	452				
6	May	212	299	401	453				
7	Jun	239	317	413	457				
8	Jul	249	350	427	460				
9	Aug	263	354	448	468				
10	Sep	291	373	367	472				
11	Oct	294	401	392	479				
12	Nov	302	437	495	484				
13	Dec	305	466	504	490				
14									
15									

Figure 167-2: This small pivot table can be expanded.

To finish up, double-click the cell that contains the total (17147, in this example). Excel creates a new sheet that displays the original data in the form of a table. Figure 167-3 shows part of this 48-row table.

The column headings display generic descriptions (Row, Column, and Value), so you probably want to change these headings to make them more descriptive.

	A	B	C	D	E
1	Row	Column	Value		
2	Jan	North	132		
3	Jan	South	233		
4	Jan	East	314		
5	Jan	West	441		
6	Feb	North	143		
7	Feb	South	251		
8	Feb	East	314		
9	Feb	West	447		
10	Mar	North	172		
11	Mar	South	252		
12	Mar	East	345		
13	Mar	West	450		
14	Apr	North	184		
15	Apr	South	290		
16	Apr	East	365		
17	Apr	West	452		
18	May	North	212		
19	May	South	299		
20	May	East	401		
21	May	West	453		
22	Jun	North	239		
23	Jun	South	317		
24	Jun	East	413		

Figure 167-3: The summary table has been successfully converted to a table.

Finding Duplicates by Using Conditional Formatting

You might find it helpful to identify duplicate values within a range of cells. For example, take a look at Figure 168-1. Are any of the values duplicated?

One approach to identifying duplicate values is to use conditional formatting. After applying a conditional formatting rule, you can quickly spot duplicate cell values.

	A	B	C	D	E	F	G	H
1	624	366	828	521	438	382	317	
2	456	361	837	839	561	710	487	
3	346	620	546	867	809	771	538	
4	709	660	586	661	539	333	408	
5	706	675	339	405	395	557	811	
6	645	850	780	543	623	750	222	
7	650	399	731	352	549	592	644	
8	812	716	728	792	488	455	825	
9	888	575	595	597	589	367	540	
10	855	643	495	394	233	570	349	
11	338	881	405	532	501	545	508	
12	569	390	476	535	427	635	735	
13	667	704	721	891	774	441	382	
14	673	867	799	728	429	853	451	
15	762	669	890	643	351	883	692	
16	766	629	414	459	318	810	584	
17	896	389	775	678	423	884	350	
18	784	821	861	572	871	865	639	
19	343	844	683	314	752	602	618	
20	814	550	501	336	763	435	505	
21	695	697	780	322	628	368	878	
22	793	803	310	719	788	610	823	
23								

Figure 168-1: You can use conditional formatting to quickly identify duplicate values in a range.

Here's how to set up the conditional formatting:

1. Select the cells in the range (in this example, A1:G22).

2. Choose Home➔Conditional Formatting➔New Rule to display the Conditional Formatting dialog box.

3. In the Conditional Formatting dialog box, select the option labeled Use a Formula to Determine Which Cells to Format.

4. For this example, enter this formula (change the range references to correspond to your own data):

```
=COUNTIF($A$1:$G$22,A1)>1
```

5. Click the Format button and specify the formatting to apply when the condition is true. Changing the fill color is a good choice.

6. Click OK.

Figure 168-2 shows the result. The six highlighted cells are the duplicate values in the range.

	A	B	C	D	E	F	G	H
1	624	366	828	521	438	382	317	
2	456	361	837	839	561	710	487	
3	346	620	546	867	809	771	538	
4	709	660	586	661	539	333	408	
5	706	675	339	405	395	557	811	
6	645	850	780	543	623	750	222	
7	650	399	731	352	549	592	644	
8	812	716	728	792	488	455	825	
9	888	575	595	597	589	367	540	
10	855	643	495	394	233	570	349	
11	338	881	405	532	501	545	508	
12	569	390	476	535	427	635	735	
13	667	704	721	891	774	441	382	
14	673	867	799	728	429	853	451	
15	762	669	890	643	351	883	692	
16	766	629	414	459	318	810	584	
17	896	389	775	678	423	884	350	
18	784	821	861	572	871	865	639	
19	343	844	683	314	752	602	618	
20	814	550	501	336	763	435	505	
21	695	697	780	322	628	368	878	
22	793	803	310	719	788	610	823	

Figure 168-2: Conditional formatting causes the duplicate cells to be highlighted.

You can extend this technique to identify entire rows within a list that are identical. The trick is to add a new column and use a formula that concatenates the data in each row. For example, if your list is in A2:G500, enter this formula in cell H2:

```
=A2&B2&C2&D2&E2&F2&G2
```

Copy the formula down the column and then apply the conditional formatting to the formulas in column H. In this case, the conditional formatting formula is

```
=COUNTIF($H$2:$H$500,H2)>1
```

Highlighted cells in column H indicate duplicate rows.

Cross-Ref

A feature introduced in Excel 2007 makes it easy to delete duplicate rows. See Tip 33.

Creating a Quick Frequency Tabulation

This tip describes a quick method for creating a frequency tabulation for a single column of data. Figure 169-1 shows a small part of a range that contains more than 20,000 rows of city and state data. The goal is to tally the number of times each state appears in the list.

Although you can tally the states in a number of ways, a pivot table is the easiest choice for this task.

	A	B	C	D	E
1	City	State			
2	Tacoma	WA			
3	Duxbury	MA			
4	Riverside	CA			
5	Fort Worth	TX			
6	Hanover	MA			
7	Merritt Island	FL			
8	Mountain View	CA			
9	Sterling	IL			
10	Miami	FL			
11	Richardson	TX			
12	Homer	AK			
13	Bridgewater	NJ			
14	Sierra Madre	CA			
15	Lansing	MI			
16	New York	NY			
17	Columbus	OH			
18	Chicago	IL			
19	Sacramento	CA			
20	Keymar	MD			
21	Portage	MI			
22	Larchmont	NY			
23	Weston	CT			
24	Denton	TX			

Figure 169-1: You can use a pivot table to generate a frequency tabulation for these state abbreviations.

Before you get started on this task, make sure that your data column has a heading. In this example, it's in cell B1.

Activate any cell in column A or B and then follow these steps:

1. Choose Insert➜Tables➜PivotTable to display the Create PivotTable dialog box.

2. If Excel doesn't correctly identify the range, change the Table/Range setting.

3. Specify a location for the pivot table.

4. Click OK.

   Excel creates an empty pivot table and displays the PivotTable Field List.

5. In the PivotTable Field List, drag the State field into the Row Labels section.

6. Drag the State field into the Values section.

Excel creates the pivot table, which shows the frequency of each state (see Figure 169-2).

	A	B	C	D	E	F	G	H
1	**City**	**State**			**Row Labels** ↴	**Count of State**		
2	Tacoma	WA			AK	113		
3	Duxbury	MA			AL	204		
4	Riverside	CA			AR	104		
5	Fort Worth	TX			AZ	363		
6	Hanover	MA			CA	3150		
7	Merritt Island	FL			CO	408		
8	Mountain View	CA			CT	388		
9	Sterling	IL			DC	84		
10	Miami	FL			DE	96		
11	Richardson	TX			FL	1001		
12	Homer	AK			GA	577		
13	Bridgewater	NJ			HI	71		
14	Sierra Madre	CA			IA	115		
15	Lansing	MI			ID	106		
16	New York	NY			IL	954		
17	Columbus	OH			IN	348		
18	Chicago	IL			KS	160		
19	Sacramento	CA			KY	138		
20	Keymar	MD			LA	193		
21	Portage	MI			MA	603		
22	Larchmont	NY			MD	517		
23	Weston	CT			ME	74		
24	Denton	TX			MI	652		
25	Ashaway	RI			MN	348		
26	Freehold	NJ			MO	300		
27	Birmingham	AL			MS	77		
28	Duncannon	PA			MT	56		

Figure 169-2: A quick pivot table shows the frequency of each state abbreviation.

This pivot table can be sorted by using the Home→Editing→Sort & Filter command. In addition, you can even create a pivot chart to display the counts graphically (as shown in Figure 169-3). Just select any cell in the pivot table and choose PivotTable Tools→Options→Tools→PivotChart.

Figure 169-3: A few mouse clicks creates a chart from the pivot table.

Controlling References to Cells within a Pivot Table

If you work with pivot tables, you've probably noticed that if you write a formula that refers to a cell within the pivot table, the cell reference is converted automatically to a GETPIVOTDATA function with a number of arguments.

Figure 170-1 shows an example. The formula in cell I4 (which I created by pointing) is a simple reference to cell G4 in the pivot table. But rather than display the simple formula, Excel converts it to

```
=GETPIVOTDATA("Score",$F$2,"Gender","Female","District","District 1")
```

Figure 170-1: A formula that references a cell in a pivot table might result in a complex formula.

This type of referencing ensures that your formulas still return the correct result if the structure of the pivot table is changed. If you prefer to avoid this automatic conversion, don't use the pointing technique when creating formulas that reference cells in a pivot table. Just enter the cell reference by typing its address.

You can also turn off the Generate GetPivotData option by choosing PivotTable Tools➔Options➔ PivotTable➔Options➔Generate GetPivotData.

The Generate GetPivotData button is a toggle. Click it once, and Excel stops generating GETPIVOTTABLE formulas. Click it again, and Excel starts generating those formulas again. This command doesn't affect existing formulas.

Grouping Items by Date in a Pivot Table

One of the more useful features of a pivot table is the ability to combine items into groups. Grouping items is simple: Select them and choose PivotTable Tools➔Options➔Group➔ Group Selection.

You can go a step further, though. When a field contains dates, Excel can create groups automatically. Many users overlook this helpful feature. Figure 171-1 shows a portion of a table that has two columns of data: Date and Sales. This table has 731 rows and covers dates between January 1, 2008, and December 31, 2009. The goal is to summarize the sales information by month.

	A	B	C	D	E
1	**Date**	**Sales**			
2	1/1/2008	1,983			
3	1/2/2008	1,991			
4	1/3/2008	2,041			
5	1/4/2008	1,978			
6	1/5/2008	2,006			
7	1/6/2008	2,003			
8	1/7/2008	1,908			
9	1/8/2008	1,972			
10	1/9/2008	1,892			
11	1/10/2008	1,908			
12	1/11/2008	1,890			
13	1/12/2008	1,932			
14	1/13/2008	1,888			
15	1/14/2008	1,988			
16	1/15/2008	2,026			
17	1/16/2008	2,082			
18	1/17/2008	1,999			
19	1/18/2008	1,956			
20	1/19/2008	2,011			

Figure 171-1: You can use a pivot table to summarize the sales data by month.

Figure 171-2 shows part of a pivot table (in columns D:E) created from the data. Not surprisingly, it looks exactly like the input data because the dates haven't been grouped.

To group the items by month, right-click any cell in the Date column of the pivot table and select Group from the shortcut menu. You see the Grouping dialog box, shown in Figure 171-3. In the list box, select Months and Years and verify that the starting and ending dates are correct. Click OK.

The Date items in the pivot table are grouped by years and by months (as shown in Figure 171-4).

	A	B	C	D	E	F
1	**Date**	**Sales**		**Row Labels** ▾	**Sum of Sales**	
2	1/1/2008	1,983		1/1/2008	1983	
3	1/2/2008	1,991		1/2/2008	1991	
4	1/3/2008	2,041		1/3/2008	2041	
5	1/4/2008	1,978		1/4/2008	1978	
6	1/5/2008	2,006		1/5/2008	2006	
7	1/6/2008	2,003		1/6/2008	2003	
8	1/7/2008	1,908		1/7/2008	1908	
9	1/8/2008	1,972		1/8/2008	1972	
10	1/9/2008	1,892		1/9/2008	1892	
11	1/10/2008	1,908		1/10/2008	1908	
12	1/11/2008	1,890		1/11/2008	1890	
13	1/12/2008	1,932		1/12/2008	1932	
14	1/13/2008	1,888		1/13/2008	1888	
15	1/14/2008	1,988		1/14/2008	1988	
16	1/15/2008	2,026		1/15/2008	2026	
17	1/16/2008	2,082		1/16/2008	2082	
18	1/17/2008	1,999		1/17/2008	1999	
19	1/18/2008	1,956		1/18/2008	1956	
20	1/19/2008	2,011		1/19/2008	2011	
21	1/20/2008	2,109		1/20/2008	2109	
22	1/21/2008	2,169		1/21/2008	2169	
23	1/22/2008	2,206		1/22/2008	2206	
24	1/23/2008	2,137		1/23/2008	2137	
25	1/24/2008	2,236		1/24/2008	2236	

Figure 171-2: The pivot table, before grouping by months and years.

Figure 171-3: Use the Grouping dialog box to group items in a pivot table.

Note

If you select only Months in the Grouping list box, months in different years are combined. For example, the June item would display sales for both 2008 and 2009.

	A	B	C	D	E	F
1	**Date**	**Sales**		**Row Labels** ▼	**Sum of Sales**	
2	1/1/2008	1,983		⊟2008		
3	1/2/2008	1,991		Jan	65,101	
4	1/3/2008	2,041		Feb	72,792	
5	1/4/2008	1,978		Mar	71,899	
6	1/5/2008	2,006		Apr	60,936	
7	1/6/2008	2,003		May	57,732	
8	1/7/2008	1,908		Jun	57,531	
9	1/8/2008	1,972		Jul	68,532	
10	1/9/2008	1,892		Aug	67,448	
11	1/10/2008	1,908		Sep	65,195	
12	1/11/2008	1,890		Oct	66,568	
13	1/12/2008	1,932		Nov	68,045	
14	1/13/2008	1,888		Dec	68,254	
15	1/14/2008	1,988		**2008 Total**	**790,033**	
16	1/15/2008	2,026		⊟2009		
17	1/16/2008	2,082		Jan	70,240	
18	1/17/2008	1,999		Feb	61,386	
19	1/18/2008	1,956		Mar	65,107	
20	1/19/2008	2,011		Apr	65,983	
21	1/20/2008	2,109		May	70,297	
22	1/21/2008	2,169		Jun	69,794	
23	1/22/2008	2,206		Jul	64,058	
24	1/23/2008	2,137		Aug	57,798	
25	1/24/2008	2,236		Sep	46,533	
26	1/25/2008	2,331		Oct	40,488	
27	1/26/2008	2,350		Nov	38,588	
28	1/27/2008	2,349		Dec	45,826	
29	1/28/2008	2,452		**2009 Total**	**696,098**	
30	1/29/2008	2,381		**Grand Total**	**1,486,131**	
31	1/30/2008	2,459				

Figure 171-4: The pivot table, after grouping by months and years.

Notice that the Grouping dialog box contains other time-based units. For example, you can group the data into quarters. Figure 171-5 shows the data grouped by quarters and years.

	A	B	C	D	E	F
1	**Date**	**Sales**		**Row Labels** ▼	**Sum of Sales**	
2	1/1/2008	1,983		⊟2008		
3	1/2/2008	1,991		Qtr1	209,792	
4	1/3/2008	2,041		Qtr2	176,199	
5	1/4/2008	1,978		Qtr3	201,175	
6	1/5/2008	2,006		Qtr4	202,867	
7	1/6/2008	2,003		**2008 Total**	**790,033**	
8	1/7/2008	1,908		⊟2009		
9	1/8/2008	1,972		Qtr1	196,733	
10	1/9/2008	1,892		Qtr2	206,074	
11	1/10/2008	1,908		Qtr3	168,389	
12	1/11/2008	1,890		Qtr4	124,902	
13	1/12/2008	1,932		**2009 Total**	**696,098**	
14	1/13/2008	1,888		**Grand Total**	**1,486,131**	
15	1/14/2008	1,988				

Figure 171-5: The pivot table, after grouping by quarters and years.

Unlinking a Pivot Table from Its Source

You may have a situation in which you need to send someone a pivot table summary report, but you don't want to include the original data. In other words, you want to "unlink" the pivot table from its data source.

Excel doesn't provide a direct way to unlink a pivot table, but if you follow a few easy steps, you'll end up with a perfect copy of the pivot table.

Figure 172-1 shows a nicely formatted pivot table. If you select the pivot table and copy it to another location, the copied range is also a pivot table. The solution is to copy and paste values.

	A	B	C	D	E	F	G
1							
2							
3		Sales Summary					
4			Eastern	Southern	Western	Grand Total	
5		Qtr1	811,861	454,819	308,050	1,574,730	
6		Qtr2	823,789	385,722	388,670	1,598,181	
7		Qtr3	799,865	320,012	505,327	1,625,204	
8		Qtr4	854,555	298,569	684,478	1,837,602	
9		Grand Total	3,290,070	1,459,122	1,886,525	6,635,717	
10							
11							

Figure 172-1: This pivot table will be unlinked from its data source.

Follow these steps to create an unlinked copy of the pivot table:

1. Select the pivot table cells (B3:F9 in this example) and press Ctrl+C to copy the range.

2. Choose Home➔Clipboard➔Paste➔Values.

   The pivot table is replaced by its values, but the nice pivot table formatting is gone (see Figure 172-2).

	A	B	C	D	E	F	G
1							
2							
3		Sales Summary					
4			Eastern	Southern	Western	Grand Total	
5		Qtr1	811,861	454,819	308,050	1,574,730	
6		Qtr2	823,789	385,722	388,670	1,598,181	
7		Qtr3	799,865	320,012	505,327	1,625,204	
8		Qtr4	854,555	298,569	684,478	1,837,602	
9		Grand Total	3,290,070	1,459,122	1,886,525	6,635,717	
10							(Ctrl) ▾
11							
12							

Figure 172-2: This pivot table is unlinked, but the formatting is no longer present.

To get the pivot table formatting back, you need to perform two additional steps:

1. Display the Office Clipboard by clicking the dialog box launcher icon in the bottom right corner of the Home➔Clipboard group.

2. With the unlinked pivot selected, click the item on the Office Clipboard that corresponds to the pivot table copy operation.

   It will be the last item, unless you copied something else.

   After you perform these steps, the pivot table is unlinked from its data source, yet retains all of its original formatting.

Using Pivot Table Slicers

If you work with pivot tables, you've probably discovered that you can apply filters to control what's shown in the pivot table. Figure 173-1 shows a pivot table (and a pivot chart) that summarizes sales by state and by month.

Sales Totals	Months						
States	**Jan**	**Feb**	**Mar**	**Apr**	**May**	**Jun**	**Total**
Arizona	1,345	1,375	1,075	1,736	1,555	1,372	8,458
California	1,118	1,960	1,252	1,271	1,557	1,679	8,837
Florida	1,705	1,792	1,225	1,946	1,327	1,357	9,352
Illinois	1,539	1,493	1,211	1,165	1,013	1,445	7,866
Kansas	1,973	1,560	1,243	1,495	1,125	1,387	8,783
Kentucky	1,109	1,078	1,155	1,993	1,082	1,551	7,968
Massachusetts	1,099	1,233	1,110	1,637	1,512	1,006	7,597
Missouri	1,511	1,744	1,414	1,243	1,493	1,820	9,225
New Jersey	1,735	1,406	1,224	1,706	1,320	1,290	8,681
New York	1,429	1,316	1,993	1,832	1,740	1,191	9,501
Oklahoma	1,309	1,045	1,641	1,924	1,499	1,941	9,359
Oregon	1,460	1,954	1,726	1,461	1,764	1,144	9,509
Washington	1,247	1,238	1,028	1,345	1,784	1,574	8,216
Total	**18,579**	**19,194**	**17,297**	**20,754**	**18,771**	**18,757**	**113,352**

Figure 173-1: An unfiltered pivot table and pivot chart.

You can filter the pivot table to show only specific months or specific states. Just click the drop-down arrow in the field label, and specify your filtering. Figure 173-2 shows a filter being applied to the States field. Clicking OK will change the pivot table (and pivot chart) to show data only for Arizona and California.

Filters are useful because you can temporarily hide irrelevant information and focus only on data that's of interest. In addition, filtering the pivot table to show only two states makes the pivot chart much more legible.

A problem with pivot table filtering is that it's easily overlooked. Not everyone understands that clicking those little arrows displays a filtering pane. Excel 2010 introduced a new feature called Slicers, which makes pivot table filtering easy and very discoverable.

⊿	F	G	H	I	J	K	L
1							
2			Sales Totals		Months ▾		
3			States	▾	Jan	Feb	Mar
4	A↓ Sort A to Z				1,345	1,375	1,075
5	Z↓ Sort Z to A				1,118	1,960	1,252
6	More Sort Options...				1,705	1,792	1,225
7					1,539	1,493	1,211
8	⊽ Clear Filter From "State"				1,973	1,560	1,243
9	Label Filters		▸		1,109	1,078	1,155
10	Value Filters		▸		1,099	1,233	1,110
11	Search		◡		1,511	1,744	1,414
12	▣ (Select All)				1,735	1,406	1,224
13	☑ Arizona				1,429	1,316	1,993
14	☑ California				1,309	1,045	1,641
15	☐ Florida				1,460	1,954	1,726
16	☐ Illinois ☐ Kansas				1,247	1,238	1,028
17	☐ Kentucky				18,579	19,194	17,297
18	☐ Massachusetts						
19	☐ Missouri						
20	☐ New Jersey						
21	☐ New York						
22	☐ Oklahoma						
23	☐ Oregon						
24	☐ Washington						
25							
26	OK	Cancel					
27							

Figure 173-2: Applying a filter to a pivot table.

To add one or more Slicers to a pivot table, select any cell in the pivot table and choose Insert➔ Filter➔Slicer. Excel displays its Insert Slicers dialog box, which allows you to choose one or more fields. Click OK, and the Slicers are added to your worksheet.

Figure 173-3 shows the pivot table after I added two Slicers. The pivot table is filtered to show data for three months for two states. Notice that the pivot chart is also filtered, making it much easier to read.

To filter using a Slicer, just click the item in the Slicer. Press Ctrl to select multiple items. To clear the filters (and show all data in a field), click the Clear Filter icon in the upper right corner of the Slicer.

Slicers are highly customizable. You can adjust their dimensions, change their colors, and specify multiple columns. When you select a Slicer, you have access to the tools on the Slicer Tools➔ Options contextual tab.

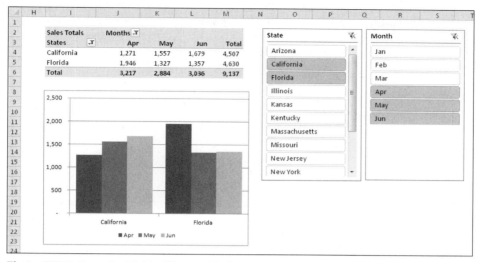

Figure 173-3: Two pivot table Slicers added to a worksheet.

## PART IX

Working with Files

In this part, you'll find tips that deal with files — information that every Excel user should know (but many don't).

Tips and Where to Find Them

Understanding the New Excel File Formats

Perhaps one of the most confusing aspects of Excel is the nearly overwhelming number of file formats that it can read and write. With the introduction of Excel 2007, things got even more confusing because it has quite a few new file formats.

This tip describes the new file formats used by Excel 2007 and Excel 2010.

Recognizing the new Excel file formats

Excel's new file formats are

> **XLSX:** A workbook file that doesn't contain macros

> **XLSM:** A workbook file that contains macros

> **XLTX:** A workbook template file that doesn't contain macros

> **XLTM:** A workbook template file that contains macros

> **XLSA:** An add-in file

> **XLSB:** A binary file similar to the old XLS format but able to accommodate the new features

> **XLSK:** A backup file

With the exception of XLSB, these are all *open* XML file formats, which means that other applications can read and write these types of files.

Note

The XML files are ZIP-compressed text files. If you rename one of these files so that it has a ZIP extension, you can examine the contents by using any of several ZIP file utilities — including the ZIP file support built into Windows.

The Office compatibility pack

Normally, those who use an earlier version of Excel can't open workbooks saved in the new Excel file formats. But, fortunately, Microsoft has released the free Compatibility Pack for Office 2003 and Office XP.

An Office 2003 or Office XP user who installs the Compatibility Pack can open files created in Office 2007 and Office 2010 and also save files in the new formats. The Office programs that are affected are Excel, Word, and PowerPoint.

To download the Compatibility Pack, search the Web for **Microsoft Office Compatibility Pack**.

Saving a file for use with an older version of Excel

To save a file for use with an older version of Excel, choose File➔Save As and select one of these options from the Save As Type drop-down list:

➤ **Excel 97–2003 Workbook (*.xls):** If the file will be used by someone who has Excel 97, Excel 2000, Excel 2002, or Excel 2003

➤ **Microsoft Excel 5.0/95 Workbook (*.xls):** If the file will be used by someone who has Excel 5 or Excel 95

When you save a file by using one of these file formats, Excel displays its Compatibility Checker dialog box. This dialog box lists all potential compatibility problems.

Note

If the workbook will be used only by someone who has installed the Office Compatibility Pack, you don't need to save it by using an earlier file format. However, it's a good idea to run the Compatibility Checker to make sure that you're not using features that aren't supported by earlier versions of Excel. To check potential compatibility problems in the active workbook, choose File➔Info➔Check For Issues➔Check Compatibility.

If you would like to use one of the older file formats as your default format, choose File➔Option and click the Save tab. Specify the default file format in the Save Files in This Format drop-down list.

Importing a Text File into a Worksheet Range

If you need to insert a text file into a specific range in a worksheet, you might think that your only choice is to import the text into a new workbook (by choosing Office➜Open) and then to copy the data and paste it to the range where you want it to appear. However, you can do it in a more direct way.

Figure 175-1 shows a small CSV (*comma separated value*) file. The following instructions describe how to import this file beginning at cell C4.

```
monthlydata.csv - Notepad
File  Edit  Format  View  Help
City,Jan,Feb,Mar,Apr,May,Jun,Jul,Aug,Sep,Oct,Nov,Dec
"ABERDEEN,  SD",10.10,16.70,29.80,45.20,57.10,66.60,72.80,70.60,59.60,47.30,30.30,15.30
"ABILENE,  TX",42.80,47.40,56.10,65.40,72.70,80.20,84.00,83.20,76.00,66.40,54.90,45.50
"AKRON,  OH",24.80,27.40,38.00,48.50,59.00,67.80,71.90,70.30,63.70,52.40,42.00,30.70
"ALAMOSA,  CO",14.70,22.40,32.30,41.10,50.40,59.40,64.90,62.40,54.80,43.50,29.90,17.50
"ALBANY,  NY",20.60,23.50,34.30,46.40,57.60,66.90,71.80,69.60,61.30,50.20,39.70,26.50
"ALBUQUERQUE,  NM",34.20,40.00,46.90,55.20,64.20,74.20,78.50,75.90,68.60,57.00,44.30,35.30
"ALLENTOWN,  PA",26.60,29.30,39.40,49.70,60.30,69.40,74.10,72.20,64.70,53.20,43.10,31.80
"ALPENA,  MI",17.60,18.30,28.00,40.90,52.00,61.30,67.10,64.80,57.30,46.90,35.70,23.70
"AMARILLO,  TX",35.10,39.20,47.10,56.80,65.40,74.10,78.60,76.50,69.10,58.50,46.00,36.90
"ANCHORAGE,  AK",14.90,18.70,25.70,35.80,46.60,54.40,58.40,56.30,48.40,34.60,21.20,16.30
"ANNETTE,  AK",34.30,37.00,39.30,43.30,49.00,54.30,58.30,58.60,54.20,46.90,39.30,35.70
"APALACHICOLA,  FL",52.20,54.50,60.70,67.30,74.00,79.70,81.40,81.30,78.60,70.20,61.90,55.30
"ASHEVILLE,  NC",35.70,38.70,47.40,55.20,63.00,69.40,72.80,72.00,66.20,55.90,47.50,39.50
"ASTORIA,  OR",41.90,44.20,45.70,48.20,52.50,56.90,60.00,60.70,58.40,52.60,46.90,42.40
"ATHENS,  GA",41.80,45.50,53.60,61.60,69.30,76.40,79.60,78.50,72.90,62.20,53.40,45.10
"ATLANTA,  GA",41.00,44.80,53.50,61.50,69.20,76.00,78.80,78.10,72.70,62.30,53.10,44.50
"ATLANTIC CITY AP, NJ",30.90,33.00,41.50,50.00,60.40,69.40,74.70,73.40,66.10,54.90,45.80,35.80
"AUGUSTA,GA",43.90,47.40,55.50,62.70,70.70,77.50,80.80,79.70,74.50,63.80,55.00,47.20
"AUSTIN,  TX",48.80,52.80,61.50,69.60,75.60,81.30,84.50,84.80,80.20,71.10,60.90,51.60
"AVOCA,  PA",24.70,26.80,36.90,48.00,58.80,67.20,71.70,69.90,62.60,51.50,41.40,30.00
"BAKERSFIELD,  CA",47.80,53.30,57.40,63.00,71.00,78.20,84.10,82.60,76.80,67.80,55.80,47.50
"BALTIMORE,  MD",31.80,34.80,44.10,53.40,63.40,72.50,77.00,75.60,68.50,56.60,46.80,36.70
"BARROW,  AK",-13.40,-17.80,-15.10,-2.20,19.30,34.00,39.30,37.90,30.50,13.50,-1.70,-11.20
```

Figure 175-1: This CSV file will be imported into a range.

1. Choose Data➜Get External Data➜From Text to display the Import Text File dialog box.

2. Navigate to the folder that contains the text file.

3. Select the file from the list and then click the Import button to display the Text Import Wizard.

4. Use the Text Import Wizard to specify how the data will be imported.

   For a CSV file, specify Delimited, with a Comma Delimiter.

5. Click the Finish button.

   Excel displays the Import Data dialog box.

6. In the Import Data dialog box, click the Properties button to display the External Data Range Properties dialog box.

7. In the External Data Range Properties dialog box, deselect the Save Query Definition check box and click OK to return to the Import Data dialog box.

8. In the Import Data dialog box, specify the location for the imported data.

   It can be a cell in an existing worksheet or a new worksheet.

9. Click OK, and Excel imports the data (see Figure 175-2).

Note   You can ignore Step 7 if the data you're importing will be changing. By saving the query definition, you can quickly update the imported data by right-clicking any cell in the range and choosing Refresh.

	A	B	C	D	E	F	G	H	I	J	K	L	M	N	O
1															
2															
3															
4			City	Jan	Feb	Mar	Apr	May	Jun	Jul	Aug	Sep	Oct	Nov	Dec
5			ABERDEEN, SD	10.1	16.7	29.8	45.2	57.1	66.6	72.8	70.6	59.6	47.3	30.3	15.3
6			ABILENE, TX	42.8	47.4	56.1	65.4	72.7	80.2	84	83.2	76	66.4	54.9	45.5
7			AKRON, OH	24.8	27.4	38	48.5	59	67.8	71.9	70.3	63.7	52.4	42	30.7
8			ALAMOSA, CO	14.7	22.4	32.3	41.1	50.4	59.4	64.9	62.4	54.8	43.5	29.9	17.5
9			ALBANY, NY	20.6	23.5	34.3	46.4	57.6	66.9	71.8	69.6	61.3	50.2	39.7	26.5
10			ALBUQUERQUE, NM	34.2	40	46.9	55.2	64.2	74.2	78.5	75.9	68.6	57	44.3	35.3
11			ALLENTOWN, PA	26.6	29.3	39.4	49.7	60.3	69.4	74.1	72.2	64.7	53.2	43.1	31.8
12			ALPENA, MI	17.6	18.3	28	40.9	52	61.3	67.1	64.8	57.3	46.9	35.7	23.7
13			AMARILLO, TX	35.1	39.2	47.1	56.8	65.4	74.1	78.6	76.5	69.1	58.5	46	36.9
14			ANCHORAGE, AK	14.9	18.7	25.7	35.8	46.6	54.4	58.4	56.3	48.4	34.6	21.2	16.3
15			ANNETTE, AK	34.3	37	39.3	43.3	49	54.3	58.3	58.6	54.2	46.9	39.3	35.7
16			APALACHICOLA, FL	52.2	54.5	60.7	67.3	74	79.7	81.4	81.3	78.6	70.2	61.9	55.3
17			ASHEVILLE, NC	35.7	38.7	47.4	55.2	63	69.4	72.8	72	66.2	55.9	47.5	39.5
18			ASTORIA, OR	41.9	44.2	45.7	48.2	52.5	56.9	60	60.7	58.4	52.6	46.9	42.4
19			ATHENS, GA	41.8	45.5	53.6	61.6	69.3	76.4	79.6	78.5	72.9	62.2	53.4	45.1
20			ATLANTA, GA	41	44.8	53.5	61.5	69.2	76	78.8	78.1	72.7	62.3	53.1	44.5
21			ATLANTIC CITY AP, NJ	30.9	33	41.5	50	60.4	69.4	74.7	73.4	66.1	54.9	45.8	35.8
22			AUGUSTA, GA	43.9	47.4	55.5	62.7	70.7	77.5	80.8	79.7	74.5	63.8	55	47.2
23			AUSTIN, TX	48.8	52.8	61.5	69.6	75.6	81.3	84.5	84.8	80.2	71.1	60.9	51.6
24			AVOCA, PA	24.7	26.8	36.9	48	58.8	67.2	71.7	69.9	62.6	51.5	41.4	30
25			BAKERSFIELD, CA	47.8	53.3	57.4	63	71	78.2	84.1	82.6	76.8	67.8	55.8	47.5

Figure 175-2: This range contains data imported directly from a CSV file.

Getting Data from a Web Page

This tip describes three ways to capture data contained on a Web page:

➤ Paste a static copy of the information.

➤ Create a refreshable link to the site.

➤ Open the page directly in Excel.

Pasting static information

One way to get data from a Web page into a worksheet is to simply highlight the text in your browser, press Ctrl+C to copy it to the Clipboard, and then paste it into a worksheet. The results will vary, depending on what browser you use. If you use Microsoft Internet Explorer, the pasted results will probably look very similar to the original — complete with formatting, hyperlinks, and graphics.

If you use a browser other than Internet Explorer, choosing Home→Clipboard→Paste might put everything you copied from the Web page into a single cell — probably not what you want. The solution is to choose Home→Clipboard→Paste→Paste Special and then try various paste options.

Pasting refreshable information

If you need to regularly access updated data from a Web page, create a Web query. Figure 176-1 shows a Web site that contains currency exchange rates, in a three-column table.

These steps create a Web query that allows this information to be retrieved and then refreshed at any time with a single mouse click:

1. Choose Data→Get External Data→From Web to display the New Web Query dialog box.

2. In the Address field, enter the URL of the Web site and click Go.

   For this example, the URL for the Web page shown in Figure 176-1 is

   ```
   http://moneycentral.msn.com/investor/market/exchangerates.aspx
   ```

   Notice that the New Web Query dialog box contains a minibrowser (Internet Explorer). You can click links and navigate the Web site until you locate the data you're interested in.

   When a Web page is displayed in the New Web Query dialog box, you see one or more yellow arrows, which correspond to various elements in the Web page.

3. Click a yellow arrow, and it turns into a green check box, which indicates that the data in that element will be imported.

You can import as many elements as you need. For this example, I clicked the arrow next to the rate table (see Figure 176-2).

4. Click the Import button to display the Import Data dialog box.

5. In the Import Data dialog box, specify the location for the imported data.

    It can be a cell in an existing worksheet or a new worksheet.

6. Click OK, and Excel imports the data (see Figure 176-3).

Figure 176-1: This site contains information that changes frequently.

Figure 176-2: Using the New Web Query dialog box to specify the data to be imported.

By default, the imported data is a Web query. To refresh the information, right-click any cell in the imported range and choose Refresh from the shortcut menu.

If you don't want to create a refreshable query, specify this choice in Step 5 of the preceding step list. In the Import Data dialog box, click the Properties button and deselect the Save Query Definition check box.

Opening the Web page directly

Another way to get Web page data into a worksheet is to open the URL directly, by using Excel's File➜Open command. Just enter the complete URL into the File Name field and click Open. The results will vary, depending on how the Web page is laid out. Most of the time, you'll get satisfactory results. In some cases, you'll retrieve quite a bit of extraneous information.

	A	B	C	D	E	F
1						
2		Currency Rates				
3		Currency	In US Dollar	Per US Dollar		
4		Argentine Peso	0.26082	3.834		
5		Australian Dollar	0.88992	1.1237		
6		Brazilian Real	0.53879	1.856		
7		British Pound	1.5949	0.627		
8		Canadian Dollar	0.94073	1.063		
9		Chinese Yuan	0.14656	6.823		
10		Euro	1.39218	0.7183		
11		Hong Kong Dollar	0.12877	7.7659		
12		Indian Rupee	0.02161	46.28		
13		Japanese Yen	0.01101	90.79		
14		Korean Won	0.00086	1,169.45		
15		Mexican Peso	0.07756	12.894		
16		Russian Rouble	0.03296	30.3404		
17		Swedish Krona	0.13762	7.2662		
18		Swiss Franc	0.94527	1.0579		
19		US Dollar	1	1		
20						

Figure 176-3: The data, imported from a Web page.

Displaying a Workbook's Full Path

If you have lots of files open in Excel, you might need to know the full path of the active workbook. Oddly, Excel provides no direct way to get this information. This tip describes several methods to enable you to determine the path of the active workbook.

Go backstage

One way to see the path of the active workbook is to choose File➞Info. The active workbook's path is displayed at the top of the Backstage View.

Use a formula

Another option is to enter the following formula into a cell:

```
=CELL("filename")
```

The formula displays the workbook's path, including the name of the worksheet that contains the formula.

Add a control to your Quick Access toolbar

A control named Document Location isn't available on the Ribbon, but you can add it to your Quick Access toolbar. Figure 177-1 shows what this control looks like. Unfortunately, you can't change the width of this control, but if you click the displayed name, you can see the entire path.

Figure 177-1: The Document Location control added to the Quick Access toolbar displays the full path of the active workbook.

To add this control to your Quick Access toolbar, follow these steps:

1. Right-click the Quick Access toolbar and choose Customize Quick Access Toolbar.

2. In the Quick Access Toolbar tab of the Excel Options dialog box, choose Commands Not in the Ribbon from the drop-down list on the left.

3. Scroll down the list and select Document Location.

4. Click the Add button to add the selected control to the Quick Access toolbar.

5. Click OK to close the Excel Options dialog box.

Display the Document panel

Yet another way to view the path of the active workbook is to display the Document Properties panel. Choose File➔Info➔Properties➔Show Document Panel. The Document Properties panel is displayed above the Formula bar. Unfortunately, the Document Properties panel takes up quite a bit of space, and it can't be moved or resized.

You might want to add the Properties control to your Quick Access toolbar. See the instructions in the previous section. In this case, choose File Tab in Step 2 and Properties in Step 3. The Properties control toggles the Document Panel display, so you can click once to see the workbook's path and then click again to hide it.

Use a macro

If you're comfortable using VBA macros, enter this Sub procedure in a VBA module in your Personal Macro Workbook:

```
Sub ShowPath()
    MsgBox ActiveWorkbook.Path
End Sub
```

Then, add the ShowPath macro to your Quick Access toolbar. When this procedure is executed, the path of the active workbook is displayed in a message box.

Using Document Properties

If you have many Excel files — and have trouble keeping them organized — this tip might be helpful. You can specify a number of properties for each workbook file. The properties describe the workbook and can be useful when searching.

Figure 178-1 shows the Document Properties panel, located above the Formula bar. To display this panel, choose File➜Info➜Properties➜Show Document Panel.

Figure 178-1: The Document Properties panel.

You can enter information in any of these fields:

> ➤ Author
> ➤ Title
> ➤ Subject
> ➤ Keywords

➤ Category

➤ Status

➤ Comments

When you use Excel's Open or Save As dialog box, you can specify which properties to display for the files. Right-click the column header (which normally displays Name, Size, Type, and Date Modified). You see a number of additional file properties that you can display. Click the More option, and you get the Choose Details dialog box. When these additional properties are displayed, you can sort the file list by any property. Make sure that you choose Details view.

Note

You can also specify some of the properties when you save a workbook for the first time. Excel's Save As dialog box displays file properties at the bottom. Just click and start typing.

Inspecting a Workbook

When you send an Excel workbook to someone (or post it on the Internet), it's a good idea to examine the workbook using Excel's Document Inspector before you save for the last time. The Document Inspector checks for these types of content:

> ➤ Comments and annotations

> ➤ Document properties and personal information

> ➤ Custom XML data

> ➤ Headers and footers

> ➤ Hidden rows and columns

> ➤ Hidden worksheets

> ➤ Invisible content

To display the Document Inspector dialog box (shown in Figure 179-1), choose File➜Info➜Check For Issues➜Inspect Document.

Figure 179-1: Use the Document Inspector to identify hidden information in your workbook.

When you click the Inspect button, Excel searches the workbook for the items that are selected in the dialog box. If any items are found, you can remove them all.

Unfortunately, this tool leaves much to be desired. For example, it doesn't provide you with any specific information or generate a report that contains the details. But, it's better than checking those items manually.

Finding the Missing No to All Button When Closing Files

Assume that you have a dozen or so workbooks open, and you want to close Excel without saving any changes. Excel displays the dialog box shown in Figure 180-1. And it does it for every changed workbook that is open.

Figure 180-1: Excel displays this prompt for every unsaved file.

As you can see, this dialog box has a Save All button but lacks a No to All button. Here's the secret: Press Shift while you click the Don't Save button. That action functions exactly like clicking a No to All button — if one existed.

By the way, this tip works in many of the Windows dialog boxes as well. For example, if you're copying a group of files and some of the files already exist, Windows makes you verify your overwrite intentions. That dialog box also lacks a No to All button, but you can Shift+click the No button.

Getting a List of Filenames

You might think that putting a list of filenames into a worksheet range would be fairly straightforward: Just instruct Windows to generate a list of files for a directory and then import the list into an Excel worksheet. Unfortunately, it's not that easy. Many users are surprised to discover that Windows doesn't provide a direct way to export a list of filenames to a file.

Perhaps the best solution is to write a VBA macro to create a list of files. The method described here doesn't require a macro. However, it does require that you go back in time and use an old-fashioned command line interface.

The following instructions assume that you want to generate a list of files contained in a directory named upper :

1. Click the Windows Start button and choose Run.

2. In the Run dialog box, type **cmd** and click OK.

   This step displays the Windows command shell.

   If you don't see the Run command, type **cmd** in the search box.

3. Navigate to the directory that you're interested in by typing **cd**, followed by the full path.

   In this example, enter this line:

   ```
   cd c:\my files\excel
   ```

4. Type the following command and press Enter:

   ```
   dir > filelist.txt
   ```

Figure 181-1 shows what the command prompt window looks like as you work through the preceding set of steps.

Figure 181-1: Using the Windows command prompt to generate a list of files.

In response to your command, Windows creates a file named upper in the current directory (the one you specified in Step 3). You can then use Excel's File→Open command to import this file, which starts the File Import Wizard. (Make sure to specify fixed-width data.) Figure 181-2 shows some data that I imported.

	A	B	C	D	E	F
1	Volume in	drive	C is	OS		
2	Volume Se	rial Nu	mber	is AAAE-8(EE		
3						
4	Directory	of c:\	my f	iles\excel		
5						
6	2/1/2010	1:41 PM	<DIR>			.
7	2/1/2010	1:41 PM	<DIR>			..
8	7/28/2009	1:41 PM			14,126	annuity calculator.xlsx
9	7/31/2009	12:37 PM			16,824	area charts.xlsx
10	11/13/2006	12:00 PM			96,670	atp examples.xlsx
11	7/24/2009	3:47 PM			13,937	basic counting.xlsx
12	7/28/2009	11:05 AM			22,793	basic lookup examples.xlsx
13	8/3/2009	3:12 PM			20,399	budget.xlsx
14	11/13/2006	12:00 PM			10,505	cell references.xlsx
15	11/13/2006	12:00 PM			21,885	circular reference.xlsx
16	7/31/2009	11:48 AM			21,594	column charts.xlsx
17	8/3/2009	10:01 AM			18,808	conditional colors.xlsx
18	11/13/2006	12:00 PM			8,821	count unique.xlsx
19	11/13/2006	12:00 PM			8,940	counting text in a range.xlsx
20	7/28/2009	10:47 AM			14,671	cumulative sum.xlsx
21	11/13/2006	12:00 PM			14,139	data validation examples.xlsx
22	11/13/2006	12:00 PM			14,732	doughnut charts.xlsx
23	2/1/2010	1:41 PM			0	filelist.txt
24	7/28/2009	10:42 AM			34,014	frequency distribution.xlsx
25	11/13/2006	12:00 PM			16,048	hands-on example.xlsx
26	7/24/2009	3:28 PM			15,001	jogging log.xlsx

Figure 181-2: This file listing was imported from a text file.

As you can see, the listing needs to be cleaned up a bit, but all the information is there, including the date, time, and size of each file.

Note

The DIR command has quite a few options. For example, you can get a list of the files in all subdirectories as well as the current directory by using this statement:

```
dir/s > filelist.txt
```

Search online for DOS DIR command, and you'll find lots of information about the DIR command.

Using Workspace Files

If you have a project that uses multiple workbooks, you probably get tired of opening the same files every time you work on the project.

The solution? Create a workspace file:

1. Open all the files used for your project.

2. Arrange the workbook windows the way you like them.

3. Choose View➜Window➜Save Workspace to display the Save Workspace dialog box.

4. Excel proposes the name upper, but you can specify any name you like. Just make sure that you use the XLW extension.

5. Click Save, and the workspace file is created.

After creating a workspace file, you can open it by choosing File➜Open. In the Open dialog box, specify Workspaces (upper) in the Files of Type drop-down list.

Note

A workspace file contains *only* the filenames and window position information — not the workbooks. Saving the workspace file does not save the workbooks.

## PART X

Printing

We haven't quite reached the paperless office yet, so it's still important to get your work on paper in a way that looks good. The tips in this part deal with printing and previewing your work.

Tips and Where to Find Them

Controlling What Gets Printed

This tip deals with some printing basics.

Displaying the Quick Print button

No, your eyes don't deceive you. It's true that Excel 2010, by default, doesn't display a Print button on the Ribbon. The "normal" way of printing a document is to choose the File➜Print➜Print command.

If you like the idea of one-click printing, make a change to your Quick Access toolbar:

1. Click the downward-pointing arrow to the right of the Quick Access toolbar.

2. Choose Quick Print.

After you complete these steps, the Quick Access toolbar displays a new icon. Click the icon, and Excel prints the entire contents of the active worksheet. But sometimes you want a bit more control over the documents you send to your printer.

Adjusting common page setup settings

Clicking the Quick Print button (or choosing File➜Print➜Print) may produce acceptable results in many cases, but a little tweaking of the print settings can often improve your printed reports. You can adjust print settings in three places:

> ➤ The Print screen in Backstage View, displayed when you choose File➜Print

> ➤ The Page Layout tab of the Ribbon

> ➤ The Page Setup dialog box, displayed when you click the dialog launcher in the bottom-right corner of the Page Layout➜Page Setup group on the Ribbon

Table 183-1 summarizes the locations where you can make various types of print adjustments in Excel 2010.

Table 183-1: Where to Change Printer Settings

Setting	Print Screen (Backstage)	Page Layout Tab of Ribbon	Page Setup Dialog Box
Number of copies	X		
Printer to use	X		
What to print	X		
Specify worksheet print area		X	X
1-sided or 2-sided	X		
Collated	X		
Orientation	X	X	X
Paper size	X	X	X
Adjust margins	X	X	X
Specify manual page breaks		X	
Specify repeating rows and/or columns			X
Set print scaling		X	X
Print or hide gridlines		X	X
Print or hide row and column headings		X	X
Specify the first page number			X
Center output on page			X
Specify header/footer and options			X
Specify how to print cell comments			X
Specify page order			X
Specify black-and-white output			X
Specify how to print error cells			X
Launch dialog box for printer-specific settings	X		X

Table 183-1 might make printing seem more complicated than it really is. The key point to remember is this: If you can't find a way to make a particular adjustment, it's probably available from the Page Setup dialog box.

Displaying Repeated Rows or Columns on a Printout

You might be familiar with the Excel View→Window→Freeze Panes command, which you can use to specify rows or columns, or both, that will remain fixed while you scroll the worksheet.

The View→Window→Freeze Panes command has no effect on printed output. If you want your printout to display one or more fixed rows at the top and/or one or more fixed columns along the left, you need to set up this task separately:

1. Select Page Layout→Page Setup→Print Titles to display the Sheet tab of the Page Setup dialog box.

2. To specify one or more rows to repeat at the top, click the icon on the far right side of the Rows to Repeat at Top field and then point to the rows in your worksheet.

3. To specify one or more columns to repeat on the left, click the icon on the far right side of the Columns to Repeat at Left field and then point to the columns in your worksheet.

4. Click OK to close the Page Setup dialog box and then print the worksheet.

Printing Noncontiguous Ranges on a Single Page

Excel lets you specify a print area that consists of noncontiguous ranges. Press Ctrl while you select the ranges to print and then choose Page Layout➔Page Setup➔Print Area➔Set Print Area. After you've defined a print area, you can use Page Layout➔Page Setup➔Print Area➔Add to Print Area to specify additional ranges to print.

When you set up a noncontiguous print area, Excel always starts printing each range on a separate sheet of paper. This tip describes a technique that allows you to print multiple ranges on a single page.

The trick involves creating a linked picture of each of the ranges to be printed and then arranging these pictures on a separate worksheet. Here's one way to create a linked picture:

1. Select the range.
2. Press Ctrl+C.
3. Activate a different cell.
4. Choose Home➔Clipboard➔Paste➔Linked Picture.

Fortunately, Excel has a much more efficient tool for the job: the Camera tool (which, for some reason, Microsoft keeps rather hidden).

Breaking out the Camera tool

To add the Camera tool to your Quick Access toolbar, follow these steps:

1. Right-click the Quick Access toolbar and choose Customize Quick Access Toolbar to display the Quick Access Toolbar tab of the Excel Options dialog box.
2. In the drop-down list on the left, choose Commands Not in the Ribbon.
3. Select Camera in the list.
4. Click Add to add the Camera tool to your Quick Access toolbar.
5. Click OK to close the Excel Options dialog box.

The Camera tool creates a linked picture of a range. Therefore, if the data in the linked range changes, the picture is updated automatically.

Figure 185-1 shows a worksheet. The goal is to print two ranges (A3:C10 and E13:G20) on a single page.

	A	B	C	D	E	F	G	H
1	**Call Volume Stats**							
2								
3	**Date**	**Calls**	**Weekday**		107	102	166	
4	1-Mar	156	Monday		126	166	189	
5	2-Mar	283	Tuesday		142	185	110	
6	3-Mar	254	Wednesday		183	169	193	
7	4-Mar	301	Thursday		101	171	106	
8	5-Mar	287	Friday		155	116	178	
9	6-Mar	132	Saturday		197	163	125	
10	7-Mar	73	Sunday		116	195	105	
11								
12								
13	153	98	182		**Date**	**Calls**	**Weekday**	
14	180	180	180		1-Apr	283	Thursday	
15	165	125	170		2-Apr	254	Friday	
16	165	183	196		3-Apr	109	Saturday	
17	128	196	102		4-Apr	56	Sunday	
18	153	152	114		5-Apr	176	Monday	
19	117	113	150		6-Apr	293	Tuesday	
20	118	187	195		7-Apr	271	Wednesday	
21								

Figure 185-1: It's normally impossible to print ranges A3:C10 and E13:G20 on a single page.

Shooting with the Camera

The following steps show you how to use the Camera tool to print multiple ranges on one piece of paper:

1. Make sure that the Camera tool is available on your Quick Access toolbar.

   Refer to the preceding steps if it's not.

2. Insert a new worksheet (Sheet2) to hold the linked pictures.

3. Select A3:C10 and click the Camera tool.

4. Activate Sheet2 and click to insert the linked picture.

5. Return to the previous worksheet, select E13:G20, and click the Camera tool.

6. Activate Sheet2 and click to insert the linked picture.

7. Use your mouse to arrange the linked pictures any way you like.

   You might want to turn off the gridline display in the worksheet that holds the linked pictures.

Figure 185-2 shows the worksheet that contains the linked pictures. If the data in Sheet1 changes, the linked pictures are updated. When you print Sheet2, both ranges appear on the same page.

	Date	Calls	Weekday
	1-Mar	156	Monday
	2-Mar	283	Tuesday
	3-Mar	254	Wednesday
	4-Mar	301	Thursday
	5-Mar	287	Friday
	6-Mar	132	Saturday
	7-Mar	73	Sunday

	Date	Calls	Weekday
	1-Apr	283	Thursday
	2-Apr	254	Friday
	3-Apr	109	Saturday
	4-Apr	56	Sunday
	5-Apr	176	Monday
	6-Apr	293	Tuesday
	7-Apr	271	Wednesday

Figure 185-2: Using linked pictures makes it possible to print the two ranges on a single page.

Preventing Objects from Printing

You can place a wide variety of objects on a worksheet — charts, shapes, pictures, SmartArt, and controls (such as check boxes), for example. By default, all these objects are printed when you print the worksheet.

You can, of course, specify that a particular object *doesn't* print. However, the procedure varies with the type of object.

The following list describes how to keep a particular object from printing. In all cases, start by clicking the object to select it.

> **Chart:** Select the Chart Area (the background), right-click, and choose Format Chart Area. In the Format Chart Area dialog box, click the Properties tab and deselect the Print Object check box.

> **SmartArt:** Right-click the background of the SmartArt object and choose Format Object. In the Format Shape dialog box, click the Properties tab and deselect the Print Object check box.

> **WordArt:** Right-click the object and choose Format Shape. In the Format Shape dialog box, click the Properties tab and deselect the Print Object check box.

> **Shape, Textbox, Picture, or Clipart:** Right-click the object and choose Size and Properties (or Format Shape) from the shortcut menu. In the Format Shape dialog box, click the Properties tab and deselect the Print Object check box.

> **Form control:** (You insert it by choosing Developer➡Controls➡Insert➡Form Controls.) Right-click the control and choose Format Control from the shortcut menu. In the Format Control dialog box, click the Properties tab and deselect the Print Object check box.

> **ActiveX control:** (You insert it by choosing Developer➡Controls➡Insert➡ActiveX Controls.) Make sure that Excel is in Design mode. (Click the Developer➡Controls➡ Design Mode button.) Right-click the control and choose Format Control from the shortcut menu. In the Format Control dialog box, click the Properties tab and deselect the Print Object check box.

Page-Numbering Tips

For lengthy printouts, you probably want to add page numbers to help keep the pages in order. This tip describes your page numbering options.

Applying basic page numbering

To add page numbering, follow these steps:

1. Choose View➡Workbook Views➡Page Layout, to switch to Page Layout view.

   Notice that each page has a header at the top and a footer at the bottom. Each header and footer is divided into three sections: left, center, and right.

2. Click the header or footer area where you want the page number to appear.

3. Choose Header & Footer Tools➡Design➡Page Number.

   Excel inserts a code that represents the page number.

4. Click any cell in the worksheet to see the actual page numbers.

In Step 3, the code that Excel adds simply inserts a number. You can add text to the page numbering code. For example, if you want your page numbers to read Page 3, type **Page** (followed by a space) before the code. This type of header or footer entry looks like this:

```
Page &[Page]
```

You might prefer to include the total number of pages so that the page numbering reads like this: Page 3 of 20. In Step 3, choose Header & Footer Tools➡Design➡Number of Pages to insert the code. You also need to enter the word *of.* The complete code looks like this:

```
Page &[Page] of &[Pages]
```

Changing the starting page number

If your printout will be part of a larger report, you might want to begin page numbering with a number other than 1. To do so, follow these steps:

1. Choose File➡Print, and Excel displays the Print settings in Backstage View.

2. Click the Page Setup link to display the Page Setup dialog box.

3. In the Page Setup dialog box, click the Page tab.

4. Enter the starting page number in the field labeled First Page Number.

Note

If you specify a starting page number other than 1, you probably don't want to use the &[Pages] code in your header or footer. If you do, you might see text that reads Page 18 of 3.

Adding and Removing Page Breaks

One way to approach page breaks on printed output is to just let the pages break where they break. That situation might be acceptable most of the time, but sometimes you need to control page breaks. This tip describes how.

Normally, Excel handles page breaks automatically. After you print or preview your worksheet, Excel displays dashed lines to indicate where page breaks occur. Sometimes, however, you want to force a page break — either vertical or horizontal— so that the worksheet prints the way you want. For example, if your worksheet consists of several distinct sections, you might want to print each section on a separate sheet of paper.

Forcing a page break to appear where you want it

To insert a horizontal page break line, move the cell pointer to the cell that will begin the new page and make sure to place the pointer in column A; if you don't, you'll insert a vertical page break and a horizontal page break. For example, if you want row 14 to be the first row of a new page, select cell A14. Then choose Page Layout➜Page Setup➜Breaks➜Insert Page Break. Excel displays a dashed line to indicate the page break.

To insert a vertical page break line, move the cell pointer to the cell that will begin the new page, but in this case make sure that you place the pointer in row 1. Choose Page Layout➜Page Setup➜Breaks➜Insert Page Break to create the page break.

Removing page breaks you've added

To remove a manual page break, move the cell pointer to the first row beneath (or the first column to the right of) the manual page break and then choose Page Layout➜Page Setup➜Breaks➜Remove Page Break. (This command has an effect only when you place the cell pointer adjacent to a manual page break.)

To remove all manual page breaks in the worksheet, choose Page Layout➜Page Setup➜Breaks➜Reset All Page Breaks. After you issue this command, the only page breaks that remain are those that occur naturally.

Saving to a PDF File

The Adobe PDF (Portable Document Format) file standard has become increasingly popular, for several reasons:

> ➤ PDF files can be read on many different platforms by using Adobe Acrobat Reader (a free product).

> ➤ The information looks the same, regardless of the computer or printer used.

> ➤ The document cannot be easily modified.

PDF is a good choice if you need to send information to someone who doesn't have a copy of Excel. Nowadays, just about everyone has software installed that can display PDF files.

Excel 2010 includes a built-in option to save to a PDF file. When your workbook is finalized, choose File➔Save & Send➔Create PDF/XPS Document. Then click the Create a PDF/XPS button, and Excel displays the Publish as PDF or XPS dialog box where you can specify the location for the file.

Note

XPS is a Microsoft file format, and it's not nearly as popular as the PDF format. In fact, many people don't even have software that displays these documents. So, unless you have a good reason to do otherwise, choose the PDF option instead.

Making Your Printout Fit on One Page

If you need to ensure that your printed output fits on a single page, you can spend time adjusting the font sizes — or you can let Excel do the work for you.

Figure 190-1 shows a worksheet in Page Layout view. This workbook will print on six pages.

Figure 190-1: This worksheet will print on six pages.

To force Excel to print the entire worksheet on a single sheet, choose Page Layout➜Scale To Fit and specify 1 Page for the Width and 1 Page for the Height. Excel will shrink the output to your specifications.

Figure 190-2 shows the worksheet after specifying these values. I also changed the orientation to landscape so that it would fit better on the page.

Obviously, you need to consider the legibility of the printout. If you force too much information on a single sheet, it's printed so small that you need a magnifying glass to read it.

Note

The Page Layout➜Scale To Fit settings affect the worksheet's Zoom level. These settings do not change the font size. To return to normal view, specify Automatic for the Width and Height settings.

Figure 190-2: Excel shrunk the output to fit on a single page.

Printing the Contents of a Cell in a Header or Footer

The Excel Header and Footer options are fairly flexible, but you have no direct way to display the contents of a cell in a page header or footer. The solution is a simple VBA macro.

Figure 191-1 shows a worksheet with some values. Cell A1 contains a simple formula that calculates the sum of the values. The goal is to display the value in cell A1 in the center header of the page.

Figure 191-1: A simple VBA macro displays the contents of cell A1 in the page header.

To create the macro, follow these steps:

1. Make sure that the workbook's window isn't maximized.

2. Right-click the workbook window's title bar and choose View Code.

    The (empty) code module for the ThisWorkbook object is displayed in the Visual Basic Editor.

3. Type the following macro (see Figure 191-2):

```
Private Sub Workbook_BeforePrint(Cancel As Boolean)
    With ActiveSheet.PageSetup
        .CenterHeader = Sheets("Sheet1").Range("A1").Text'
    End With
End Sub
```

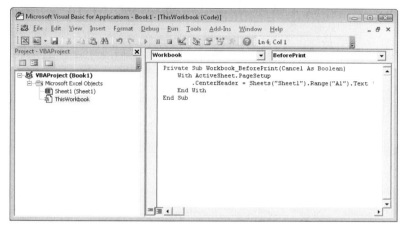

Figure 191-2: This macro is executed before the workbook is printed.

This macro is executed whenever the workbook is printed. The macro copies the contents of cell A1 (on Sheet1) into the center header. You can, of course, adjust the sheet name or range address so that the header displays the contents of a different cell.

To put the cell contents in a different header or footer position, substitute one of the following names for CenterHeader:

➤ LeftHeader

➤ RightHeader

➤ LeftFooter

➤ CenterFooter

➤ RightFooter

Unfortunately, Excel 2010 does not display the new header or footer when the workbook is previewed.

Note If your workbook has an XLSX extension, you need to resave it with an XLSM extension. Otherwise, Excel will discard the macro.

Copying Page Setup Settings Across Sheets

Each Excel worksheet has its own printing options (orientation, margins, and headers and footers, for example). These options are specified in the Page Setup group on the Page Layout tab.

When you add a new sheet to a workbook, the sheet contains the default Page Setup settings. Here's an easy way to transfer the settings from one worksheet to additional worksheets:

1. Activate the sheet that contains the setup information you want.

   This is the *source* sheet.

2. Select the target sheets.

   Ctrl+click the sheet tabs of the sheets you want to update with the settings from the source sheet.

3. Click the dialog box launcher in the Page Layout➜Page Setup group.

   It's the small icon to the right of the Page Setup group name. Clicking this icon displays the Page Setup dialog box.

4. When the Page Setup dialog box appears, click OK to close it.

5. Ungroup the sheets by right-clicking any selected sheet and choosing Ungroup Sheets from the shortcut menu.

   The Page Setup settings of the source sheet are transferred to all the target sheets.

Note

Two settings located on the Sheet tab of the Page Setup dialog box are not transferred: Print Area and Print Titles. In addition, pictures in the header or footer are not transferred.

Printing Cell Comments

Normally, when you print a worksheet that contains cell comments, the comments are not printed. If you want to print the comments, follow these steps:

1. Click the dialog box launcher in the Page Layout→Page Setup group.

   It's the small icon to the right of the Page Setup group name. Clicking this icon displays the Page Setup dialog box.

2. In the Page Setup dialog box, click the Sheet tab.

3. Make your choice from the Comments drop-down control: At End of Sheet or As Displayed on Sheet (see Figure 193-1).

   If you choose the As Displayed on Sheet option, the comments will not print unless they are visible. Use Review→Comments→Show All Comments to toggle the visibility of cell comments.

4. Click OK to close the Page Setup dialog box.

   Or, click the Print button to print the worksheet.

Figure 193-1: Specifying how to print cell comments.

Printing a Giant Banner

Excel really wasn't designed for this task, but if you need to print a giant banner — and you have no other way to do it — follow these instructions to create a workbook that prints one large character per page.

1. Start with a new workbook and make sure that all other workbooks are closed.

2. Type your message, one character per cell, in column A.

3. Select the cells and make the text bold and centered vertically and horizontally.

4. Set the font size to 409 (the largest allowable font).

5. Select column A, choose Home➜Cells➜Format➜Column Width, and set the column width to 84.

   Or, adjust as needed. Your goal is to make column A occupy an entire horizontal page.

6. Choose Page Layout➜Page Setup➜Margins➜Custom Margin to display the Margins tab of the Page Setup dialog box.

7. In the Page Setup dialog box, place a checkmark in both the Horizontally and the Vertically check boxes.

8. Choose View➜Workbook Views➜Page Layout to enter Page Layout view.

9. Use the Zoom control on the status bar to set the worksheet zoom to 10 percent.

   Then you can see many complete pages.

10. Use the Page Layout➜Scale To Fit➜Scale control to increase the scale factor to 150 percent.

11. Adjust, if necessary, until each page displays a large character.

Make sure to look at your sheets in Print Preview mode before printing to ensure that each character is as large as possible on the page.

Figure 194-1 shows the word *Congrats* in Page Layout view.

Figure 194-1: Printing one character per page to create a banner.

## PART XI

Spotting, Fixing, and Preventing Errors

Just because your spreadsheet doesn't display an error value doesn't mean that it's accurate. The tips in this part will help you identify, fix, and prevent errors.

Tips and Where to Find Them

Using the Excel Error-Checking Features

If your worksheets use a lot of formulas, you might find it helpful to take advantage of the auto-matic error-checking feature. You enable this feature on the Formulas tab of the Excel Options dialog box (see Figure 195-1). To display this dialog box, choose File➜Options.

You turn error checking on or off by using the Enable Background Error Checking check box. In addition, you can specify which types of errors to check by selecting check boxes in the Error Checking Rules section.

Figure 195-1: Excel can check your formulas for potential errors.

When error checking is turned on, Excel continually evaluates your worksheet, including its for-mulas. If a potential error is identified, Excel places a small triangle in the upper left corner of the cell. When the cell is activated, a Smart Tag appears. Clicking it provides you with some options. Figure 195-2 shows the options that appear when you click the Smart Tag in a cell that contains a #DIV/0! error. The options vary, depending on the type of error.

In many cases, you choose to ignore an error by choosing the Ignore Error option, which elimi-nates the cell from subsequent error checks. However, all previously ignored errors can be reset so that they appear again. (Click the Reset Ignored Errors button in the Excel Options dialog box.)

	A	B	C	D	E	F	G
1	**Telemarketing Results**						
2							
3	**Day**	**Calls Made**	**Sales**	**Percentage**			
4	3–Aug	754	21	2.79%			
5	4–Aug	732	31	4.23%			
6	5–Aug	655	18	2.75%			
7	6–Aug	934	35	3.75%			
8	7–Aug	1,022	38	3.72%			
9	8–Aug			#DIV/0!			
10	9–Aug			#DIV/0!			
11	10–Aug		◈ ▾	#DIV/0!			
12				Divide by Zero Error			
13				Help on this error			
14				Show Calculation Steps...			
15				Ignore Error			
16							
17				Edit in Formula Bar			
18				Error Checking Options...			
19							
20							
21							

Figure 195-2: Clicking an error Smart Tag gives you a list of options.

Even if you don't use the automatic error checking option, you can choose the Formulas→ Formula Auditing→Error Checking command to display a dialog box that displays each potential error cell in sequence, much like using a spell-checking feature. Figure 195-3 shows the Error Checking dialog box. Note that because it's a modeless dialog box, you can still access your worksheet when the Error Checking dialog box is displayed.

Error Checking	? ✕
Error in cell D9	Help on this error
=C9/B9	
Divide by Zero Error	Show Calculation Steps...
The formula or function used is dividing by zero or empty cells.	Ignore Error
	Edit in Formula Bar
Options...	Previous Next

Figure 195-3: Using the Error Checking dialog box to cycle through potential errors identified by Excel.

Caution Understand that the error-checking feature isn't perfect. In fact, it's not even *close* to perfect. In other words, you can't assume that you have an error-free worksheet simply because Excel doesn't identify any potential errors! Also, be aware that this error-checking feature doesn't catch a common type of error — overwriting a formula cell with a value.

Identifying Formula Cells

A common spreadsheet problem occurs when a formula is accidentally replaced with a value. This type of error is often difficult to spot, especially if your worksheet contains a large number of formulas. This tip describes two ways to quickly identify the formulas in a worksheet by highlighting them. Then, if you zoom out (make the cells appear very small), you might be able to spot gaps in groups of formulas.

Using Go To Special

This method of identifying formula cells is easy, but it's not dynamic. In other words, it's good for a one-time check:

1. Select any single cell in your worksheet.

2. Choose Home➔Editing➔Find & Select➔Go to Special to display the Go to Special dialog box.

3. In the Go to Special dialog box, click the Formulas option and make sure that all check boxes below it are selected.

4. Click OK.

   Excel selects all formula cells.

5. Click the Fill Color control in the File➔Font group

   Select any color that's not already being used.

6. Use the Zoom control and zoom your worksheet to a small percentage (25 percent is a good choice).

7. Check the sheet carefully and look for any unshaded cells in a group of shaded cells.

   It might be a formula that was overwritten by a value.

If you didn't make any edits, you can click Undo (or press Ctrl+Z) to remove the fill colors you applied in Step 6.

Using conditional formatting

This method of identifying formula cells takes a bit of setup work, but it has a distinct advantage over the previous method: It's dynamic. Formula cells are identified immediately when they're entered.

To set up conditional formatting, follow these steps:

1. Choose Formulas➔Defined Names➔Define Name to display the New Name dialog box.

2. In the New Name dialog box, enter the following line in the Name field:

   ```
   CellHasFormula
   ```

3. Enter the following formula in the Refers To field:

   ```
   =GET.CELL(48,INDIRECT("rc",FALSE))
   ```

4. Click OK to close the New Name dialog box.

5. Select all cells to which you want to apply the conditional formatting.

   Generally, they comprise a range from A1 down to the lower right corner of the used area of the worksheet.

6. Choose Home➔Conditional Formatting➔New Rule to display the New Formatting Rule dialog box.

7. In the top part of the dialog box, select the option labeled Use a Formula to Determine Which Cells to Format.

8. Enter this formula in the bottom part of the dialog box (see Figure 196-1):

   ```
   =CellHasFormula
   ```

9. Click the Format button to display the Format Cells dialog box and select the type of formatting you want for the cells that contain a formula.

   An unused fill color is a good choice.

10. Click OK to close the Format Cells dialog box and click OK again to close the New Formatting Rule dialog box.

After you complete these steps, every cell that contains a formula and is within the range you selected in Step 5 displays the formatting of your choice. In addition, if you enter a formula within the range that has the conditional formatting, the cell immediately displays the formatting. This formatting lets you easily identify a cell that should contain a formula but doesn't.

Note The formula you enter in Step 3 is an XLM macro. Consequently, you must save the workbook as a macro-enabled file (using an XLSM extension). If you save the workbook as an XLSX file, Excel deletes the CellHasFormula name.

Figure 196-1: Using conditional formatting to highlight formula cells.

Dealing with Floating-Point Number Problems

Excel users are often baffled by Excel's apparent inability to perform simple math. It's not the program's fault: Computers, by their nature, don't have infinite precision. Excel stores numbers in binary format by using 8 bytes, which can handle numbers with 15-digit accuracy. Some numbers can't be expressed precisely by using 8 bytes, so the number is stored as an approximation.

To demonstrate how this limitation might cause problems, enter the following formula into cell A1:

```
=(5.1-5.2)+1
```

The result should be 0.9. However, if you format the cell to display 15 decimal places, you discover that Excel calculates the formula with a result of 0.899999999999999 — a value that's *close to* 0.9, but certainly *not* 0.9. This result occurs because the operation in parentheses is performed first, and this intermediate result is stored in binary format by using an approximation. The formula then adds 1 to this value, and the approximation error is propagated to the final result.

In many cases, this type of error doesn't present a problem. However, if you need to test the result of that formula by using a logical operator, it might present a problem. For example, the following formula (which assumes that the previous formula is in cell A1) returns FALSE:

```
=A1=.9
```

One solution to this type of error is to use the ROUND function. The following formula, for example, returns TRUE because the comparison is made by using the value in A1 rounded to one decimal place:

```
=ROUND(A1,1)=0.9
```

Here's another example of a precision problem. Try entering the following formula:

```
=(1.333-1.233)-(1.334-1.234)
```

This formula should return 0 but instead returns $-2.22045E-16$ (a number very close to zero).

If that formula were in cell A1, the following formula would return Not Zero:

```
=IF(A1=0,"Zero","Not Zero")
```

One way to handle these "very close to zero" rounding errors is to use a formula like this:

```
=IF(ABS(A1)<1E-6,"Zero","Not Zero")
```

This formula uses the less-than operator to compare the absolute value of the number with a very small number. This formula would return Zero.

Another option is to instruct Excel to change the worksheet values to match their displayed format. To do this, access the Excel Options dialog box (choose File➜Options) and click the Advanced tab. Select the Set Precision as Displayed check box (which is located in the When Calculating This Workbook section).

Caution

Selecting the Precision as Displayed option changes the numbers in your worksheets to permanently match their appearance on-screen. This setting applies to all sheets in the active workbook. Most of the time, this option is not what you want. Make sure that you understand the consequences of using the Set Precision as Displayed option.

Removing Excess Spaces

A common type of error involves something that you can't even see: a space character. Consider the example shown in Figure 198-1. Cell B2 contains a formula that looks up the color name in cell B1 and returns the corresponding code from a table. The formula is

```
=VLOOKUP(B1,D2:E9,2,FALSE)
```

▲	A	B	C	D	E
1	Enter a color name:	Green		Color	Code
2	The code:	65280		Black	0
3				Blue	16711680
4				Cyan	16776960
5				Green	65280
6				Magenta	16711935
7				Red	255
8				White	16777215
9				Yellow	65535
10					

Figure 198-1: A simple lookup formula returns the code for a color entered in cell B1.

In Figure 198-2, the formula in cell B2 returns an error — indicating that *Red* wasn't found in the table. Hundreds of thousands of Excel users have spent far too much time trying to figure out why this sort of thing doesn't work. In this case, the answer is simple: Cell D7 doesn't contain the word *Red*. Rather, it contains the word *Red* followed by a space. To Excel, these text strings are completely different.

▲	A	B	C	D	E	F
1	Enter a color name:	Red		Color	Code	
2	The code:	#N/A		Black	0	
3				Blue	16711680	
4				Cyan	16776960	
5				Green	65280	
6				Magenta	16711935	
7				Red	255	
8				White	16777215	
9				Yellow	65535	
10						

Figure 198-2: The lookup formula can't find the word *Red* in the table.

If your worksheet contains thousands of text entries — and you need to perform comparisons using that text — you might want to identify the cells that contain excess spaces and then fix those cells. The term *excess spaces* means a text entry that contains any of the following: one or more leading spaces, one or more trailing spaces, or two or more consecutive spaces.

One way to identify this type of cell is to use conditional formatting.

To set up conditional formatting, follow these steps:

1. Select all text cells to which you want to apply conditional formatting.

2. Choose Home➜Conditional Formatting➜New Rule to display the New Formatting Rule dialog box.

3. In the top part of the dialog box, select the option labeled Use a Formula to Determine Which Cells to Format.

4. Enter a formula like the following in the bottom part of the dialog box:

```
=A1<>TRIM(A1)
```

Note: This formula assumes that cell A1 is the upper left cell in the selection. If that's not the case, substitute the address of the upper left cell in the selection you made in Step 1.

5. Click the Format button to display the Format Cells dialog box and select the type of formatting you want for the cells that contain excess spaces.

    A yellow fill color is a good choice.

6. Click OK to close the Format Cells dialog box, and click OK again to close the New Formatting Rule dialog box.

After you complete these steps, every cell that contains excess spaces and is within the range you selected in Step 1 displays the formatting of your choice. You can then easily spot these cells and remove the spaces.

Note

Because of the way the TRIM function works, the formula in Step 4 also applies the conditional formatting to all numeric cells. A slightly more complex formula that doesn't apply the formatting to numeric cells is

```
=IF(NOT(ISNONTEXT(A1)),A1<>TRIM(A1))
```

Viewing Names Graphically

If your worksheet has lots of range names, it might be helpful to identify the location of the ranges. Excel can help: Just zoom the worksheet to 39 percent or less (using the Zoom control on the status bar), and the names are displayed.

Figure 199-1 shows an example of a worksheet that has three named ranges: Monthly, Pmt_ Breakdown, and Annual.

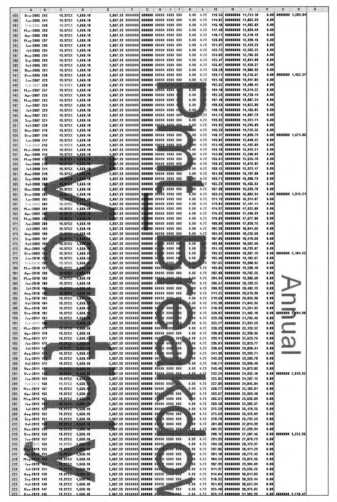

Figure 199-1: Excel displays the range names when you zoom a worksheet to 39 percent or less.

Locating Phantom Links

You might open a workbook and see a message like the one shown in Figure 200-1. If the workbook contains links, you expect to see this message. But sometimes this message appears even when a workbook contains no linked formulas.

Figure 200-1: The Excel way of asking whether you want to update links in a workbook.

To get rid of these phantom links, first try clicking the Edit Links button in the dialog box (or choose File➜Info➜Edit Links to Files) to display the Edit Links dialog box. Then select each link and click Break Link. Save the workbook and reopen it. Note that the Edit Links to Files command is not available if your workbook contains no links.

If breaking the links doesn't solve the problem, the phantom link might be caused by an erroneous name. Erroneous names might be created when you copy a worksheet that contains names. Choose Formulas➜Defined Names➜Name Manager and scroll through the list of names. If you see a name that refers to #REF!, delete the name. There's an excellent chance that your phantom link will disappear.

Understanding Displayed versus Actual Values

You might encounter a situation in which values in a range don't appear to add up correctly. For example, Figure 201-1 shows a worksheet with the following formula entered into each cell in the range B3:B5:

```
=1/3
```

◢	A	B	C	D
1				
2				
3		0.33		
4		0.33		
5		0.33		
6		1.00		
7				
8				
9				

Figure 201-1: A simple demonstration of numbers that appear to add up incorrectly.

Cell B6 contains the following formula:

```
=SUM(B3:B5)
```

All the cells are formatted to display with two decimal places. As you can see, the formula in cell B6 appears to display an incorrect result. (You might expect it to display 0.99.) The formula, of course, returns the correct result. The formula uses the actual values in the range B3:B5, not the displayed values.

You might be tempted to instruct Excel to use the displayed values. You do this by selecting the Set Precision As Displayed check box on the Advanced tab of the Excel Options dialog box. (Choose File➡Options to display this dialog box.)

Generally, using the Set Precision As Displayed check box isn't the best way to handle this type of problem. Checking the Set Precision As Displayed check box also affects normal values (not formulas) that have been entered into cells. For example, if a cell contains the value 4.68 and is displayed with no decimal places (that is, 5), selecting the Set Precision as Displayed check box converts 4.68 to 5.00. This change is permanent, and you can't restore the original value if you later deselect the Set Precision as Displayed check box.

A better approach is to use the Excel ROUND function to round the values to the number of decimal places you want. In the example shown here, the range B3:B5 would contain this formula:

```
=ROUND(1/3,2)
```

Summing the three values results in 0.99.

Tracing Cell Relationships

In many worksheets, the cells might contain complex interrelationships. Trying to debug a formula can be easier if you understand two key concepts: cell precedents and cell dependents:

> **Cell precedents:** Applicable only to cells that contain a formula, a formula cell's precedents are all the cells that contribute to the formula's result. A *direct precedent* is a cell that you use directly in the formula. An *indirect precedent* is a cell that isn't used directly in the formula, but is used by a cell that you refer to in the formula.

> **Cell dependents:** These formula cells depend on a particular cell. A cell's dependents consist of all formula cells that use the cell. Again, the formula cell can be a *direct dependent* or an *indirect dependent*.

Identifying cell precedents for a formula cell often sheds light on why the formula isn't working correctly. Conversely, knowing which formula cells depend on a particular cell is also helpful. For example, if you're about to delete a formula, you might want to see whether it has any dependents.

Identifying precedents

You can identify cells used by a formula in the active cell in a number of ways:

> **Press F2.** The cells that are used directly by the formula are outlined in color, and the color corresponds to the cell reference in the formula.

> **Display the Go To Special dialog box** (choose Home➜Editing➜Find & Select➜Go To Special). Select the Precedents option and then select either Direct Only (for direct precedents only) or All Levels (for direct and indirect precedents). Click OK, and Excel selects the precedent cells for the formula.

> **Press Ctrl+[** to select all direct precedent cells on the active sheet.

> **Press Ctrl+Shift+[** to select all precedent cells (direct and indirect) on the active sheet.

> **Choose Formulas➜Formula Auditing➜Trace Precedents,** and Excel draws arrows to indicate the cell's precedents. Click this button multiple times to see additional levels of precedents. Choose Formulas➜Formula Auditing➜Remove Arrows to hide the arrows.

Note that all of these techniques are limited to identifying precedent cells only on the sheet that contains the formula. Figure 202-1 shows a worksheet with precedent arrows drawn to indicate the precedents for the formula in cell C13.

	A	B	C	D	E	F	G	H
1	Commission Rate	5.50%	Normal commission rate					
2	Sales Goal	15%	Improvement from prior month					
3	Bonus Rate	6.50%	Paid if Sales Goal is attained					
4								
5	Sales Rep	Last Month	This Month	Change	Pct. Change	Met Goal?	Commission	
6	Murray	101,233	108,444	7,211	7.1%	TRUE	7,049	
7	Knuckles	120,933	108,434	-12,499	-10.3%	FALSE	5,964	
8	Lefty	139,832	165,901	26,069	18.6%	TRUE	10,784	
9	Lucky	98,323	100,083	1,760	1.8%	FALSE	5,505	
10	Scarface	78,322	79,923	1,601	2.0%	FALSE	4,396	
11	Total	538,643	562,785	24,142	4.5%		33,697	
12								
13	Average Commission Rate:		5.99%					
14								
15								

Figure 202-1: This worksheet displays arrows that indicate cell precedents for the formula in cell C13.

Identifying dependents

You can identify formula cells that use a particular cell in a number of ways:

> **Display the Go to Special dialog box.** Select the Dependents option and then select either Direct Only (for direct dependents only) or All Levels (for direct and indirect dependents). Click OK. Excel selects the cells that depend on the active cell.

> **Press Ctrl+]** to select all direct dependent cells on the active sheet.

> **Press Ctrl+Shift+]** to select all dependent cells (direct and indirect) on the active sheet.

> **Choose Formulas➜Formula Auditing➜Trace Dependents,** and Excel draws arrows to indicate the cell's dependents. Click this button multiple times to see additional levels of dependents. Choose Formulas➜Formula Auditing➜Remove Arrows to hide the arrows.

Again, these techniques are limited to identifying dependent cells only on the active worksheet.

## PART XII

Basic VBA and Macros

Even if you know nothing about VBA and macros, you may find that some of the tips in this section whet your appetite to learn more. And, if you're just starting out with macros, you'll find some useful tips in this part.

Tips and Where to Find Them

Learning about Macros and VBA

The terms *macro* and *VBA* remain a mystery to most Excel users. This tip provides a broad overview to help you decide whether learning to create Excel macros would be useful.

What is a macro?

A *macro* is a sequence of instructions that automates some aspect of Excel so that you can work more efficiently and with fewer errors. You use the scripting language Visual Basic for Applications (VBA) to create macros. You might create a macro, for example, to import data from a text file, format it, and save it as a workbook. After the macro is developed, you can then execute the macro to perform many time-consuming procedures automatically.

You need not be a power user to create and use simple VBA macros. Casual users can simply turn on the Excel macro recorder: Excel records your actions and converts them into a VBA macro. When you execute this macro, Excel performs the actions again.

More advanced users can write code that tells Excel to perform tasks that can't be recorded. For example, you can write procedures that display custom dialog boxes, add new commands to the Excel menus, or process data in a series of workbooks.

What can a macro do?

VBA is an extremely rich programming language with thousands of uses. The following list describes just a few things you can do with VBA macros:

> **Insert a text string or formula:** If you need to enter your company name into worksheets frequently, you can create a macro to do the typing (and even format the cell) for you. The Excel AutoCorrect feature can insert text, but it can't do any formatting.

> **Automate a procedure that you perform frequently:** For example, you might need to prepare a month-end summary. If the task is straightforward, you can develop a macro to do it for you.

> **Automate repetitive operations:** If you need to perform the same action in 12 different workbooks, you can record a macro while you perform the task once — and then let the macro repeat your action in the other workbooks.

> **Create a custom command:** For example, you can combine several Excel commands so that they're executed from a single keystroke or from a single mouse click.

> **Create a custom button:** You can customize the Excel Ribbon or Quick Access toolbar with your own buttons to execute macros that you write.

➤ **Respond to events automatically:** You can create macros that execute automatically when a particular event occurs. For example, you can write a macro that responds to the WorksheetChange event — which is triggered whenever a cell in a worksheet is changed. Excel supports many other events.

➤ **Create a simplified "front end" for users who don't know much about Excel:** For example, you can set up a foolproof data entry template.

➤ **Develop a new worksheet function:** Although Excel includes a wide assortment of built-in functions, you can create custom functions that can greatly simplify your formulas.

➤ **Create complete, macro-driven applications:** Excel macros can display custom dialog boxes and be executed from commands you add to the Ribbon.

➤ **Create custom add-ins for Excel:** Most add-ins that are shipped with Excel were created with Excel macros.

Recording a Macro

The easiest way to get started learning about Excel macros is to use the macro recorder to record a sequence of actions. Then you can play back the sequence — otherwise known as *running* the macro.

The following hands-on demonstration gives newcomers a feel for how macros work. This example demonstrates how to record a simple macro that inserts your name in the active cell.

Creating the macro

To create the macro, follow these steps:

1. Activate an empty cell.

2. Click the Record Macro button on the left side of the status bar.

   Excel displays the Record Macro dialog box.

3. Enter a new single-word name for the macro, to replace the default Macro1 name.

   A good name is MyName.

4. Assign this macro to the shortcut key Ctrl+Shift+N by typing an uppercase **N** in the edit box labeled Shortcut Key.

5. Click OK to close the Record Macro dialog box and begin recording your actions.

6. Type your name in the selected cell and press Enter.

7. The macro is finished, so click the Stop Recording button on the status bar.

This macro is very simple. Most of the time, you record more actions than in this example.

Examining the macro

The macro was recorded in a new VBA module named Module1. If you're interested, you can take a look at the instructions that were recorded. To view the code in this module, you must activate the Visual Basic Editor (VBE). Press Alt+F11 to toggle between the VBE and the Excel window.

In the VBE, the Project window displays a list of all open workbooks and add-ins. This list is displayed as a tree diagram, which you can expand or collapse. The code that you recorded previously is stored in Module1 in the current workbook. When you double-click Module1, the code in the module is displayed in a Code window.

Figure 204-1 shows the recorded macro, as displayed in the Code window.

Figure 204-1: The MyName macro was generated by Excel's macro recorder.

Notice that Excel inserted some comments at the top of the procedure. This is some of the information that appeared in the Record Macro dialog box. These comment lines (which begin with an apostrophe) aren't necessary, and deleting them has no effect on how the macro runs.

Testing the macro

Before you recorded this macro, you set an option that assigned the macro to the Ctrl+Shift+N shortcut key combination. To test the macro, return to Excel by pressing Alt+F11.

When Excel is active, activate a worksheet. (It can be in the workbook that contains the VBA module or in any other workbook.) Select a cell or range and press Ctrl+Shift+N. The macro immediately enters your name into the cell.

Note

In this example, notice that you selected the cell before you started recording your macro. This is important. If you select a cell while the macro recorder is turned on, the actual cell that you selected is recorded into the macro. In such a case, the macro always enters your name into that cell, so the macro isn't a "general-purpose" macro.

Executing Macros

If you create a macro, you need a way to execute it. This tip describes all the ways to execute a macro in Excel 2010.

Use the Macro dialog box

All available macros are listed in the Macro dialog box. For a macro to be available, the workbook that contains the macro must be open. To display the Macro dialog box, choose View➜Macros➜ Macros (or press Alt+F8). The Macro dialog box displays the macros in a list. Just select the macro and click Run.

Use the Visual Basic Editor window

You can execute macros directly from the VBE — although it's certainly not the most convenient method. Press Alt+F11 to activate the VBE. Then locate the project and the code module that contains the macro. Place the cursor anywhere within the macro code, and choose Run➜Run Sub/UserForm (or press F5).

Use a shortcut key

When you begin recording a macro, the Record Macro dialog box gives you an opportunity to provide a shortcut key for the macro. If you later want to change the shortcut key or provide a shortcut key for a macro that doesn't have one, follow these steps:

1. Press Alt+F8 to display the Macro dialog box.

2. In the Macro dialog box, select the macro name from the list.

3. Click the Options button. Excel displays the Macro Options dialog box.

4. Specify the shortcut key and click OK to return to the Macro dialog box.

5. Click Cancel to close the Macro dialog box.

Assign the macro to a button

You can add a button to a worksheet and then execute a macro by clicking the button.

Note

To add a button to a worksheet, the Developer tab must be present. To display this tab, choose File➜Options. In the Excel Options dialog box, select the Customize Ribbon tab, and place a checkmark next to Developer.

Perform these steps to add a button to your worksheet and to assign a macro to the button:

1. Choose Developer➔Controls➔Insert and click the Button control in the Form Controls section.

2. Draw the button on the worksheet.

   Excel displays the Assign Macro dialog box.

3. In the Assign Macro dialog box, select the macro from the list.

4. Click OK to close the Assign Macro dialog box.

5. If you want to change the text that appears on the button, to make it descriptive, right-click the button, choose Edit Text from the shortcut menu, and make your changes.

After you complete these steps, clicking the button executes the assigned macro.

Assign the macro to a shape

You can also assign a macro to a shape object on a worksheet. Just right-click the shape and choose Assign Macro from the shortcut menu. Select the macro from the Assign Macro dialog box and click OK.

After you perform these steps, clicking the shape runs the macro.

Add a button to your Quick Access toolbar

Another way to execute a macro is to assign it to a button on the Quick Access toolbar:

1. Right-click the Quick Access toolbar and choose Customize Quick Access Toolbar to display the Excel Options dialog box.

2. In the drop-down list on the left, choose Macros.

   A list of available macros is displayed.

3. Select the macro from the list and click Add.

4. Optionally, you can click the Modify button, select a different icon, and provide a different name for the Quick Access Toolbar button.

Add a button to the Ribbon

Excel 2010 allows users to modify the Ribbon, and that includes adding buttons that execute macros. You need to add a new group, though. (You can't add a button to a built-in Ribbon group.) To assign a macro to a button on the Ribbon:

1. Right-click the Ribbon and choose Customize the Ribbon to display the Excel Options dialog box.

2. In the list on the right, click a tab and then click New Group to create a new group in the selected tab.

3. In the drop-down list on the left, choose Macros.

   A list of available macros is displayed.

4. Select the macro from the list and click Add.

You can use the Rename button to provide a name for your button and the new group you created.

Understanding Functions Versus Subs

Excel VBA macros come in two distinct varieties: Sub procedures and Function procedures. This tip describes how they differ.

VBA Sub procedures

You can think of a *Sub procedure* as a new command. You can have any number of Sub procedures in an Excel workbook. Figure 206-1 shows a simple VBA Sub procedure. When this code is executed, it toggles the page break display for the active worksheet.

Figure 206-1: A simple, but useful, VBA procedure.

Sub procedures always start with the keyword Sub, the macro's name, and then a pair of parentheses. The End Sub statement signals the end of the procedure. The lines between this keyword and statement comprise the procedure's code.

You execute a VBA Sub procedure in several ways. For example, you can press Alt+F8 and then select the macro from the Macros dialog box. For other ways to execute Sub procedures, see Tip 205.

When you record a macro, it's always a Sub procedure.

Note

VBA functions

A second type of VBA procedure is a *Function* procedure, which always returns a single value (just as a worksheet function always returns a single value). A VBA Function procedure can be executed by other VBA procedures or used in worksheet formulas, just as you would use the built-in Excel worksheet functions.

Figure 206-2 shows the listing of a custom function named User. This function simply returns the name of the user (as specified in the Excel Options dialog box). A Function procedure looks much like a Sub procedure. Notice, however, that Function procedures begin with the keyword Function and end with an End Function statement.

Here's an example of a worksheet formula that uses this function:

```
=PERSONAL.XLSB!User()
```

This formula assumes that the User function is defined in your Personal Macro Workbook. If the function is defined in the workbook that contains the formula, you can omit the file reference and use this formula:

```
=User()
```

Figure 206-2: A Function procedure that returns the user's name.

Creating Simple Worksheet Functions

Excel provides many worksheet functions, but sometimes you need something other than what's available by default. This tip provides a few examples of custom functions that can be used in worksheet formulas.

Note **Function procedures must be placed in a normal VBA module. If your workbook doesn't have any VBA modules, activate the Visual Basic Editor, select your workbook from the Project list, and choose Insert→Module.**

Returning the user name

The following USERNAME function simply displays the name of the user — the name listed on the General tab of the Options dialog box:

```
Function USERNAME()
    USERNAME = Application.USERNAME
End Function
```

Here's a worksheet formula that uses this function:

```
=USERNAME()
```

Determine whether a cell contains a formula

The following CELLHASFORMULA function accepts a single-cell argument and returns TRUE if the cell has a formula:

```
Function CELLHASFORMULA(cell) As Boolean
'    Returns TRUE if cell has a formula
    CELLHASFORMULA = cell.Range("A1").HasFormula
End Function
```

If a multicell range argument is passed to the function, the function works with the upper left cell in the range.

Returning a worksheet name

The following SHEETNAME function accepts a single argument (a range) and returns the name of the worksheet that contains the range:

```
Function SHEETNAME(rng) As String
'    Returns the sheet name for rng
     SHEETNAME = rng.Parent.Name
End Function
```

Returning a workbook name

The following function, WORKBOOKNAME, returns the name of the workbook:

```
Function WORKBOOKNAME() As String
'    Returns the workbook name of the cell
'    that contains the function
     WORKBOOKNAME = Application.Caller.Parent.Parent.Name
End Function
```

Reversing a string

The following REVERSETEXT function returns the text in a cell backward:

```
Function REVERSETEXT(text) As String
'    Returns its argument, reversed
     REVERSETEXT = StrReverse(text)
End Function
```

Extracting the nth element from a string

The EXTRACTELEMENT function extracts an element from a text string based on a specified separator character. Assume that cell A1 contains the following text:

```
123-456-789-9133-8844
```

The following formula returns the string 9133, which is the fourth element in the string. The string uses a hyphen (-) as the separator.

```
=EXTRACTELEMENT(A1,4,"-")
```

The EXTRACTELEMENT function uses three arguments:

> **Txt:** The text string from which you're extracting (can be a literal string or a cell reference)

> **n:** An integer that represents the element to extract

> **Separator:** A single character used as the separator

Here's the VBA code for the EXTRACTELEMENT function:

```
Function EXTRACTELEMENT(Txt, n, Separator) As String
'    Returns the nth element of a text string, where the
'    elements are separated by a specified separator character
    Dim AllElements As Variant
    AllElements = Split(Txt, Separator)
    EXTRACTELEMENT = AllElements(n - 1)
End Function
```

Describing Function Arguments

When you use Excel's Insert Function dialog box to insert a built-in worksheet function, clicking OK leads to the Function Arguments dialog box, which assists you with entering the arguments for the function.

You can use the Insert Function dialog box to insert a custom VBA function in a formula, but the Function Arguments dialog box doesn't display descriptions for the arguments. However, a new feature in Excel 2010 lets you create argument descriptions for your custom VBA functions.

To demonstrate how this works, I'll use the EXTRACTELEMENT function, listed in Tip 207:

```
Function EXTRACTELEMENT(Txt, n, Separator) As String
'    Returns the nth element of a text string, where the
'    elements are separated by a specified separator character
     Dim AllElements As Variant
     AllElements = Split(Txt, Separator)
     EXTRACTELEMENT = AllElements(n - 1)
End Function
```

To provide function descriptions for this function, you must create and execute a macro. The following macro, when executed, provides a description for the function, plus a description for each of the three arguments:

```
Sub SpecifyDescriptions()
    Dim D0 As String, D1 As String
    Dim D2 As String, D3 As String
    D0 = "Returns a specified element from a string that uses a separator
  character"
    D1 = "The text string from which you're extracting"
    D2 = "An integer that represents the element to extract"
    D3 = "A single character used as the separator"
    Application.MacroOptions _
        Macro:="EXTRACTELEMENT", _
        Description:=D0, _
        ArgumentDescriptions:=Array(D1, D2, D3)
End Sub
```

Figure 208-1 shows how the function appears in the Function Arguments dialog box. Note that you need to run this macro only one time. The descriptions are stored in the workbook that contains the function definition.

Figure 208-1: Inserting a custom VBA function that has argument descriptions.

Making Excel Talk

This tip describes how to make Excel monitor a particular cell and give a verbal report using the text-to-speech feature when the value changes. The tip uses an event-handler macro — specifically, a macro named Worksheet_Calculate.

 See Tip 38 for more about using the text-to-speech options in Excel.

Cross-Ref

The Worksheet_Calculate macro must be placed in the code module for the worksheet that contains the cell that's being monitored. The easiest way to activate that code module is to right-click the sheet tab and choose View Code from the shortcut menu.

The following code assumes that cell A1 contains a total and is the cell that's being monitored. The listing uses a different phrase for each of six conditions. For example, if cell A1 contains the value 1,050, Excel says "You're over the budget."

You can, of course, add as many conditions as you like and adjust the numeric ranges to handle other conditions.

```
Private Sub Worksheet_Calculate()
    With Application.Speech
    Select Case Range("A1")
        Case Is < 600: .Speak "Way below the budget"
        Case 601 To 900: .Speak "Within the budget"
        Case 901 To 999: .Speak "Getting close to the budget"
        Case 1000: .Speak "You are exactly at the budget"
        Case 1001 To 1100: .Speak "You are over the budget"
        Case Is > 1100: .Speak "You are going to get fired"
    End Select
    End With
End Sub
```

Understanding Custom Function Limitations

Almost all users who start creating custom worksheet functions by using VBA make a fatal mistake: They try to get the function to do more than what is possible.

A worksheet function returns a value, and the function must be completely *passive:* In other words, the function cannot change anything on the worksheet.

For example, you might write a function like the following. This function takes one argument (a cell reference) and attempts to change the formatting of the cell. Although the following function contains perfectly valid VBA code, it does *not* make the referenced cell bold:

```
Function MakeBold(cell)
    If cell.Value > 100 Then
        cell.Font.Bold = True
    Else
        cell.Font.Bold = False
    End If
End Function
```

In many cases, you can use an event macro rather than a custom function. The following macro, located in the module for a worksheet, is executed whenever the sheet is calculated. If cell A1 contains a value greater than 100, the cell is made bold; otherwise, it isn't bold:

```
Private Sub Worksheet_Calculate()
    If Range("A1").Value > 100 Then
        Range("A1").Font.Bold = True
    Else
        Range("A1").Font.Bold = False
    End If
End Sub
```

Note

This simple example is for illustration only. A more efficient solution is to use Excel's conditional formatting feature.

Executing a Ribbon Command with a Macro

This tip describes how to write VBA code that mimics clicking a command on the Excel Ribbon. For example, you can write a macro that executes the Home→Alignment→Align Text Left command.

To execute a Ribbon command, you must know the command's name. One way to find a control's name is to use the Customize Ribbon tab of the Excel Options dialog box. Choose File→ Options and click the Customize Ribbon tab. Then locate the command in the list on the left and hover your mouse over the command. A ToolTip displays the command's name (in parentheses).

In Figure 211-1, for example, the ToolTip indicates that the command name for Home→ Alignment→Align Text Left is AlignLeft. The following VBA macro, when executed, has the same effect as choosing the Home→Alignment→Align Text Left command:

```
Sub ExecuteAlignLeft()
    CommandBars.ExecuteMso "AlignLeft"
End Sub
```

Figure 211-1: Using ToolTips to determine command names.

You can download a workbook from the Microsoft site that lists all Excel Ribbon command names — more than 1,700 of them. Try searching the Web for *Office 2010 Ribbon commands*.

Note

Here's another example that displays the Font tab of the Format Cells dialog box:

```
Sub ShowFontTab()
    CommandBars.ExecuteMso "FormatCellsFontDialog"
End Sub
```

Attempting to execute a command in an incorrect context generates an error. For example, this statement executes the command that displays the Insert Function dialog box:

```
CommandBars.ExecuteMso "FunctionWizard"
```

If you execute this statement when something other than a range is selected (for example, a chart), you get an error. Here's a procedure that checks for such an error and displays a friendly message:

```
Sub ShowInsertFunction()
    On Error Resume Next
    CommandBars.ExecuteMso "FunctionWizard"
    If Err.Number <> 0 Then
        MsgBox "That command is not appropriate.", vbInformation
    End If
End Sub
```

Understanding Security Issues Related to Macros

Recent versions of Excel have made macro security a key priority. The reason is that macros are powerful — so powerful that they can do serious damage to your computer and even to other computers on your network. Unfortunately, lots of people in the world find it entertaining to see how much harm they can accomplish from their computer desks.

Security settings are specified in the Trust Center dialog box. Figure 212-1 shows the Macro Settings section of the Trust Center dialog box. To display this dialog box, follow these steps:

1. Choose File➜Options.

2. In the Excel Options dialog box, click the Trust Center tab.

3. Click the Trust Center Settings button.

4. Click the Macro Settings tab.

Figure 212-1: The Macro Settings section of the Trust Center dialog box.

By default, Excel uses the Disable All Macros with Notification option. With this setting in effect, if you open a workbook that contains macros (and the file isn't digitally "signed" or in a trusted location), the macros are disabled, and Excel displays a security alert above the Formula bar. If you're certain that the workbook comes from a trusted source, click Enable Content to enable the macros.

Note

If the Visual Basic Editor window is open when you open a workbook that contains macros, Excel doesn't display the security alert above the formula bar. Rather, it displays a dialog box with two buttons: Enable Macros and Disable Macros.

Perhaps the best way to handle macro security is to designate one or more folders as "trusted locations." All the workbooks in a trusted location are opened without a macro warning. You designate trusted folders in the Trusted Locations section of the Trust Center dialog box.

Using a Personal Macro Workbook

When you start recording a macro, the Record Macro dialog box prompts you for a location to store the macro (see Figure 213-1). Your choices are

➤ Personal Macro Workbook

➤ New Workbook

➤ This Workbook

Figure 213-1: The Record Macro dialog box lets you choose where to store the recorded macro.

Most user-created macros are designed for use in a specific workbook, but you might want to use some macros in all your work. You can store these general-purpose macros in the Personal Macro Workbook so that they are always available to you.

The Personal Macro Workbook is loaded whenever you start Excel. The file, named personal.xlsb, doesn't exist until you record a macro by using Personal Macro Workbook as the destination.

Note   The Personal Macro Workbook normally is in a hidden window (to keep it out of the way).

To record the macro in your Personal Macro Workbook, select the Personal Macro Workbook option in the Record Macro dialog box before you start recording. This is one of the options on the Store Macro In drop-down list.

If you store macros in the Personal Macro Workbook, you don't have to remember to open the Personal Macro Workbook when you load a workbook that uses macros. Excel automatically opens it.

If you made any changes to your Personal Macro Workbook, you're prompted to save the file when you close Excel.

Index

Special Offer . . . Save $30.00!

Power Utility Pak v7

"The Excel tools Microsoft forgot"

A $39.95 value. Yours for only $9.95.

Pro-Quality Tools

PUP v7 is a handy collection of 60 general purpose Excel utilities, plus 50 new worksheet functions. Download a trial version from the URL at the bottom of this page. If you like it, use this coupon and save $30 on the licensed version.

VBA Source Code is Available

You can also get the complete VBA source files for only $20.00 more. Learn how the utilities and functions were written, and pick up useful tips and programming techniques in the process. This is a must for all VBA programmers.

YES! I want Power Utility Pak v7

Name: _____

Company: _____

Address:_____

City:_____ State: _____ Zip: _____

Check one:

❑ PUP v7 Licensed Version $9.95

❑ Developer's Pak: Licensed Version ($9.95) + VBA Source ($20.00) $29.95

Upon receipt of this coupon, you will receive download instructions via e-mail. Please make your e-mail address legible.

E-mail: _____

Credit Card:_____ Expires:_____

Make check or money order (U.S. funds only) payable to:

JWalk & Associates Inc.
P.O. Box 68797
Tucson, AZ 85737 (USA)

Download a free 30-day trial version of PUP from:

http://spreadsheetpage.com

PUP v7 is compatible only with Excel 2007 and Excel 2010. For earlier versions of Excel, use PUP v6.